THE HOUSE ON PALMER STREET

THE HOUSE ON PALMER STREET

by

HELEN CONSTANTINE DRACOS

HELLENIC COLLEGE PRESS
Brookline, Massachusetts

© Copyright 1993 by Helen Constantine Dracos

Published by Hellenic College Press
50 Goddard Avenue
Brookline, Massachusetts 02146

Cover design by Mary C. Vaporis

Library of Congress Cataloging-in-Publication Data

Dracos, Helen.
    The house on Palmer Street / by Helen Dracos
        p.   cm.
    ISBN 0-917653-41-6. --ISBN 0-917653-42-4 (pbk.)
    1. Greek Americans--Biography. 2. Douropoulos family.
3. Douropoulos, Constantine--Family.   I. Title.
E184.G7D73   1993
973'.048'93--dc20   93-20851
                                                            CIP

In memory of Arthur

They told me, Heraclitus, they told me you were dead,
They brought me bitter news to hear and bitter tears to shed.
I wept as I remember'd how often you and I
Had tried the sun with talking and sent him down the sky.

William (Johnson) Cory

Acknowledgements of Gratitude

To my late husband, Harry, to my daughter, Alexandra Penney, and my son, Ted Dracos, to my grandchildren, John B. Penney and Erin Dracos, for the constancy of their patience, their loyalty, their love.

To friends, old and new, whose understanding helped in my continuing to write as best I could during a most trying period of my life. They know who they are, and they know of my appreciation for their many kindnesses.

To Fr. N. Michael Vaporis, distinguished Director of the Hellenic College Press, and his patient and tireless staff for the production of this book.

To Ernest A. Villas, Director of the Archdiocese Department of Religious Education, Dr. Sophronia Tomaras, Mrs. Rose Golden, and Mr. Morton C. Bradley, Jr., who gave invaluable assistance in furthering the publication of this book.

I am strongly moved to mention specifically the Very Reverend George Poulos, dearly loved pastor of the Church of the Archangels in Stamford, Connecticut, and dearest of friends, the late Fredrick S. "Barney" Troy, Professor Emeritus of English at the University of Massachusetts.

Fr. Poulos believed that the memoir I wrote for my family would be of interest to a wider readership. This dedicated man of the cloth is also a man of parts: a bibliophile of breadth and depth, a writer of notable biographies, and a writer of compelling secular and religious articles. The ceaseless demands on his time did not deter him in his efforts to insure the publication of this book.

Fred "Barney" Troy never failed to admonish me during his visits to our home "to finish the opus." But for his loving concern and support this book would have remained an incomplete manuscript.

Even without the limitations of space imposed by acknowledgements, I confess my inability to do justice to the patrician quality of Fred's presence, his mind and his spirit. I can only quote a statement of a former student of his—William Manchester, eminent author and historian of our times: "I studied at three universities and have long been associated with a fourth, yet I have never known a teacher who brought such vigor, such clarity, and such passion to the classroom."

Principal Characters

Constantine Douropoulos	One of the Greek Orthodox pioneer priests in America
Alexandra	Wife of Constantine
Their Children:	
Dion (Dionysios)	Demetra
Angela (Angeliki)	Catherine (Katina)
Sophia	Christine (Christina)
Arthur (Athanasios)	The two American-
Helen (Elly)	born offspring
Athanasios (Thanasi) Douropoulos	Father of Constantine
Christina	Mother of Constantine
Their Children:	
Constantine	Theone
Nicholas	John
Panos Regas	Father of Alexandra
Angeliki Regas	Mother of Alexandra
Costakis Thanopoulos	Maternal grandfather of Alexandra
Katerina Karanicholas	Maternal grandmother of Alexandra
Nicoletta	Ancestress of Constantine's mother, Christina
Captain Dimitri Hadjichristos	Godfather of Constantine's mother Christina
Saint Nektarios	Orthodoxy's 20th century Saint, canonized in 1961

ix

Chapter One

One day I would go back again to see the house on Palmer Street. I often wondered if the maple trees that lined the sidewalks were still there. I was waiting for time to ease the memories of childhood pain, to soften the heartaches of youth and most of all, to lighten the sorrows of parting. I was waiting for remembrances to filter gently through the years and render less vivid and overwhelming the panorama of a family in its halcyon days.

As the youngest member of that family, separated from most of my seven siblings by a good many years, I was, at first, more an observer from my special vantage point than a participant within that extraordinary microcosm. It was, in fact, a unique phenomenon in its time and place and way of life. For we were, as far as I know, the first Greek family to live in Arlington, Massachusetts, an old historic New England town settled in 1635 and located six miles northwest of Boston.

Our arrival was of little if any consequence to this middle class suburb, but for the residents of Palmer Street it was undoubtedly a trauma. To have suddenly thrust within their comfortable insularity a family of foreigners, and of all people, Greeks, must have been a fearful threat to the pattern of their subdued, well-regulated lives. And all of it happened so quickly, so unexpectedly. Who could have imagined that Mr. Angus MacNeill, a sensible Scotsman, an elder of the Presbyterian Church, no less, would do anything so unorthodox as to sell his fine old house to a Greek Orthodox priest with a flock of children of all sizes and ages that seemed more like an outlandish tribe than a decent family?

But the die was cast. With typical New England fortitude the inhabitants of that quiet little street accepted the inevitable. Grim but calm, they retreated behind the barricade of their sturdy front porches to the security of their rocking chairs from where they could watch the invasion of the Greeks.

When the Reverend Constantine Douropoulos came to Boston as pastor of the Greek Orthodox Church, he decided to forego the convenience of living close to his parish. Both he and the *Presbytera*, the formal title of a Greek priest's wife, felt that a house in one of the Boston suburbs would be more suitable for their large family.

Most of the Greeks in Boston, who had come to America in the immense surge of immigration during the early part of the nineteen hundreds, were still living in crowded sections of the city. Survival could be insured only by brutal working hours that often began before the light of day and extended into the dark of night. The startling statement carried by letter to those back home that "the sun never shines in America," was more unconsciously poignant than intentionally ironic.

In view of the ordeals that these pioneer immigrants were facing, it was not surprising that they would feel resentful if not envious that their pastor had fled "to the country" where he lived like a squire among the *Amerikanoi*. His parishioners would have been even more acerbic in their criticism had they known that the priest had been elevated from the status of a squire to the office of a bishop by the members of the Arlington Firehouse. A fellow clergyman who was coming to pay a call on Father Douropoulos lost his way and stopped at the firehouse for help.

"I don't know of a Greek priest around here," said one of the firemen, "you must mean the Greek bishop who lives on Palmer Street, just a few blocks from here. I'll show you on the map. It's the third house in on the right. I was there just yester-

2

day for a fire inspection and met the bishop. Fine man, your bishop. Give him my regards—from the Fire Chief," he added pompously.

Father Seraphim Alenopoulos headed for Palmer Street in great distress. The large beak-like nose that dominated his narrow wizened face drooped more than usual towards his straggly beard that now bristled with indignation.

Bishop—*your* bishop! How did Constantine Douropoulos, a mere parish priest and a married one, no less, dare to assume that noble title! What a travesty, what a desecration of the canon laws that demand the vow of celibacy from those appointed hierarchs of the Church!

He would never have believed his old friend capable of such a sacrilege had he not heard it with his very own ears. He wondered with sorrow how it could have happened, how this good man could have been led so far astray. And then he had a revelation—why, of course, it was the Presbytera who had helped to promote this most sinful impression! She was a clever, spirited woman with none of the meekness one expected to find in a cleric's wife . . . a dominating personality that the Reverend Alenopoulos considered unbecoming to a female and particularly offensive in the wife of a priest. Besides such an attractive woman had no business becoming a Presbytera. But in all fairness (for he considered himself a man of dispassionate judgment), he admitted that Mrs. Douropoulos was ever kind and gracious to him or to any guest who enjoyed the festive board of a hostess excelling in the art of Greek hospitality.

But all this largess, that overpowering warmth, that overwhelming charm of hers, he was now beginning to see in a different light. It was but a means of creating a captivating setting for herself and her husband, for her two sons and her six daughters, all of whom sooner or later she would undoubtedly marry off with enviable success.

He shook his head. Women were ambitious and crafty and none were to be trusted—a conclusion he had reached long ago and one that never failed to comfort him.

How wise he had been in his decision to be wedded to The Holy Church! But few outside of the celibate order to which he

3

belonged could appreciate the sacrifices he had made in order to attain the ultra-mundane bliss of this sacred union. He recalled the tail-end of a sickening conversation he had heard by chance between two women who were waiting, ironically enough, for the sacrament of confession. They were apparently discussing some celibate priest or other and amid indecent giggling and snickering one of them said, "It's just as well he's wedded to The Church for what women in her right mind would ever marry such a miserable specimen of manhood?" The other's response was so lewd, so unspeakably profane that Reverend Alenopoulos could not bear to repeat it even within the privacy of his innermost mind.

A tremor passed through his scrawny frame as he thought of those coarse creatures with their monstrous breasts and buttocks and their filthy tongues and souls, maligning some poor priest who had sacrificed his virility in order to serve The Faith in purity.

Riled further by these sordid recollections, the Reverend had gone well beyond Palmer Street. Realizing his error, he angrily retraced his steps and finally arrived at his destination in a most disagreeable state of mind.

Ignoring the customary exchange of cordial greetings that still begin with the ancient Greek salutation χαίρετε, "Rejoice," he returned his host's staunch handclasp by barely extending his cold limpid fingers. And without so much as a word of apology or explanation to the Presbytera for his considerable delay (which had, indeed, jeopardized the perfection of the dinner she had prepared), he directly opened fire.

"Aha, Father Constantine, I wouldn't mind living so far out if I could pass for a *bishop* as you do!"

Father Douropoulos looked puzzled. His friend had anticipated a reaction of feigned surprise and continued with a mordant smile. "I had no idea, of course, of your present exalted status until I was informed of it at the fire station where I stopped to get clearer directions to your house. The Fire Chief himself told me that it was not a Greek priest who lived on Palmer Street but the Greek *Bishop*! He asked me, in fact, to convey his regards 'to your fine *Bishop*.' Those were his words, his very words."

The Reverend was trying desperately to control his voice, but it rose in the air like the phrenetic shriek of a wounded bird, and his long thin nose quivered helplessly. It had actually turned, Mrs. Douropoulos later recalled, into a most peculiar shade of magenta.

The priest's expression of surprise changed to one of shock. For a moment his eyes grew dark with anger and then filled with pity. What an anguished soul this must be to reveal compulsively the consuming guilt of envy, the relentless torment of regret for his irrevocable choice of celibacy—to disclose publicly what properly belonged in the merciful privacy of confession!

The uncomfortable silence that followed was broken by Mrs. Douropoulos. Casting a bewildered glance towards her husband, she asked to be excused so that she might attend to serving dinner. The mention of dinner and, no doubt, an exquisite one such as the Presbytera was capable of producing, had an instantaneous salutary affect on Father Alenopoulos.

"My good Presbytera," he said, in a tone unexpectedly dulcet, "I hope you have not gone to any trouble on my account. The simplest of foods prepared by your hands would be ambrosial!"

Father Douropoulos was amused by the mercurial change in his guest—a minor miracle which he credited to his wife's charisma. Now he could approach and try to clarify the absurd matter which had exploded so senselessly in their midst a few moments ago.

"I must say, Father Seraphim, what you have just reported is the first I have heard of this nonsense. It's a mistake, of course, but made in good faith by an ignorant fireman —ignorant, I mean, of the rules of our religion.* One could hardly expect those outside of our Church to be aware that a Greek Orthodox priest who is married cannot become a bishop or aspire to any

---

*The Greek Church permits candidates for the priesthood to marry *before* ordination. Married clerics may not rise higher than the rank of priesthood. The unmarried may become Archimandrites, the highest order of celibate priesthood from which bishops are usually chosen. The Greek Church recognizes three religious orders: deacons, priests and bishops. Metropolitans, archbishops and patriarchs are, in effect, bishops. The Greek Orthodox Patriarch of the Great Church of Constantinople is regarded as "the first among equals," and is considered the world-wide spiritual leader of Orthodoxy. He still bears the ancient title: His All Holiness, Archbishop of Constantinople, New Rome and Ecumenical Patriarch.

5

higher post above his humble station, and that our prelates are culled only from the ranks of the celibates.''

"Now *I*," continued Father Constantine, as he led his guest towards the dining room, "cannot become a bishop, but at most be mistaken for one, while *you*, my friend, may actually become one."

Father Douropoulos could never be sure whether his words had mollified their guest, or whether the benign, almost seraphic look on his face was due to the sight and aroma of the Presbytera's celebrated "egg-lemon" soup awaiting him on the table.

The words that Father Douropoulos spoke that night were prophetic. His fellow priest's obsessive ambition was fulfilled. In due time, the Reverend Seraphim Alenopoulos became a bishop, and a bitter enemy of Father Douropoulos.

Chapter Two

A short time before the United States entered the First World
War, when the Douropoulos family came to Arlington, only a
few of the large tracts of privately owned land were still operating
as truck garden farms. As early as 1850 this type of agriculture
had been a lucrative source of income for the town. The vegetable
produce from these farms was acknowledged as the finest of its
kind all along the North Atlantic seaboard.

Arlington's proximity to Boston, however, had made the town
a highly desirable suburb. These farmlands inherited by a small
group of descendants from the town's early seventeenth century
settlers were being rapidly and profitably sold for residential purposes. A few of the more astute and fortunate landowners who
could afford the continually increasing taxes were waiting with
a sharp and joyful eye for the most propitious time to sell their
properties at a dazzling profit.

One of the largest of these valuable parcels of land still functioned as a truck garden farm and bordered on Massachusetts
Avenue a few hundred yards south of Palmer Street. It was this
unexpected expanse of dark, rich soil in long, precise furrows
burgeoning with tender heads of lettuce and slender stalks of
celery that enchanted Dionysios when by chance he came across
it. Dion, as he was called outside of his Greek environment, was
the oldest of the priest's children, and he had undertaken the task
of finding a suitable dwelling place for the household. He was a

tall, elegantly slim young man in his mid-twenties. Like his mother, he had clean-cut features, a clear fair skin and a similar shade of medium brown hair and eyes. Dion did not possess, however, his mother's ebullient nature, but had inherited more of his father's quiet, dignified manner which was softened by his youthful amiability and pleasant smile. Yet, when he smiled his eyes remained grave. His female admirers interpreted this peculiarity as appealingly "wistful" or "pensive"—as though, they said, he suffered from some secret unrequited love. But beneath Dion's polished sociability and his romantic air was a brilliant scholarly mind that had yet to find a meaningful or satisfying outlet for his talents.

Since its arrival from Pittsburgh, Pennsylvania, the family was temporarily lodged in cramped quarters at the "Apollo," a small hotel in Boston, whose proprietor was a compatriot and admirer of Father Douropoulos. Along with other prominent members of the Hellenic society of that era, he had successfully arranged the transfer of the priest from the relatively provincial parish in Pittsburgh to the more sophisticated one of Boston. This would be the third and last parish the priest would serve since he had come to America in 1907. He had been sent by the Holy Synod to establish a church in Baltimore, Maryland. Sixty-eight families had settled in that city and had formed a small community whose initial goal was to establish a church of their own. Father Douropoulos organized the church and remained four years in Baltimore until he was assigned to Pittsburgh and after spending another four years there, he was transferred to the Greek Church in Boston. In this superior milieu—for the Greek community of Boston was acknowledged as outstanding in comparison to the other Greek settlements in America—Father Douropoulos' spiritual qualities and worldly wisdom were valuable assets; moreover, he was a handsome man of commanding presence—like an Anglican cleric—who would not affront the aesthetic sensibilities of the proper Bostonians.

Dion was anxious to find a comfortable house for the family. The ultimate choice would, of course, be his parents' but he could spare them the tedious groundwork of locating the proper area and then a suitable place in which to settle. Even if the time and effort involved in the search proved arduous, he would, nevertheless, attend to it conscientiously. The first-born son in the Greek family is committed by tradition to a position of responsibility and trust that demands on his part the concommitants of devotion and loyalty to his parents—to assume, if necessary, their care in illness or old age; he is expected to inspire and guide his younger brothers and to protect and defend, at all cost, the honor of his sisters.

As a result of this special concern for the daughters of the family, it was not unusual to find the oldest son postponing indefinitely and sometimes permanently his own matrimonial aspirations, in order to assure his sisters' marriages in the correct chronological sequence from the oldest to the youngest.

The powerful influence of Hellenic tradition which is continually exerted on the Greek ethos was not in Dion's case mainly responsible for the abiding sense of duty towards his parents. The desire to be of use to them stemmed rather from the great regard he had for his father and the deep affection he felt for his mother. Dion was closer to her in spirit than his sisters, and closer to her in age than he was to his two American-born siblings, Arthur and Elly. Of all the Douropoulos offspring, Dion could best recall his mother as a young woman—a slender vibrant being who captivated his schoolmates and impressed his teachers.

Among those who thought highly of her and honored her by becoming a family friend was the Director of the pre-eminent Rezarios Theological Seminary in Greece which is situated in Athens. Dion had entered and graduated from the Seminary as one of the youngest and brightest students during the Directorship of Bishop Nektarios Kefalas, Titular Metropolitan of Pentapolis. Now he is revered as SAINT NEKTARIOS—an Orthodox Saint proclaimed in the twentieth century a few decades after his death.

This friendship was to have a profound effect on the lives of Alexandra and Constantine and their children.

The moment he mentioned it Dion realized he had made a mistake to announce he was going househunting that morning.

His sisters instantly pounced on him like a flock of magpies, clattering that one of them, at least, should accompany him on so important a mission. Only Angela, the oldest of the girls, did not join the cacophany.

Angela had been christened *Angeliki*, which in Greek means "angelic." No other name could have suited her better. Angela moved in a gentle, innocent world of her own with a delicate grace that set her apart from her more worldly sisters and from the eager nubile maidens of those days. The appeal of her chaste femininity prompted the most eligible bachelors to seek her hand in marriage.

But those who sang her praises the loudest were the libertines in the Greek community which had its share of the married and unmarried species. For them Angela represented the ideal of pure womanhood, the fair vision of a *virgo intacta*. This recognition of her worth was comforting proof to them and adequate evidence for the *cosmos*, the Greek expression for people at large, that they could still discriminate between the gold and the dross.

Dion would have gladly chosen Angela to join him, but if he made a concession in favor of one of his sisters he feared he might end up escorted by a convoy. To avoid such a disaster, Dion flatly rejected his sisters' demands.

In the momentary lull that followed Dion's blunt refusal, Mrs. Douropoulos found, at last, an opening to express her views. She had tried to take command of the situation but to her chagrin her voice, vigorous as it was, failed in this instance to rise above the concerted vocality of her five grown-up daughters. She was about to make herself heard when her husband entered the room with two Greek newspapers, the *Atlantis* and the *National Herald*, tucked under his arm. For a Greek the perusal of a newspaper, or as many as he can possibly lay his hands on, is a time-honored ritual faithfully observed each day up to the time of his demise.

He was greeted with a courteous but somewhat dispirited chorus of "Good morning, Babá." His children were not in the habit of addressing him as "father" but by the less staid equivalent of "babá," an indication that their tender affection for him was not overshadowed by his innate dignity or by the

10

respect which the cloth he wore commanded.

He sensed a tension in the atmosphere. He glanced around him and only his son, Dion, appeared to be at ease. Whatever the problem might be, Father Douropoulos wanted no part of it. He would find some other spot in the hotel where he could read his paper in peaceful solitude. But before he had a chance to escape, his daughters with the exception of Angela, surrounded him and started in unison to air their grievances and decry their brother's stubborn stand.

This display of sisterly solidarity did not elicit any support, or even a word of response from their father. As a result, his daughters' frustrations increased and their voice mounted to a dissonant crescendo—a deplorable performance that offended the Reverend's finer sensibilities. All he had wanted was a place to pursue his reading in peace, and instead he had blundered into a gynaeceum of malcontent females.

The Presbytera glanced apprehensively at her husband. He had, she would sigh, a sharp but fortunately short-lived temper— the only flaw in an otherwise exemplary disposition. She conceded gratefully, however, that this was a relatively minor failing in view of the equanimity and benevolence he exercised in a household of a dozen or so individuals, the greater part of whom were members of the distaff side. The Reverend and his two sons, Dion and Arthur, were the only males in the family; the rest consisted of his wife, six daughters, a maid who was considered part of the familial unit, and, at any given time, one and sometimes two unmarried female relatives. The Presbytera felt a responsibility towards any of her kinswomen who, for one reason or another, had difficulty in finding a husband. She would take them into her fold until such time as she could arrange a suitable match for them. All Greeks have a talent for matchmaking. The Presbytera had a genius for it.

Annoyed as he may have been, Father Douropoulos had no intention of losing his temper. It was hardly worth risking the enjoyment of reading his paper by upsetting himself over this puerile outburst of his daughters. They were normally respectful and considerate, and their father was grateful in having been blessed with six healthy, virtuous girls. He had heard them praised

11

more than once as "the priest's bright and beautiful daughters." But he did not allow himself to succumb to pride at these "encomia." He felt rather a deep sense of gratitude for the qualities his children had thus far displayed. As a father confessor he knew only too well how easily, how swiftly, the fragile equilibrium of morality could be destroyed in a reckless moment of passion.

The Greeks, on the whole, refrain from extolling their possessions and attainments, and, especially, from exulting in the God-given gifts of their children. Beneath this respect for the Christian virtues of humility and modesty lies a haunting ancestral fear of *hubris*—the sin of overweening pride that aroused the relentless wrath of the pagan gods. The ancient Greek tragedies remain as terrifying testimonials of the nemesis awaiting those who dare to indulge in arrogance.

Father Douropoulos decided not to break his silence. It would be wiser to leave before the effect of his wordless presence wore off and someone or other broke the blessed quietude that for the moment prevailed. He caught his son's eye and gave him an understanding nod and a conspiratorial wink, then with magesterial dignity made his exit and closed the door firmly behind him.

A perfect pantomime, thought Dion, the way his father had quelled a rising rebellion without uttering a single word. He glanced at his mother who seemed disconcerted rather than pleased at her husband's performance. She did not consider the "silent treatment" an effective method of discipline. She believed silence created ambiguity since it could be interpreted as approval or disapproval. She preferred to make her stand perfectly clear by *speaking* her mind. Besides, she considered silence an affront to God who had blessed mankind with the gift of speech.

It is unlikely that a Greek had coined the phrase "silence is golden," for, on the whole, Greeks are a highly articulate peo-
~d Alexandra was no exception. She would have been con-
·he episode in *The Education of Henry Adams* regard-
˜ President Adams towards his young grand-
⁄ against going to school one hot summer
ntleman who was close to eighty at the time

12

had taken the boy's hand without saying a word and walked with him for nearly a mile over a shadeless road and did not stop until the boy was seated inside the school. "He had shown no temper, no irritation, no personal feeling, and had made no display of force. Above all, he had held his tongue."

That was the last thing that poor old man should have done—to hold his tongue—Alexandra would have said. He had foolishly risked getting a sunstroke or apoplexy at his advanced age when a few firm words or even a good many of them, if necessary, would have saved him a dangerous trip by making that little rascal of a grandson come to his senses.

Although Alexandra was most anxious to give her daughters a piece of her mind, she restrained herself admirably. She waited a few moments in deference to her husband's impressive departure before she gave a deep sigh and exclaimed, "Po, po, po!" an expression by which the Greeks vent their dismay. She had a naturally husky voice that gave it a dramatic quality, especially in contrast to the high-pitched tones the provincially bred females of her time cultivated as a sign of gentility.

She paused and looked reproachfully at her daughters. None of them, however, seemed particularly uneasy or remorseful. Irked by their apparent lack of contrition, she resorted to sarcasm in the hope of stinging them into shame. "*Euge*, well done, my girls! You certainly showed your father how much respect and affection you have for him. Ah, yes, he was so moved at the way you crowded around him, the one trying to outdo the other in your solicitude for his comfort, he couldn't speak and left the room overwhelmed by your concern for him."

Dion saw his two younger sisters, Katina and Christine, exchange glances. They are amused, thought Dion, at their mother's heavy-handed sarcasm. The truth was, he admitted, she was inept in its use, for she lacked spitefulness or bitterness on which sarcasm can be finely honed.

Angela was the only one who took polite notice of her mother's remarks and took the trouble to respond to them. "Mother, you know we all love Bábá and respect him more than anyone else. We didn't force him to go elsewhere to read his papers. Even at home he always went to his study when he wanted to read.''

It was typical of Angela to defend her younger sisters in the face of her mother's disapproval of their actions. She was by far the kindest, the gentlest, the sweetest of the sisters, but not at the price of meekness or blandness; she had a mind and convictions of her own that despite the softness of her disposition were to prove in the near future strong enough to resist the most vigorous pressures.

It suddenly struck Dion that his mother's powerful personality had not inhibited the development of a decided individuality which each of her daughters possessed. Their good looks and vigor, of course, helped them to maintian a certain poise and confidence. The three older sisters, Angela, Sophia, and Demetra, were undeniably beauties in full bloom; the two younger ones, Katina and Christine, although still in the awkward stage of mid-adolescence were following closely in their older sisters' footsteps. As for Elly, ''the baby'' of the family, it was too early to pass any judgment, but one thing about her was certain; of all of his sisters, she was the closest to her mother's heart. But it wasn't fair, thought Dion, to give his mother all the credit for the attributes with which her daughters were endowed. His father was an exceptionally handsome man who had an impressive amount of elegance and grace. And if his children possessed these qualities to a considerable extent (which in all honesty he had to admit was the case) they were beholden to their father for them.

Dion could not but attribute the prepotency of vitality to his mother which her offspring had inherited in some degree or other. Yet, the amount of energy she had retained was still by far greater than that which all of her children had collectively acquired from her. Dion had arrived at a point from which he could see his mother as a person and not simply as a parent (a point which only his youngest two siblings, Arthur and Elly, would eventually reach). He now realized that his mother possessed an infinite amount of vitality which in turn had produced in her an enormous *élan vital*—a quality that is universally recognized and admired. In his reading Dion had come across Herbert Spencer whose statement that ''men's character must be in part determined by their visceral structures" was clearly applicable to his mother. The powerful physique she had acquired through natural selection of hardy Arcadian mountaineer stock functioned superbly. But her physical vitality accounted only in part for her character. She also possessed a strong and simple faith in the greatness of God and the goodness of man. These two gifts, one physical and the other spiritual, had combined to create in Dion's mother a powerful force which operated steadily throughout her lengthy life.

Dion was beginning to understand why his mother was described time and again as "a most remarkable woman."

Mrs. Douropoulos appeared to take no notice of her eldest daughter's comments, but Dion noted that his mother fell back from her first line of attack to a second line of defense which usually consisted of praise for other peoples' children. It did her heart good, she said, when she visited some stranger's home on a mission of mercy. The Presbytera could always be counted on to offer whatever help she could to any parishioner in need. Yes, it did her heart good to see the love and respect, the devotion and consideration that these children, these "angels," as she called them, showered on their poor parents who could not give them any of the advantages that more fortunate parents could provide for their offspring.

This time the two younger sisters went further than exchanging glances. Katina giggled outright when Christine declaimed *sotto voce*, "How sharper than a serpent's tooth it is to have such thankless daughters." Dion could not resist grinning at his sister's paraphrase. Shakespeare had not been wasted on her, he thought.

Their mother heard but did not understand what was said since her English was limited. She was about to rebuke the two girls for their rudeness when she saw Dion look at his watch and start for the door. The sisters saw this as a sign to disband. But before Christine had a chance to escape, her mother gave her a Parthian shot: "You seem to have forgotten—in *this* family we speak Greek," and turned hurriedly toward her son.

"Wait a minute, Dionysios," she cried, lest her son leave on his mission without one or two good wishes which abound in the

15

Greek language for every conceivable occasion or event.

"May the good hour be with you, my boy, and help you find a nice little house for us."

"I don't think a 'little house' would do for us," said Dion with a smile, "but don't worry, something sooner or later will show up now that I have narrowed the search to Arlington." Dion had come to Boston several weeks ahead of the family to find a house worth buying. His father had decided it was about time to stop paying out money for another man's property.

"I have to take Elly to the dentist again this afternoon, otherwise I would go along with you. That would have put a stop to all the fuss your sisters made."

"Where are the children?" asked Dion, "I haven't seen them around this morning." The "children" specifically meant Arthur and Elly, the two youngest members of the family and the only ones who were born in America. Elly's five older sisters were referred to as "the girls" and Dion was simply Dion or Dionysios as he was called by his parents.

"Oh, the children—they've gone to get some milk with Eleni. Now that there's so little for her to do in the hotel, Eleni has taken full charge of them."

"They couldn't be in better hands," said Dion. "She's so devoted to them—to all of us," he added. "By the way, I'll be glad to take Arthur with me since he doesn't have to see the dentist."

"He will prefer to stay with Elly; he's worried that the dentist will hurt her. You know those two are practically inseparable! But Dr. Lydakis won't hurt her. He is so gentle and considerate and polite, you can't imagine. How nice it is to have a Greek dentist available right here in Boston!"

Dion looked again at his watch. "It's getting late . . . if you will excuse me, mother . . . I have to be in Arlington by noon to look at a house that just came on the market, and I want to see it."

His mother interrupted him hastily. "Must you go *today*?" she asked in an anxious tone.

"Yes, of course. I have an appointment with Mr. Hilliard, a real estate agent, to see a house in Arlington. But why," he asked, "Why did you say 'must you go today'?"

"Today is Tuesday," she answered gravely.

"Yes, I know it's Tuesday. But what's wrong with Tuesday, if you don't mind telling me?"

"It's the day of ill omen," replied his mother.

"Tuesday? I thought Friday was a day of bad luck . . . but Tuesday?"

She answered solemnly. "It's considered as bad, if not worse than Friday. Have you forgotten what happened to the Greeks on that ill-fated day?"

Dion suddenly realized what she meant and burst out laughing. "Oh, mother, you are priceless, you and all the Greeks who still mourn the 'Fall of Constantinople' on Tuesday the 29th of May in 1453!"

"You may laugh, my boy, but let me tell you, our forefathers did not think it was funny when the infidel conquered our land on that wretched day."

Dion tried to control his laughter when he realized his mother was upset because he made fun of a tradition apparently respected in the past. "I promise you, mother, if you and father should like the house I am going to see today, we'll make sure, if you decide to buy it that it won't be on a *Tuesday.*"

"Now, don't waste your time trying to cajole me! You better run along if you don't want to be late." She couldn't resist adding one more wish: "*Sto kalo*"—in other words, "Go and may 'the good' be with you."

Dion watched his mother march down the corridor in her usual brisk fashion with shoulders straight and head held high. The weight she had added since the birth of her last two offspring did not detract from the litheness or the swiftness of her steps; it had replaced the slim lines of her youthful years with a womanliness befitting the wife of a cleric and the mother of eight children. Although she was a little above average in height her naturally elegant carriage gave one the impression she was tall and stately. She was already in her middle years but her face had not lost any of its early freshness and her skin was as fine as that which a young girl less than half her age would covet. She had the typical leucomelanous coloring of the Arcadian highlanders—

a fair skin combined with brown eyes and hair which in her instance was fine but thick and which she wore throughout her adult life coiled around the top of her head like a crown. It had been the color of honey in her early youth, but slowly turned to brown as she grew older. Not until she was nearly eighty years old did her hair become white without the usual interim of gray—a curious, lovely kind of white with a pronounced golden cast to it, a phenomenon she explained as a reversion to her girlhood when she was considered a beautiful blonde.

Although Alexandra was a very handsome woman up to the end of her long life, she lacked the narcissism often found in those who possess, or believe they possess, pulchritude. Nevertheless, in her old age she relished the memories of her youthful charms which had brought her a husband (and what a husband!) without the benefit of matchmakers who flourished in her day.

The morning was still young and the Reverend had no trouble finding a quiet corner with a comfortable chair in the hotel lobby. A splendid spot for reading, since it was practically hidden from view by a rubber plant that stood a few feet away. It had grown to a monstrous size under the personal ministrations of Mr. Solon Macris, proprietor of the Apollo Hotel. He held the ungainly plant in high regard, for he believed it gave the establishment a certain "class."

The priest normally had an aversion to such gross vegetation. He had developed a simple, orderly taste from his youth when he had served as a *dokimos*, a novice, in the ancient Arcadian monastery of St. John the Forerunner, and later at the Tripolis Seminary where nothing pretentious, superfluous or exaggerated met the eye—only the honest beauty of simplicity. But he forgave the grotesque plant, in this instance, for it afforded him privacy from the well-meaning interruptions of passers-by. He made his way to a chair but when he sat down, instead of reading his papers he tossed them aside on a nearby table. Since the family's arrival in Boston a few days ago, he had not had a moment to call his own. This was the first opportunity to sit quietly by himself with his thoughts that demanded attention rather than distraction.

His mind went back to the minor crisis he had witnessed a few moments ago. Obviously his children's contentiousness was the result of fatigue. The upheaval involved in moving a considerable distance had taken a toll of all the family save for his wife—may God keep her well—whose vigor was phenomenal. Their present confinement in the small hotel added, as well, to a general state of irritability. The panacea for this strain was, of course, obvious—a roomy, comfortable house of their own. That was a matter Dion could handle far more ably than any one else in the family. He had a greater grasp of "the American way" than his sisters—or his mother, whose world was and would remain Greek to the core. Furthermore, his son had mastered to an admirable degree the English language and spoke it with the grace and style that marks a man of letters.

While attending the Rizarios Theological Seminary in Athens, Dion had undertaken on his own to learn the English language. His reason for doing so was based on a nebulous hope that one day he would go to America where his father's two younger brothers had migrated several years ago. This hope materialized far sooner than he had anticipated when his Uncle Nicholas offered him a trip to America as a present for graduating with high honors from the Seminary.

Dion had expected to stay only a few months in America before returning home to further his education at the University of Athens. But "the changes and chances of this mortal life" radically altered Dion's plans for the future when his father made the irrevocable decision to enter the priesthood.

In less than a year from the time Dion's holiday began, the Reverend Constantine Douropoulos sailed from Patras, Greece, in May 1907 with his family on the Austro-American boat, *S. S. Sophia Hohenzollern*, and arrived in Baltimore, Maryland, to serve his compatriots as one of the first Greek Orthodox priests in the New World.

As soon as the family had settled, Dion became concerned as to how he could best acquire a sound American education. As a Baltimore resident, he was eligible for a Baltimore City Senatorial Scholarship which would be most helpful financially. His father, born in 1858, was now almost fifty years old, and he alone was carrying the burden of providing for a large family in an alien world on an income determined by the precarious earnings from a humble community of struggling immigrants. Even with the limited aid of the pension he received for his twenty-five years of service in the teaching profession, Dion marveled how his parents maintained a relatively high standard of living. Their incredible courage inspired him to apply for a scholarship at St. John's College in Annapolis, Maryland, where he would enrich his knowledge of English and increase his chances of entering an American university.

Dion's essay entitled *Et in Arcadia Ego* won him a scholarship at St. John's college. The following year he entered John Hopkins in Baltimore, Maryland, as a medical student. The desire to become a doctor had taken hold of him.

The newspapers were forgotten as Father Douropoulos' mind leafed through those early years of the past decade when he had brought his family to America. Dion was a mere youth then, yet all of them had depended on him in a thousand different ways. Without Dion's help the family's adjustment in that early period of transition from an old world to a new one, would have been infinitely harder to bear.

Constantine's affection for his son and the appreciation of his worth did not efface but intensified a sense of sadness that this firstborn son, the most promising thus far of his offspring, had yet to find a direction to his life. This was his hidden sorrow compounded by a sense of remorse that the expectations which they had for Dion and the demands they had made on him, proved to be excessive. For within two years after the family's arrival in America Dion's health broke down. He withdrew from the Medical School, his world shattered—and with it the world of dreams that a father and mother had nurtured for their son.

A routine physical examination during Dion's second year as a medical student at Johns Hopkins revealed that he was suffering from pulmonary tuberculosis. This insidious disease which up to the end of the first decade of this century was the foremost cause of death in the United States and in Europe, condemned most of its prey to a limited reprieve to be suffered in isolation. Its contagiousness was such as to annihilate whole families and entire villages, as well. The only means known, at the time, to escape further contagion, was to segregate the consumptive as completely as possible. This procedure was as cruel for those who were required to enforce it as for those on whom it was enforced.

Father Douropoulos was not only deeply disturbed by his son's condition, but also greatly concerned as to the effect this sudden blow would have on his wife. Alexandra had experienced first hand the fearful havoc wrought by "the white plague," for it had caused the death of her favorite brother, Leonidas—and in its tragic aftermath had claimed her father's life.

Leonidas had gone to Russia where he had prospered as a wheat merchant. After an absence of fifteen years, he returned to his birthplace, unaware that he had contracted tuberculosis.

Within a year of his homecoming, Leonidas died. After the funeral his father undertook the task of reducing to ashes Leonidas' clothing and personal belongings.* One by one he cast them to the flames until he came to the fur coat that Leonidas had brought as a gift to him—a much too elegant gift, his father had protested. At his son's insistence, he tried it on. It fitted him to perfection, for he had the same tall, lean frame as his son. He could not remember how the matter had ended, but it no longer mattered. The old man held the coat in his trembling arms, pressing it close to him as he had done when he had embraced his son on that long awaited hour of his return. He closed his eyes and threw it into the blazing fire. The sickening smell of burning skin and hair enveloped him, and with a moan he fell to the ground. A few days later he was buried beside his son. These tragic events did not, however, weaken Alexandra's valiant spirit which faithfully served her for a lifetime that spanned two centuries for nearly a hundred years.

In the dark days that followed the verdict on Dion's state of health, his mother was sustained by prayer and hope—the hope that "the spot" on Dion's lung was not an indication of tuberculosis, but the result of pneumonia he had suffered as a child. Dr. Pournaras, a kinsman of Alexandra's, had taken care of Dion at the time. She was confident that if he could examine her son

---

*This grim procedure became unnecessary with the subsequent knowledge that the tubercle bacilli could be rendered harmless by a few hours exposure to sunlight.

he would not condemn him so readily as a consumptive. Her trust in this doctor was not unwarranted, for his reputation as a diagnostician had become legendary throughout the Peloponnesos.

Arrangements were made for Dion's return to Greece to undergo a series of tests and examinations to be administered by Dr. Pournaras and his colleagues.

The ceaseless prayers and supplications were answered by the doctor's report: No evidence of tuberculosis had been indicated. But what concerned him now, wrote the doctor, was Dionysios' dispiritedness which, he believed, was responsible for the loss of appetite and the ensuing loss of weight. He recommended that Dion remain in Greece for several months—specifically in the Arcadian village where he was born, where "the invigorating mountain air and its rugged beauty are the finest balm for body and soul." The doctor knew whereof he spoke, for as he reminded his young patient, " *'Et in Arcadia ego'*— I, too, come from Arcadia."

Dion was of a different mind, however. He would return to America and put an end to his parasitical existence by earning his keep or, a least, part of it until he felt stronger. For the present he could do some tutoring since he was proficient both in Greek and English. He had already been asked by Dr. Miller, a professor of classics at Johns Hopkins, to give him lessons in Modern Greek. He knew the language of the dead Greeks, the professor said, but wanted to learn the language of the living ones. Dion also hoped to find among his emigrated countrymen those who, as a matter of pride or necessity, wished to improve their English or Greek. And surely he would be able to relieve his father of the additional duties that he would soon be expected to undertake. For after the members of a Greek community establish a House of God, their next objective is an afternoon parochial school, so that their children would learn to read and write in Greek. The parishioners had given what they could spare, and often what they could not afford to spare for a church; and they had no means to hire a teacher, let alone finding a competent one among the immigrant population. Dion would not only be helping his father but the small and admirably ambitious Greek community of Baltimore.

As for furthering his own education, under the existing circumstances, Dion could not consider it—later, perhaps—but at the present time it was out of the question.

The family was overjoyed at Dion's return without a Damoclean sword over his head. But when his mother expressed concern about his future, Father Douropoulos would remind his wife that the Lord had answered their prayers. For His infinite mercy they should be everlastingly grateful; to ask for more of Him was to commit the shameful sin of ingratitude.

The Priest's somber recollections were interrupted by the sound of Dion's footsteps, which came to a halt in front of a full-length mirror in the lobby. From the well-hidden corner where his father had taken refuge, he could see his son appraising his appearance. He was apparently satisfied with it, save for the way he wore his hat. He removed it and replaced it carefully at a rakish angle and went on his way.

The father watched this little vignette with amusement and, no less, with pleasure. His son seemed relaxed and cheerful, without a trace of that manqué expression that cut his father to the quick whenever he caught sight of it on Dion's sensitive face.

With a smile Father Douropoulos reached for one of the newspapers, but his smile faded as he read of the political situation in Greece. The rift between the Liberals, who supported Venizelos, and the Royalists, who stood steadfast by the Crown, was growing wider day by day. The Church was already becoming involved since Orthodoxy was a state religion, and as such was inextricably connected with the changing fortunes of the government. This conflict was bound to affect, as well, the Hellenic communities in the New World, for the ties of the Greek immigrants with their birthplace were still fresh and strong. Indeed, they were stronger than ever. The prodigious patriotism the Greeks normally possess was intensified to an almost mystical ferver in the expatriated by their very absence from the motherland.

In a gesture close to weariness, the priest threw the newspapers in the waste basket. He could not afford to dissipate time nor

23

energy anticipating the disasters that would tear asunder the burgeoning Orthodox communities in America and traumatize their priests. His foremost duty was to serve the Greek community of Boston to the best of his ability with the hope that Divine Providence would guide him and his countrymen on the road to righteousness.

Chapter Three

The house Mr. Hilliard wanted Dion to see was a short walk from Arlington Center. It was located on Palmer Street off of Massachusetts Avenue, a main artery that led to Boston. Trolley cars ran on this avenue from Harvard Square in Cambridge to Arlington Heights and were the means of dependable transportation to and from the city.

Palmer Street had an air of genteel respectability dear to the heart of suburban Americans in the early years of the twentieth century. It was a short street—pleasant, quiet, and tidy and flanked on either side by evenly spaced and evenly trimmed maple trees. Their symmetrical forms reminded Dion of the patterns children cut out from multi-folded paper that open into rows of identical designs. The sizeable but unpretentious clapboard houses were well-built and well kept. All of them could boast of front and back porches, neat lawns and orderly gardens which revealed the pride of private ownership.

The house with the FOR SALE sign stood on a double-sized lot halfway up the street from the corner of Massachusetts Avenue where the trolley car stop was conveniently located. The high pitched roof, the corner bay windows, and a porch that wrapped around two sides of the house gave it a somewhat Victorian flavor. Its owner, Mr. Angus MacNeil, was sitting in his wicker rocking chair on the shady side of the porch. Although Fiona had ruled he was not to smoke before mealtime, Angus was puffing away at his pipe, more from pique than pleasure. He had words with his wife after Mr. Hilliard telephoned to say he was bringing over a "good" prospect—the son of a Greek priest anxious to settle his family in Arlington. They would be coming a little before noon, he said, and hung up hurriedly.

"The nerve of him!" Fiona exclaimed. "You should have told him he's wasting his time if he thinks we'd sell our house to foreigners."

"Their money is as good as anyone else's," snapped Angus. He didn't care where it came from, Angus went on to say, as long as he was paid in honest American dollars. And she had better not care either if she wanted to move to New Jersey and buy a little bungalow near their son. . . . Hadn't he tried for months to sell the house on their own to save a broker's fee? All she had done was to snivel and squawk until he was forced to turn it over to a real estate agent. But she needn't worry about Harry Hilliard catering to riff-raff. He was a brother Kiwanian. They were both among the first to join the newly established Kiwanis Club in Arlington, whose members, he reminded her, are pledged to play the game "fair and square" and to follow the Golden Rule . . . and, to come right down to it, what was wrong about selling their house to a Greek priest, he wanted to know.

He'd know well enough, his wife retorted, if he ever saw one! Well, she had seen a picture of a Greek priest in some newspaper or magazine; he had a long black beard and he was wearing a long black robe and the strangest black thing on his head like a stove pipe, really, a stovepipe, she declared, with a nervous little laugh.

"That's what they wear in the old country, I suppose. But if they've got the guts to wear that sort of garb in this country that's their business. It's the land of the brave and the home of the free, isn't it?"

She had made him uneasy. She could tell from the way his square jaw protruded defensively. But Fiona knew better than to goad her husband further to a point of intractable stubbornness; she, therefore, gave way somewhat by saying: "I don't suppose it would do any harm if the Greek priest's son looked at the place. We've had plenty of lookers and one more won't matter." But she had no intention, she declared, of staying around to do the honors. And soon after she flounced out of the house with her large straw shopping bag and headed for the stores at Arlington Center, which was but a few blocks north of Palmer Street.

By the time she returned, the realtor and his client had come and gone and Angus seemed to be in the best of spirits. "You just missed a fine young man," he remarked amiably, "in his mid-twenties, I'd say. He's a neat, good-looking chap, well dressed, nothing flashy, you know—must be a decent fellow—looking around for a house to save the old folks the trouble. That's more than I've seen any lads doing around here these days."

"So you were taken with him, and you didn't discourage him, did you?" asked Fiona.

He avoided her question by saying that the young man seemed taken with the house and he would be bringing his parents over tomorrow to look at it.

This time, announced Fiona grimly, *she* would stay around to see for herself. If that priest looked anything like the picture she had seen of one, she would refuse to sign any contract or whatever she would have to sign in selling the house. Had he forgotten that the house was in *her* name?

"Don't get excited, girlie, they may be just lookers, as you say. Besides, judging from the son, I guess they're pretty classy folks and maybe this house won't do for the likes of them," said Angus shaking his head in studied skepticism.

She did not deign to respond to so patently ridiculous a supposition, but she gave him her most withering look. After the deed for the property on Palmer Street had been "signed, sealed and delivered," the MacNeills informed their neighbors that the purchaser was Father Constantine Douropoulos, a Greek Orthodox priest.

Palmer Street consisted of a homogeneous assortment of New Englanders who had the capacity to deal realistically with disaster. They soon absorbed the painful fact that the alien force which had found its way to their street might remain indefinitely in their midst. Fortunately, there were certain aspects of this foreign family which helped to mitigate somewhat the blow of this unexpected visitation. Judging from their appearance, at any rate, these Greeks were not the usual lowly type of immigrants. The dignified bearing of the priest also helped to allay some of the prevailing fears.

The members of the distaff side of Palmer Street were happy to note that whenever the Reverend met them, or in passing by as they sat on their porches, he did not merely tip his hat but bowed as he removed it from his head; and a fine head it was with silver hair that curled gently in the back over his Roman collar, and with a neatly groomed beard which gave him a distinguished air.

The priest's clothes were apparently custom made, for they did not conform to contemporary fashion. Except on warm days when he wore a sack-type suit made of a fine, silky, black material, his usual attire was impeccably tailored in the style of a Prince Albert frock coat. It would have appeared outmoded and a bit theatrical on another man, but it befitted him and seemed perfectly suitable for the gold-crowned ebony cane His Reverence habitually carried.

This worldly exterior, however, belied the sacerdotal qualities Father Douropoulos possessed. His priestliness was manifest at home when he discarded his secular apparel in favor of the *rason*—a long black robe somewhat similar to the Anglican or Catholic cassock. In this traditional vestment of the Greek Orthodox priest, he looked more like a patriarchal figure than the urbane cleric he appeared to his American neighbors.

He had a particular affection for this garment; he once wore a small version of it as a poor, motherless boy at the monastery where he had been placed by his father; he had worn a similar one when he studied at the Tripolis Theological Seminary. Following his graduation from the seminary he entered the Teachers' College in Athens, and thus the rason was laid aside. It came into use again when, after twenty-five years in the teaching profession, he was ordained by the Metropolitan of Pentapolis, the future Saint Nektarios. The friendship and guidance of this holy man was the essential inspiration which led Constantine to become a servant of God.

No one else, however, went as far as Dolly Endicott, the only divorcée in the neighborhood and well beyond it, to state that the Greek priest was one of the most elegant men she had seen in a long time—on Palmer Street, of all places! Thereby implying she had come across a number of such men in her day but hardly expected to find one in so parochial a milieu as her present one.

Dolly had always been prone to exaggerated statements and dramatic actions. Her transgressions were nevertheless forgiven, including her status as a divorcée even though the time had yet to come when a divorce would not be considered a social or moral stigma but a symbol of emancipated womanhood. After all, she was one of them, indeed, one of the best of their breed as far as her "Mayflower" ancestry was concerned. Besides, she had atoned for her reckless marriages by returning to the fold and devoting herself in taking care of her ailing mother.

The priest's wife was also an object of interest and of conjecture, as well. Some of the neighbors thought that Alexandra must be the priest's second wife—most likely the mother of the two or three younger daughters and of the two youngest children. She looked more like a sister than a parent of the older girls and the older son. They would not, however, have entertained this suspicion had they known that the Greek Church does not permit a widowed priest to remarry, nor by tradition rather than tenet may the widow of a Greek priest enter into a second marriage.

Although Alexandra could be judged fairly only within the natural framework of her Greek environment, yet the compelling qualities of her personality were evident even to those who merely chanced to see her at any place and at any time. From what her neighbors saw of her at a distance, as it were, she impressed them as being eminently well-suited as the cleric's wife and mother of his eight children.

The ample size of the priest's family raised, however, one question in particular. Wasn't it an unseemly number of children for a man of the cloth to have fathered? For Dolly Endicott this question was tainted with puritanical hypocrisy that exasperated her to the point of declaring, "Oh, for heaven's sake, what do you expect from a virile man, priest or not, who's married to a woman with all that vitality? These are warm-blooded human beings, and you may be sure it's not ice water that flows in *their* veins!''

The good ladies of Palmer Street tacitly agreed to overlook these gross remarks on so delicate a subject. Poor Dolly, who knows what suffering had prompted them? If only she would curb her tongue and not give cause for low-minded gossips to bandy about their titillating suspicions as to why her marriage had been so unsatisfactory.

The absorption with the divorcée's "private" life, or rather the reasons for its dissatisfaction, were, at the moment, of less interest than the present occupants of the MacNeill house. Their endless comings and goings, the constant flow of activity and the continual appearances of new faces made it difficult for the neighbors to ascertain who was who and what was what. Fortunately Bessie Potter, who lived directly opposite them, could be of help. Due to a bad hip, the poor soul was confined most of the time to a chair in the front of her living room bay window or to her wicker rocker on the porch when the weather permitted.

Mrs. Potter viewed the arrival of the Greek family as a blessing or, at least, a mixed blessing. For one thing it opened up fresh vistas on her weary horizon. After all, there was a limit to crocheting doilies and antimacassars to while away the hours. Besides, they were going out of style. She had guessed as much from the strained thanks she received of late when giving away these little "labors of love" as bridal shower gifts or simply as small remembrances to her dear friends.

Nevertheless, she could appreciate her neighbors' alarm. In all honesty, she, too, was dismayed when she first heard that foreigners were about to invade their territory. She was surprised when Fiona MacNeill had brought her a plateful of scones, simply delicious ones, something she was not in the habit of doing; indeed, she had never done so before. She had refused a cup of freshly made S. S. Pierce coffee which, if Bessie Potter had to say so, was far superior to the A&P or the S. K. Ames brand regularly brewed by the residents of Palmer Street. Her late husband would often remind her: "Bess, don't settle for the second-rate when you can get the first-rate even if it costs a bit more." What a wise, generous man he was!

Fiona had declared she couldn't stop for even a sip, much as she would like to, but there was so much to be done now that their place had been sold. Oh, yes, they had sold it the day before yesterday, in fact—to a Greek family. She had given this incredible piece of news over her shoulder, so to speak, as she darted across the street towards her house. "Do be sure to heat up the scones before trying them," she cried out from her front door and then disappeared from sight before Mrs. Potter could say "Jack Robinson."

Well, it was quite a shock, of course, yet some good had surely come of it. Not that Bessie Potter was thinking only selfishly of the pleasurable excitement that the newcomers were bringing into her lonely life, but of the salutary effect their sudden presence had exerted on the street as a whole. Their arrival had brought the neighborhood together in a solidarity such as she had not witnessed heretofore. Only when her Edwin had passed away and at the same time she was laid low by a broken hip did she have practically as many callers as she had now, concerned at the distress "those people" across the street must be causing her.

Bessie Potter, unlike her outspoken neighbor, Dolly Endicott, did not have the courage to antagonize the Establishment in which she was born and bred, nor did she desire to express views that varied considerably from those of the majority of Dalton Street's residents. They were kind and decent people who had rallied 'round her only a few months ago when she was racked by pain and grief. Yet, for all the mildness of her nature Bessie Potter was not lacking in Yankee shrewdness, which led her to give a somewhat ambiguous report on the Douropoulos family that she hoped would emphasize neither partiality nor prejudice.

So far, they really hadn't bothered her, she said, but time would tell. People put their best foot forward, you may be sure, when they first came to a new neighborhood. But they were, she admitted, a gregarious lot. Something going on all the while at that house. Nothing untoward, you understand, at least, as far as she could see, but then she went to bed early. Yet, one shouldn't be surprised by all that activity in a household with five, lively, grown-up daughters and that nice-looking older son. Besides, the father was a clergyman and perhaps the Greeks expected their churchmen to keep their door open day and night as, indeed, it seemed to be. Naturally, she was only guessing since she knew nothing about Greek customs and traditions.

But the one thing she did know—what a talkative people they were! She couldn't help hearing them when she hobbled outside to water her morning glories or when she sat on her front porch, for a spell, to get a breath of fresh air. They were forever chattering away in their native tongue—even the two youngest ones. The little girl was as cute as a button and a real chatterbox. The little boy, he was a quiet one, a shy little fellow, but as beautiful a child as she had ever seen—with those big, thoughtful, brown eyes and that curly, chestnut-colored hair. He was such a sweet child and he didn't seem spoiled but, of course, she couldn't tell from the little she had seen of him. It would be a wonder, though, if he wasn't pampered, coming after so many girls. To tell the truth, she added with a wistful sigh, she might very well have been tempted to spoil such a lovely child if she had been blessed with one herself. . . . It really was something, she continued, the way they could change from one language to the other—in a flash—although she gathered that they did not speak English in the presence of their parents. And how fast they all talked! For the life of her she couldn't make out a single word, and at this point, she would throw up her hands and exclaim, "It's all Greek to me!"

Her callers would join in laughter at Bessie's clever little *jeu de mots*, but before she caught her second breath they would say they had tired her more than enough and taking their leave they promised to drop in to see her soon again. In the meantime, if there was anything they could do for her, she shouldn't hesitate to let them know.

As they left, her neighbors were of one mind. Bessie Potter was such a dear, so good and kind and patient, and never troubling them with woeful litanies of widowhood. In view of her loneliness they were not surprised that she enjoyed that constant hub-bub just across the street from her. They were not surprised either at the way she raved about the two youngest members of the priest's family. But no one put much stock in Bessie's opinions regarding little children. She was inclined to see them as

32

veritable cherubim of sweet innocence—a view not uncommon among women who have no offspring, but one that is seldom shared by those who have them.

Yes, she was a dear but, really, the way she rambled on these days . . . and who could afford to waste time listening to all that trivia about those foreigners?

Chapter Four

The priest and his wife were not aware, it seems, that some of the neighbors were distressed by the presence of foreigners in their midst. Nor did it occur to them that they might be looked upon with disfavor because they were neither Protestants nor Catholics, but adherents of a denomination known as Orthodoxy. Moreover, they spoke in a strange tongue which had not been heard before in the area or for that matter, in any part of Arlington as far as any one could recall. That these particular reasons should be a basis for labeling them as "undesirables" was quite beyond their comprehension. Wasn't Orthodoxy the oldest Christian faith and the one which had preserved almost intact the form and substance of the original Church for over fifteen centuries to the present time? As for the Greek language, wasn't it the oldest European tongue in continuous use for nearly four thousand years, and one of the few in the world that had so lengthy an oral life? Besides, it was the very language in which the New Testament was written.

The reverence which the Greeks have for their Hellenic heritage obscures the simple fact that not every one knows or cares about the "glory that was Greece." Their touching naiveté in this respect had the value, nevertheless, of sparing Alexandra and Constantine a blow to their pride. Blissfully unconscious that they or anyone in their family could be looked upon as a *persona non grata*, they settled in the town of Arlington, which held

34

the promise of a good life for them and their children.

When the Douropoulos family came to Arlington its population was less than eighteen thousand and consisted mainly of a middle and upper-middle class. Among its inhabitants were some of the descendants of the earliest New England colonists. These first settlers were attracted by the fertile land and ample water of the area which was called Menotomy, a word whose derivation is unknown; but it is not unlikely that it was the name used to describe this particular territory by the Indians who had originally occupied it.

The survival of these pioneers depended in the early years on their small farms and mills. During the following two centuries a number of enterprises were established which expanded with time into flourishing industries. One of these developed, halfway through the nineteenth century, an international trade which extended as far as India. The commodity that reached another hemisphere was ice obtained from a picturesque body of water known as Spy Pond. By the time the twentieth century had arrived, Arlington—as the town was officially named in 1867 in commemoration of its Civil War dead—had become primarily a residential area of Greater Boston.

As an established community Arlington had more to offer besides its status as a suburb of one of America's distinguished cities and the importance of its adjacency to Cambridge, a preeminent center of learning. It had an air of respectability which was prized in the early part of the century, especially by those who were raising a family. It had, as well, a dim aura of dignity which clung to it from the time it was known as Menotomy and its name "made famous by the first great battle of the American Revolution which took place within this town's boundaries."[*] Adding further luster to Arlington's historical background were "the many handsome residences dating from the seventeenth century to the present, the homes not only of Arlington's farmers, craftsmen and industrialists, but also of noted professional men and artists."[*] The town's continuity with its Anglo-Saxon

[*] Arlington Historical Society, *Arlington, Massachusetts—Exploring Its History*. Pamphlet presented to the Community by the Arlington Co-Operative Bank, 1972.

35

heritage was also evident in the religious interests and the academic concerns of its inhabitants. The predominantly Protestant houses of worship and the sizeable Catholic church were well-attended, and the excellence of the schools consistently placed them among the foremost of Greater Boston. In the schools of this pleasant New England town, Arthur and Elly first came into contact with their American peers and among them found friends that would last a lifetime. This world beyond Palmer Street which the two of them shared in their youth would replenish through the years their mutual affection by "rememberances of things past."

In their own world within the household, "the children" shared the life of the family with their siblings. Yet, certain factors which Arthur and Elly had in common set them apart, so to speak, from the rest of the Douropoulos offspring. They were closer in age to each other than they were to their siblings, and they were the only two members in the family who were born in Baltimore, Maryland, where Father Douropoulos served as the first priest in the city's fledgling community of Greek Orthodox. Because of their status as native citizens of the United States they were often referred to as the *Amerikanakia*, the little Americans, by their parents, who felt a sense of pride in having contributed to the citizentry of the New World; moreover, their parents' devotion increased toward the country to which their American-born children would owe their allegiance.

What gave additional distinction to Arthur and Elly—in their mother's eyes, at least, was the fact that they were the only two of her children who could be called *porphyrogenites*. This high-flown expression "born to the purple" must have raised eyebrows among those who did not know its full meaning. Although it was originally applied to the children of a Byzantine emperor who were born *after* his coronation, it is the proper term to use in designating the children of a Greek Orthodox priest who are born following his ordination. In Father Douropoulos' instance, the birth of his children, with the exception of the last two, Arthur and Elly, had preceded his entry into the ministry.

The family as a whole, however, considered the similarities between the two children as inconsequential in comparison to the fundamental dissimilarity of their gender. Elly was just

36

another girl in a family surfeited by females. But Arthur was a boy and the longed-for son who finally broke a chain of seven daughters long. (One of the seven girls was stillborn, the other died of diptheria at an early age.)

By the time Alexandra had reached the last few months of her first pregnancy in America, her daughters, Angela, Sophia and Demetra were old enough to surmise the nature of their mother's condition. Their reaction to it was a mixture of hope and gloom. The dismal thought that one more female could be on the way was, however, mitigated by the exciting possibility that the forthcoming sibling might not be one of their kind.

Their conjectures on this matter soon gave way to the more fascinating ones regarding their mother's pregnancy which the older sisters pursued at length among themselves. The topic of sex in that bygone era, particularly in a Greek household, was hermetically sealed so as not to reach the innocent ears of the young.

Dion, who undertook his responsibilities as an older brother conscientiously, kept a close watch on his sisters. He soon became aware that they were unduly, not to say, morbidly preoccupied with their mother's condition. He did not, however, enlighten them on this matter. They would, no doubt, gather considerable information through the process of osmosis both at school and at home; as for specific knowledge, there would be time enough for that when they reached a marriageable age. He could understand their anxiety for a brother which he desired, no less, but for reasons that his sisters could not possibly understand. His singularity as an only son had placed him for too long a time in the epicenter of the family's attention. The presence of another and so much younger a son would challenge this position, which Dion would gladly relinquish.

At this point, however, Dion was more concerned about his mother than the gender of a future sibling. His devotion to her made him apprehensive as to her welfare; she was nearing middle age—a stranger in a strange land—whose language she had yet to learn. In each of her previous deliveries she had been in the hands of a midwife. Dion would now see to it that she had the care which the American-trained doctors offered. The time he

37

had spent in the medical school had given him a profound respect for the practice of medicine in the New World.

But Dion need not have been concerned, for Arthur was born with the swiftness and ease which were typical of his mother's deliveries thus far. As soon as her labor pains began Dion left at once to get hold of Dr. Butler, whom he had selected to care for his mother. A surprisingly short time after his arrival, the doctor informed Father Douropoulos that his wife had given birth to a boy.

Sophia could give a vivid account to the end of her days of that wondrous moment when her father announced the birth of his second son. "He bounded down the stairs more like a youth than a dignified, middle-aged man. His eyes were glowing in a way we had never seen before or since; nor had we ever heard his voice sound so joyous as it did when he cried out 'It's a boy!' As though we needed to be told," she would add laughingly, "with that glorious smile spread all over Babá's face."

The infant was christened Athanasios after his paternal grandfather. He received this name by default, however, for it is traditionally given only to the firstborn son in a Greek family. Dion who was entitled to the name by right of primogeniture failed to receive it due to a combination of circumstances which preceded his birth.

Alexandra's first two pregnancies had ended in miscarriage. Fearing lest she suffer the same misfortune in this pregnancy she appealed through prayer to St. Dionysios. Childless women and those with child sought and found relief from their respective problems through the miraculous powers of this holy man, whom they considered as the patron saint of fertility.

Convinced that her prayers *in absentia* would be less efficaceous than those she could offer directly to the saint, Alexandra decided to go to the island of Zante where the remarkably preserved body of Saint Dionysios reposes in the church bearing his name.

Warnings that the tiring journey from Arcadia to Zante could cause the very calamity she hoped to avoid did not deter Alexandra whose strong will was re-enforced by a still stronger faith. She went on her pilgrimage and returned confident that she would bear a son whose name she had vowed would be Dionysios.

Some twenty years went by before the penultimate child of Alexandra and Constantine re-established, albeit in reverse order, the time-honored tradition of bearing the name of his paternal grandfather, Athanasios. However, he became known as Arthur.

Relieved from the strain of anxious anticipation, the Douropoulos family entered into a new world of enchantment which Arthur had created by his arrival. His sisters could hardly wait for the end of each school day so they could come home and see their baby brother. But the happy hours they spent near him were suddenly suspended a few weeks after his birth when Arthur caught a cold followed by an insistent cough. Dr. Butler came at once and continued to come as the fever increased. Taking Dion aside he told him what Dion already suspected that the child was seriously ill with pneumonia.

Since antibiotics for the treatment of pneumonia had yet to come, the doctor outlined a procedure which would enable the child to receive a maximum amount of oxygen for his congested lungs. He was to be wrapped up as warmly as possible within his well-covered crib, which was to be placed in front of a wide-open window. The doctor also gave some specific instructions to Dion. "Get the room cleared of all those females that are milling around. They're only using up the clean air the child needs and not doing themselves any good either. From what I've seen, I'd say that the whole lot of them are on the verge of hysteria. Your mother and that bright servant girl you call Eleni will do well enough. By the way, how many womenfolk are there in this household, anyway?"

Dion started counting out loud on his fingers, "My mother, five sisters, Eleni and two first cousins." (Mrs. Douropoulos had sent for her sister's two eldest daughters a few months after coming to the New World. Her purpose in doing so was to find each of them a husband since they lacked a sizeable dowry which limited their chance of making a good marriage in the old country).

"So, there's nine of them," mused the doctor. "Well, I must say that mother of yours is a remarkable woman."

"That's what people say about her," replied Dion with a smile that for a moment lit up his troubled eyes.

Dr. Butler put his arm around Dion's lean shoulders. "Your little brother must have inherited some of your mother's stamina, as I suspect all of you have to some degree or other, . . . and the chances are that he will pull through."

Elly, the last child, was born a month after Arthur had reached his first birthday, and it hardly needs to be said that her birth was an anticlimax. Her sisters had taken for granted that Arthur, who had fulfilled their desire for a little brother, would be the last and the brightest star of the family constellation. Elly's presence was also a source of embarrassment to her sisters. She was irrefutable proof that their respectable, aging parents had continued to indulge in the sort of thing which had resulted in this unnecessary appendage to the family. It had been confusing and shocking that their mother would have another child and, besides, had shown no signs of contrition. If anything, Alexandra had been in a sanguine state of mind throughout her pregnancy. Arthur's birth was for her a clear indication that the law of averages at long last was once again in operation. She was, therefore, confident that when her time came she would deliver a son. How splendid that would be, and especially for Arthur to have a little brother close to his own age for companionship.

The elemental drama of birth was in Elly's case heightened by a number of unexpected developments. To begin with, she was born two months ahead of time on a stormy night in February. Alexandra and her husband were entertaining a kinsman named Spyro Kangias who had come from Buffalo, New York, to Baltimore to pay his respects. While they were chatting, a violent blast of wind tore off the limb of a nearby tree. At the sound of crashing glass that came from the second story of the house Alexandra raced in terror up the stairs to Arthur's room. She found her little son undisturbed by the havoc that had taken place in the room close to the one in which he was sleeping.

Shortly after, Alexandra felt the first sharp stabs of pain that signalled the onset of labor. A call to Dr. Butler brought the distressing information that his return from an out-of-town call had been deyaled by the storm. Her husband became alarmed.

The precipitant nature of his wife's delivery, plus the prematurity of the impending one, made it vital that she receive immediate medical attention. His anxiety was somewhat relieved when Dion suggested calling a Dr. Demarest, who lived around the corner.

At this point their guest decided to take matters in his own hands. "No, don't call him. If he's that close by, let's go and get him. Don't worry, Father, if the fellow's at home, I promise you we'll bring him back."

Dion would have preferred going alone to the doctor's house, for Spyro Kangias' appearance left much to be desired. He was, to be sure, a kindly, decent fellow, but nature had given him a neanderthal facade that belied his virtues. Spyro was short and stooped-shouldered with small beady eyes and bushy eyebrows and a simian-like forehead capped with coarse black hair. It was a standing joke among his friends that whenever Spyro visited his sister, who lived across the Canadian border, the custom officials grilled him mercilessly despite his proper credentials. His appearance, nevertheless, served him well. Men twice his size walked meekly out of his saloon when he ordered them off the premises, if their manner did not suit him. . . . Compliance was the better part of valor when confronted by a man who was a crack shot with a pistol strapped to his leg.

Dr. Demarest hardly expected on such a wretched night that any of his patients would take advantage of his evening visiting hours, least of all, the incongrous pair that arrived at his office— one of them a personable youth, the other an uncouth older man.

Dion did not waste time on introductions but hurriedly explained his mother's situation and ended his account with a plea for the doctor's immediate help. Dr. Demarest did not reply at once but drummed his fingers for a few moments on his desk, then slowly shook his head. No, he couldn't possibly leave his office. He had *regular* patients who could only come during the evening office hours and his first duty was to them. His mother was Dr. Butler's regular patient—a most reliable colleague—and, no doubt, he would return in time to care for his patient. Although he did not say so outright, it was obvious that he considered it unwise to replace another doctor, especially in a premature delivery. If anything went wrong with the mother or child, he feared that he would be blamed. "Besides," he added in a lighter tone, "your mother probably has an exaggerated notion of how quickly she gives birth. I am quite certain Dr. Butler will get to your mother with time enough to spare; he is, if I may so again, a most reliable—"

Dion was no longer listening to the doctor's specious reasoning. He turned to Spyro with a stricken look. "Let's go, we're only wasting time here."

"Not yet, my boy," replied Spyro. But as far as Dr. Demarest was concerned, the session was over. He walked briskly to the door and opened it. Spyro followed, but instead of making his exit, he slammed the door shut with the full force of his foot. He kept it firmly planted against the wood while he slowly raised the baggy leg of his trousers up to the knee.

"I don't wanna use it," he said, "so, get your coat, Doc."

In the years to come, Alexandra often recalled her husband's words—the prescient words—he spoke when Elly, their last child, was born. He had reproved her gently for the disappointment she felt at giving birth to another daughter. He reminded her that well before Arthur was born she had prayed for a son—"for *one more son* and that was all you asked of God, and He did not fail you, for was not Arthur the answer to your supplications?"

He had leaned over the newborn's crib and smiled at the sight of the infant. "How tiny she is and how brave she is to defy nature by coming into this harsh world before her time. I hope her courage will last, for I fear she may know in her early years the pain of orphanhood."

"Oh, please, please, don't say that!" cried Alexandra.

He realized how much his words had distressed her and he hurriedly tried to make amends. Oh, no, he did not mean that the child would grow up bereft of both parents. "I was speaking only for myself," he explained, "I am, after all, twelve years older than you and men, on the whole, do not outlive their wives. Besides, you are exceptionally healthy; you have never been even mildly sick save for that one fearful illness that struck you with a lethal force, and by the grace of God, Saint Nektarios was visiting us at the time and performed the miracle which saved your life. That holy man disavowed any possession of miraculous power. He only claimed that he had prayed to our Lord to restore the health with which He had so generously endowed you. Your God-given vitality led the Saint to say that you are one of those blessed mortals destined to reach a very old age. "You see, I am counting on the Saint's prophecy regarding your longevity. So, you had better prepare yourself for a long life, and during those lengthy years when I will no longer be at your side, you will have the comfort of your children. And this little girl—the Benjamin of our family—may outdo them all in her devotion to you."

Chapter Five

A consensus is hard to come by among individualists such as the members of the Douropoulos household. It was, therefore, gratifying to their father that his daughters, who tended to be critical, praised Dion's choice of the house on Palmer Street. They had not been happy in their former home in Pittsburgh even though it was quite elegant—the only one on the street that had two parlors and marble fireplaces, high carved ceilings and dark panelled walls that gave it a kind of melancholy charm. But whatever charm it might have had, the sisters lost sight of it instantly when told by their schoolmates that the fine residence in which they lived was known as "the haunted house." Following this fearful disclosure, reports abounded each morning at the breakfast table of strange sounds heard during the night—moans and shrieks, the clanging of chains and the scraping of tables and chairs as they moved across the floor of their own accord.

Father Douropoulos investigated the matter by spending a night in the part of the house where his daughters' rooms were located. The only sound he heard as he went the rounds was his children's breathing. Its gentle rhythm made him sigh . . . long ago, how long ago he could not remember, he, too, had known the blessing of youth's sweet slumber.

He did not mention his nocturnal vigil. His daughters' morbid fantasies required more than words of reassurance to prevent hysteria which would lead, no doubt, to irrational demands for exodus from the "cursed house." So, their father donned his stole, without which a Greek Orthodox priest may not perform a religious rite; he then went from room to room sprinkling holy water and reciting the prescribed prayers for the exorcism of evil spirits. After completing his task he addressed his children. "If this doesn't work, nothing will. In any case, we are *not* moving from here."

No one dared to mention the matter again—at least not in the presence of Father Douropoulos. But it had left an uneasiness that made the girls appreciate all the more the cheerful atmosphere of their new house on Palmer Street.

But what was most gratifying to the priest was his wife's satisfaction with the house. Since coming to America, it was the first one she could consider her own, her very own, for her husband had bought it in her name. A roof over her head was, at least, a basic provision for her future welfare.

That she was now a woman of property was of little consequence to the Presbytera. She was not interested in the acquisition of material possessions. Had she coveted them she would not have readily disposed of valuable personal items that were part of her dowry, as well as those she had received as gifts through the years, in order to raise money for some benevolent cause or other. But her ownership of a house was another matter. It was a material asset that gave her a sense of security, a feeling of being a legitimate member of the New World by owning a piece of it, however small. But, above all, it was a place that her children could rightfully call "home."

Since she was neither vain nor ostentatious it probably did not occur to her that the house on Palmer Street would be considered luxurious by the existing standards of her compatriots. Most of them were still living within the city proper in apartments, in double and triple 'deckers,' some of which contained several units under a single roof. These were the precursors of the multi-housing developments of the present era. Within a few years, however, the *arrivistes* in the Greek community would acquire impressive houses in the exclusive suburbs of Boston. The Presbytera genuinely admired and praised these handsome residences, but they did not diminish in the least the enjoyment

45

of her comparatively modest home in Arlington.

She liked the house from the time she had first seen it, and after she had inspected it she deemed it eminently suitable for her large family. She was no less pleased with the ample garden, which to her surprise included a grape arbor at the rear of the property. Dion had made no mention of it, most likely because it was of no consequence to him. But it was obviously of interest to his mother, who scrutinized it carefully, much to Mr. MacNeill's discomfort. He had only himself to blame for not getting rid of that eyesore before putting the house up for sale. He made light of it, however, saying it was a simple matter to do away with it . . . just a few whacks with an axe. He would be glad to—Mrs. Douropoulos raised her hand in a prohibatory gesture. "No, no," she cried, "no touch it, please!"

She had seen in a glance that the decrepit arbor could be revived. It needed but a few hours of a carpenter's time to reset the sagging posts and stakes, and to mend the laticed roof. The pruning of old canes and the trimming of errant vines she could do herself. Whatever she knew about viticulture she had learned from watching and often helping the workers on her father's vineyards, whose technique hardly differed from the one practiced by their distant ancestors in pre-Homeric times.

Soon after the household had moved to Palmer Street, the Presbytera saw to it that the grape arbor was put in good order. But this was only one of her concerns. The more pressing ones were the preparations for the first wedding in the family, which was to take place the last week in June at Palmer Street.

The die-hard conservatives in Boston's Greek community were taken aback by the news that the priest was disregarding an age-old custom by allowing his second daughter, Sophia, to marry before Angela, the first-born daughter, had been duly wed.

This now by-gone custom had its genesis in years long past when matrimony and subsequent maternity were the only worthy pursuits for women. It was a means of safeguarding the oldest daughter from being "left on the shelf" by deterring a prospective suitor from seeking the hand of a more attractive younger sister.

This matter was academic, however, as far as Angela and

Sophia were concerned, for both sisters had more than their share of pulchritude. Sophia was acknowledged as a beauty in the classical genre. She had the air of a *grande dame* which would suit her as the wife of an austerely handsome, cultivated, New Yorker called John Limpert (his last name was originally Limperopoulos, but shortened for the sake of convenience). He was a young man of means, who had already established a food processing concern that is still prospering under the direction of his oldest son. John Limpert, it was said, had done well in choosing Sophia as his wife, for she was bound to have more than a moderate success as a young matron, what with her striking presence and her flair for entertaining—a quality that she, as well as the rest of her sisters, had inherited from their mother.

Even though Sophia was greatly admired by those who saw her, Angela was truly loved by all who knew her. Everything about her—the sweet oval face framed by soft wavy hair, the fine eyebrows that arched over the large dreamy eyes, the full lips that never curled in scorn or drooped with bitterness— everything about Angela betokened a spirit of grace that transcended whatever qualities the rest of her sisters possessed.

Since no one doubted that Angela had received more proposals than most girls could ever hope for, people, or the *cosmos* as the Greeks say, began to wonder. Only one conclusion seemed to make sense, a sad one, indeed. The priest's lovely daughter must be suffering from some hidden malady. . . . Come to think of it, that slimness of hers, that delicate gardenia-white skin, surely, these were symptoms of God knows what had befallen the poor girl.

But the simple truth was that Angela was not anxious to marry. The only plausible excuse she hoped would ease her mother's anxiety was to say that she had not yet found anyone with whom she felt she could be happy. If she was waiting for the perfect husband, her mother retorted, she would never find him. Marriage was based on practicality and not on idealism. Her mother would then again outline the dire consequences in store for an unattached female, and with each of her repetitions the vision of spinsterhood became increasingly abysmal.

It remained for Father Douropoulos to put an end to this

47

untoward situation which exasperated his wife and distressed his daughter. He had a talk with Angela but he had listened more than he had spoken, and he came to the conclusion that Angela's "quest for the ideal" was not the issue. He suspected more from what he sensed than what she said, that her fastidious nature was threatened by the physical intimacy of wedlock. But whether or not his assumptions were correct, he believed that Angela's personal feelings must be respected rather than violated by any further pressure on this matter. He, for one, was rejoicing in this coming event, and he was thankful that he had been spared thus far to officiate at Sophia's wedding whether or not she was the first-born of his six daughters.

Father Douropoulos could appreciate his wife's concern, and he tried to lessen it by pointing out that Angela was still very young with plenty of time for a change of heart. He kept to himself his doubts as to such a likelihood.

Among the most appealing photographs in the family album is one of Sophia as a bride. She is not facing the camera with that stilted kind of smile often evident in bridal pictures, but is looking instead at her bouquet of white roses with a pensive expression. A narrow band of orange blossoms frames the bouffant cap that covers her hair. It is made of soft tulle which falls gently over her shoulders and flows into a graceful train. The high-waisted bodice of her white satin wedding dress has an oval neckline and short sleeves that reach to the edge of the long white kid gloves. The skirt is gently gathered and comes to a point in the front. Beneath its shortened hem, a broad border of Valenciennes lace reaches to ankle length and reveals white satin slippers with matching rosettes and "baby-Louis" heels. Her only adornment is a double strand of pearls—a gift from her husband whose infatuation for Sophia lasted through his incredibly long lifetime, which came to an end December 1984 when he had reached one hundred and four years of age.

He had known Sophia from the time she was a child, for both of them were born in the same Arcadian mountain village of Zatouna. Her father had been one of John Limpert's teachers in his early education and one which he held in high regard. He remembered his mother-in-law as a beautiful woman with a slim waist and with a queenly carriage, which she had yet to lose.

"They were an admirable pair," John Limpert would say, "and I fell in love with them first and then with their daughter."

Sophia's marriage and the subsequent marriages of her sisters were topics of considerable interest, and not in a few instances, of considerable envy in the Greek community. The Douropoulos girls had married "for love" without help from their mother or from anyone else for that matter. Three of the younger daughters married graduates of Harvard Law School, who eventually became corporate counsels in outstanding companies in America. One of them, Stephen P. Ladas, was recognized well beyond the United States as an authority and author on International Law of Copyrights and Trademarks.

The *cosmos* agreed that such fine marriages would not have come about quite so easily without "the open house" on Palmer Street and without the unstinted hospitality which was and had been a way of life for Constantine and Alexandra Douropoulos.

Sophia's attachment to her family often brought her back home during the early years of her marriage. Her visits were gleefully anticipated by Arthur and Elly, for when their married sister came to Arlington—if time and weather permitted—she would hire a car from Mr. Harvey Forest, who owned the only limousine service in the town, consisting of one enormous, glistening black Packard that he chauffered himself. For the munificent sum of ten dollars, the limousine and its driver left Palmer Street carrying a full cargo for a long, leisurely afternoon cruise.

For the birth of her first two children, Sophia came to Boston. As the size of her family increased, her trips to Arlington were not as frequent as they were in the past. But her parents and her siblings came periodically to New York to visit the Limpert family. But Angela's visits to Sophia's house were lengthy ones extending for months and seasons at a time, for since their earliest years the two sisters had been close to each other.

When Father Douropoulos brought his family to America, Angela and Sophia had already reached the early stage of adolescence while their younger sisters were still mere children. They had both entered at the same time the Notre Dame Academy in Baltimore. They would often reminisce about the gentle nuns who accepted them with such warmth and kindness, and they recalled with affection Sister Clarissa, an elegant gentlewoman, who was their favorite. She had recognized Angela's gift for handwork and had taken the time, despite her tasks as a teacher and her duties as a nun, to teach Angela the art of fine embroidery. When Sophia married, Sister Clarissa sent her as a wedding gift a piece of her own exquisite work embroidered with the words: *"Jesus Be Ever With Us."* Sophia had it framed and it remained on the wall of her room ever after.

As time passed, Angela, known as the beloved "Aunt Kiki" to her sisters' children, was no longer a lovely girl, but a lovely woman. Her friends more aptly described as "devotees"—for Angela inspired loyalty as well as love—were ever alert for a worthy bachelor who would lead her to the altar. No less than Archbishop Athenagoras, Primate of the Greek Orthodox Church of North and South America, who honored the Douropoulos family by his friendship, had a special fondness for Angela. His Eminence undertook the role of matchmaker in her behalf by personally bringing to Boston a dear friend of his from Port Arthur, Texas.

Angela with her customary graciousness managed to back out of this proposed alliance, as she had done in so many other instances—much to the Archbishop's disappointment and even more so to the regret of his friend. Her refusal did not diminish, however, His Eminence's affection for Angela nor did it lessen the regard in which her family was held by this hierarch destined to become His All Holiness Ecumenical Patriarch of Constantinople, head of world Orthodoxy.

Chapter Six

In summertime the Arcadian kinship with the pagan past is renewed in an atavistic relish of life. The visitors who came to Arlington on Sunday—the casual *jour fixe* at the Douropoulos house—found enjoyment not only in the cordial atmosphere, but in the prospect of a long leisurely *peripatos*. Walking is as pleasing an exercise to modern Greeks as it was to their ancient predecessors. Aristotle give his famous lectures as he walked with his pupils outside the Athenian Lyceum—a practice, as Dion explained to Arthur and Elly, which could account for the term "Peripatetics" given to Aristotle's followers.

The town had three choice areas—Spy Pond, the Mystic Lakes and Menotomy Rocks Park, which visitors to Arlington could freely enjoy. The areas of the lakes or the park were the ones usually chosen for a walk since their distance from Palmer Street offered an excuse for a midway rest by the edge of the lake or a chance to sit awhile on one of the large boulders in the park's cool forest.

One who remembered those walks was Basil Despotes, an old friend of the Douropoulos family. "Ah, those Sunday excursions," he said to Elly, who was paying him a visit during one of her occasional trips to Boston, "they are among my fondest recollections of Arlington. . . . You may be sure that never before or since those distant days have such sounds as our voices, raised in youthful laughter and lively conversation, in song and in poetry, echoed across the waters of the Mystic Lakes or vibrated through

Menotomy Rocks Park."

Basil Despotes was the last of the habitués at Palmer Street, and Elly always looked forward to seeing him, for the leitmotif of their conversation was the remembrance of a time that harked back to more than half a century. The intervening years had not altered significantly the colorful aspects of his personality. He was a wiry, effervescent little man with an impish face that gave him the look of a winsome gnome. His droll appearance was counterbalanced by a keen mind and a kind heart, which were hidden beneath a caustic wit that seared without mercy the pretentions of a social climber or the presumptions of an intellectual poseur.

The first member of the Douropoulos family that Basil had come across was Dion when both of them were students at the Rizarios Seminary in Athens. He had not met Dion's parents, but he had caught a glimpse of them, now and then, at some of the school functions, and he had retained an impression of them as a striking couple.

But if Basil Despotes did not know Dion's father and mother, they knew him, or rather knew about him; for Basil and a small group of his school mates were expelled from the Seminary with the grave threat of excommunication hanging over their heads. Basil evidently was a non-conformist in his adolescence. At the Seminary he became attached to a small circle of restive youths who accepted him as a potential renegade. These youths soon became known as "free thinkers." This term was first applied to them when they began questioning the blind obedience of the student body to the school's strict rules and prescriptions that were based on the Orthodox monastic system. They next attempted to undermine their schoolmates' loyalty to religious authority. And, finally, carried away by their audacity, they proceeded to publish and disseminate material upholding their belief in atheism. That such a state of affairs could have come about in the most prestigious, the most respected seminary of Greece was more than a scandal, more than a sin—it was a crime against God and His Church.

A less resilient spirit than that which Basil Despotes possessed could have been crushed by the outcome of so unfortunate a youthful indiscretion. But he accepted the penalty for his actions without breaking down under the severe onus of disgrace and alienation from the Orthodox community. He applied and was accepted at Anatolia College, presently located in Salonika, Greece. After graduating from Anatolia he came to America and entered the Harvard Dental School. He chose dentistry as a profession because he hoped it would give him a good income. He needed it badly, for he had undertaken to support his widowed sister and her young children.

In the Presbytera's eyes Basil Despotes was a true Christian.

"You were but a child then, my dear Elly, and you could not possibly realize what those days meant to us. Arlington, or more specifically Palmer Street, was not for us simply the name of a certain street in a certain town, but the eponym for your parents' house. It was a haven for those of us who had come to America as students without means, without family, and had gravitated to Boston to complete our education in the famous colleges and graduate schools in an area known as 'the Athens of America'—a designation which added to the pride we felt in our Hellenic heritage. That open house on Palmer Street was more than a haven. We thought of it as a *salon*—at least the closest to it we could hope to come across in our young lives.

"Ah, you are smiling or trying to hide your smile. I shall overlook your amusement, for you, my dear, are much younger than I am, and I dare say you consider this retrospection of mine as an oldster's tendency to view the past in a romantic light." The fact was, he declared, that romanticizing those by-gone days was to "guild the lily"; it would be more than enough if he could recapture their singular quality. He could not do so, however—not that his memory failed him—but because his remembrances, indeed, all remembrances were, at best, only shadows of former realities.

He paused for a few moments, bemused by some undercurrent of his thoughts. When he spoke again it was to say, "Perhaps what gives our reminiscences a sense of poignancy is the awareness that our past experiences become an irretrievable part of eternity; and to those of us who are old, memories are more than poignant, for they are fraught with the universal pathos of youth forever lost.''

He gave a small sigh followed by a small smile that tugged at Elly's heart, for the smile was no longer impish, but wistful. Sensing her feelings, his expression changed to a mischievous grin, and his voice took on its old tone of mockery.

"It's kind of you, dear child, to visit an old friend. You've come prepared, I hope, to endure the boredom of rambling recollections which the aged, not to say the senile, indulge in since it's an indoor sport they can enjoy with impunity.''

"But I'm not in the least bored," remonstrated Elly. "I find your recollections fascinating.''

"Now you are fibbing and you shall be punished by being subjected to a lengthy soliloquy on those memorable days in Arlington.

"If you ask me," Basil began, "what was especially gratifying at Palmer Street was the *kouventa*—conversation, the Greek national pastime which, I must say, was of a high order. Those frequent visitors were mainly young bachelors who had received the greater part of their education in Greece, and some had studied, as well, in European universities. Our corps also included a scattering of the already established professional men and their wives. Some of these ladies were well-educated and were considered or, at least, considered themselves the bluestockings in the Greek community.

"Sooner or later talk would focus on the area of *belles lettres*, for in those gatherings were some of the most promising students and scholars in the field of the humanities, who were to leave their mark in the American academic world. One of these luminaries was Aristides Phoutrides, that enormously gifted young man whose talents were already recognized at Harvard, where he was teaching the Classics. He was an exuberant activist with rare vision. An example of his foresight was the establishment of the *Helicon*, a society, or club as it is called, for Greek undergraduate and graduate students, which continues to play a notable part in upholding intellectual standards in Boston's Greek Community. Yet, farseeing as he was, I doubt if Aristides could have envisioned that today in the educational institutions of New

54

England alone, there would be several hundred eminent teachers, instructors and professors of Greek descent—and, indeed, one of them Matina Horner, the head of Radcliffe College, from which his wife, Margaret Garrison, had graduated.

"The other outstanding personality in that nucleus of very bright young people was, of course, our beloved friend, Raphael Demos, who became Harvard's Alford Professor of Natural Religion, Moral Philosophy and Civil Polity. He had the distinction of being a foremost authority on Plato, and was acknowledged as a highly popular lecturer on philosophy. A while ago I came across one of his former students who maintained that the most exciting course he had ever taken was the one given by Professor Demos. He also claimed that each of his lectures was a gem of clarity and sparkle rarely found in a classroom. Your husband had the same reaction, and I remember his saying that he felt especially fortunate to have had Raphael not only as a teacher, but as his tutor as well.

"But we who were his life-long friends cherished him not only for the grandeur of his mind but the grace of his spirit; he lived, the moral philosophy he preached, in the last chapter of his book, *The Philosophy of Plato*. No doubt, you have it."

"Yes, he was kind enough to send us a copy.'

"In that chapter, called the 'Portrait of the Philosopher,' Raphael unwittingly presents a self-portrait. He describes Plato's view of a philosopher 'as a certain sort of man . . . not so much that he thinks about truth as that he embodies it and is honest through and through, not so much that he studies universals as that his personal attitude is tinged with universality and is untainted by pettiness . . .'

"But to talk about Phoutrides and Demos and fail to mention your brother-in-law, Nicholas Culolias, would be a grievous omission of an exceptional member in our coterie. I am always moved when I think of him as a poor shepherd boy coming from Arcadia to America at the age of eleven, *entirely on his own*, without a single word of English in his vocabulary and without a single penny in his pocket. Yet, this waif—what else could you call him?—graduated from Princeton and went on to the Harvard Law School to become the first of his countrymen to graduate from that venerable institution.''

Basil stopped long enough to enjoy a little chuckle. ''I once asked Nick how was it that he, a homeless and penniless immigrant boy finally landed, of all places, in a rich man's college.''

''I never had that impression of Princeton,'' he replied.

''This was typical of your brother-in-law, true egalitarian that he was; money or material possessions made so little impression on him that he was simply not aware of their plentitude at Princeton. Nick is a thrilling example among those who fought against all odds to make 'the American dream' come true. And this he accomplished without sacrificing to the slighest degree his integrity. Nick Culolias was as honorable a man as one could hope to find.

''But to get back to Palmer Street. The conversations that took place there often centered on contemporary Greek literature written in the 'demotic' language rather than the 'puristic,' which prevailed among the highly educated and the pendants—I confess it's sometimes hard to tell these two apart. Inspired by the prose and poetry coming out of Greece, we became the apostles of that fresh exciting literature. And our enthusiasm nurtured what now is recalled as the 'neo-Hellenic renaissance' in the Greek community of Boston. . . . Incidentally, Aristides Phoutrides was a poet in his own right. His book of poetry, *Lights At Dawn*, is proof enough of his talent, and further evidence of it is in the marvelous way he translated the poetry of Kostis Palamas, the finest modern poet of Greece. As for Raphael Demos, his poetic bent led him to translate with great sensitivity some work of the Alexandrian Greek poet, C. P. Cavafy. Raphael's translations were published sometime during nineteen thirty-three or four, in the then splendid magazine, *The New Republic*. He was among the first in this country to recognize the genius of Cavafy.

''I'm afraid you may have the impression from what I've been saying that we came to Palmer Street mainly to hear ourselves discussing high-flown subjects. We could have done that at the Helicon Club or during the times we spent together, for we were a close-knit group, that is, those of us who came regularly to Arlington. But I must confess we believed we were the 'cognoscienti' in the Greek community and we could not resist playing to the gallery, especially since our audience in Arlington consisted of a number of pretty, bright girls who were, or more likely pretended to be, impressed by our erudition.

"But when our intellectual exhibitions became tiresome, Raphael would put an end to them by saying, 'How about a little gossip for a change?' He had, you know, a streak of gentle irony in him that was not so gentle in his youth. And those who took advantage of his remark to repeat a malicious scandal or to revel in vicious slander found themselves beset by a Socratic gadfly. Raphael's seemingly artless questions so befuddled the scandalmongers that they would soon retract their words or wished they had never uttered them.

"We had, of course, other diversions in Arlington besides talking and walking which, I suppose, would be considered by today's youth as 'square'—to use one of their neologisms. They would, no doubt, find it hard to believe that we found enjoyment in gathering around the piano to sing, in dancing to the tune of a hand-cranked victrola or listening to music from the fine collection of classical records that were available at Palmer Street. These were pastimes in which the whole family could join; they added a richer texture to life which is lacking today—much to the detriment of both children and parents.

"If I may digress a bit, the custom of dating (which at the present time is often a euphemism for mating) became established in this country around the early part of the twenties, when we were coming regularly to Arlington. But the early Greek families did not countenance this American custom until later, and in some cases much later, if at all. Nevertheless, Eros was not deterred from giving a helping hand to romances whose inception took place in the family setting. I would say that Nick and Demetra's marriage was sufficient proof of that. By the way, you probably have heard that Nick was smitten, at first, with your oldest sister, Angela. But it was the third sister down the line—Demetra with her pretty, round face and her tom-boyish air that finally won Nick's heart.

Basil had not forgotten how fetching Demetra looked on one particular occasion many years ago. "It was a day in January when a heavy snowstorm inspired George Demetriou—he was one of

57

the crowd at the time—to get hold somehow of a sleigh; I think he had borrowed it from some wealthy admirer of his. Demetriou, if you remember, was a sculptor—a delightful fellow with a flair for the dramatic, who made quite a name for himself in the artistic circles of Boston. It was a sight to behold, that bell-tinkling sleigh with a red *flocati* rug for a blanket. He stopped by my place and took me along with him to Arlington to treat, as he put it, 'the love-birds to a sleigh ride.' '' We rode, or rather we sleighed up Massachusetts Avenue in grand style and arrived at Palmer Street with a flourish of bells that brought the neighbors running to their windows.

"I can still remember what your sister was wearing that day— some kind of a coat with a brown fur collar and a hat and muff of the same fur that marched the color of her eyes. What sparkling eyes she had! Her cheeks were bright pink that afternoon—not, I suspect, from the sharp winter wind. Her engagement had just been announced, and sitting snugly close to her fiancé—far from the family's critical eyes—must have given her a sense of excitement . . . ah, the sweet innocence of those days!

"She was pretty as a picture, and so were all her sisters, and the two brothers—they were a mighty handsome pair." Basil remembered Dion from the time they were both attending the Rezarios Seminary in Athens. "He had entered the seminary at a much earlier age than was usual, thanks to his fine mind. Yet, he was so modest and appealing a lad, that he had won the affection of his schoolmates and his teachers. Saint Nektarios, that holy man who headed the seminary, was especially fond of him. . . . As for Arthur, he had the kind of personal beauty which, according to Aristotle, is a greater recommendation than any letter, and that bumptious old philosopher, Hobbes, acknowledged that 'good looks were a power even in a man since they predisposed women and strangers in his favor.' Yes, indeed, all of the Douropoulos offspring were a captivating lot that gave an irresistible charm to Palmer Street."

"You are much too generous in your praise," said Elly, "but I believe it was our parents who were the real 'drawing card.' ''

"They undoubtedly were," agreed Basil, "Nick, my dearly loved old friend, had come to the same conclusion. He once remarked to me that he had not realized until he became a member of the Douropoulos family that it was essentially your father and your mother who attracted that stream of visitors who came from far and near to Arlington. It goes without saying that a husband and wife primarly create the atmosphere of their surroundings. Your parents had given to the house at Palmer Street an inviting ambience that was palpable as soon as one stepped inside the door. It, also, goes without saying that hospitality is a basic tradition in the Greek household; in the Douropoulos home it became a legend—and that was in great part due to your mother. She could take in stride however large a number of visitors might appear at any time, and in a moment's notice she managed in a way that seemed effortless to prepare and serve something invariably delectable. Food at Palmer Street was not just food—*it was poetry.*"

"How nicely you put it!" exclaimed Elly. "I shall never forget those words." And she never did.

"But, I must say, what gave those memorable gatherings in Arlington a certain elegance was your father's bearing. In the role of a host his dignity was tempered with graciousness. His courtliness extended to the younger folks no less than to the older ones, and he was no more solicitious of important guests than of the ordinary run of visitors. I don't recall any instance when he pulled rank on us or questioned the avant-garde views we espoused in our salad days. The only indication of his amused tolerance at our brash youthfulness was a fugitive smile that played about his lips now and then.

"Yet, we never went so far, I'm glad to say, as to offend him—at least, not deliberately. His mere presence, apart from the cloth he wore, commanded respect. We wouldn't think of smoking in front of him. If the desire for a cigarette became too insistent we'd take a little *volta* out on the porch or around the garden, or we went to the kitchen where Eleni, that good woman, reigned, and chatted a bit with her as we recklessly puffed away. I enjoyed those little visits to the kitchen," he added, "for Eleni was a part of the unique atmosphere of Palmer Street."

His thoughts returned again to Elly's father and to the other pioneer priests who had been sent by the Greek Church to

America, and as he spoke of them his voice became somber. Whatever respect, not to mention gratitude, that was shown to these clerics was shamefully inadequate. Only now when it was too late, Basil confessed, it had become evident how heavy was the cross they carried while serving their countrymen in the New World. They were overworked and underpaid from the meager coffers of their parishes; yet they went hundreds of miles beyond their assigned posts to meet the sacramental needs of their fellow pioneers who lacked the means for a church of their own, and in many instances could not even afford to reimburse the traveling expenses of a visiting priest.

"If these early clerics had grievances or problems—and God only knows how many they endured especially during the years when the virulent political passions involving the Church were reflected in the Greek American parishes—their only recourse was the Mother Church thousands of miles away. By the time their petitions reached across the ocean and a decision rendered via the same route, the members of the local church councils had often taken it upon themselves to hire or to dismiss a priest at will. The Greek Orthodox Archdiocese was not established in the United States until 1918, and it was not until the 1930s that the ecclesiastical chaos in the Greek communities came to an end.

"Very few of these pioneer priests reached the biblical lifespan of 'three score years and ten.' Their names and their deeds are all but forgotten. Only their faded signatures remain on birth, marriage and death certificates in the archives of the churches they helped to build or in which they served."

"I used to wonder," said Elly, "why my father so seldom smiled, and when he did it was a small, sad smile that made me want to cry. It still does, even now, when I think of it."

"Oh, my dear, forgive me if my reflections make you feel sad," replied Basil. But there are recollections that are bound to evoke sorrowful thoughts and feelings of regret. For me, even my happiest recollections of Aristides Phoutrides are invariably accompanied by deep pain at his loss from a sudden heart attack in the glorious prime of his life. And speaking of that brilliant young man's death, I am reminded at the moment of how it touched in an unexpected way a member of your family.

60

Aristides' wife, Margaret Garrison, was a true humanitarian. She had inherited an everlasting concern for public service from her great-grandfather, William Lloyd Garrison, the famous Abolitionist. The first of her many benevolent acts was the establishment of a scholarship fund in her husband's memory at Harvard for students of Greek descent. Your brother, Arthur, was the first of the Aristides Phoutrides Scholarship recipients, and due to his consistently high academic standing, he was the beneficiary of it during his four years of college."

"It continued, I believe," said Elly, "while Arthur was getting his master's degree, and it was a great help, of course; but still Arthur had to work and work hard at whatever he could get in the way of a job to make ends meet—which they never did for him and for many others in the Depression."

"I remember when he worked at the 'hot dog place' which Nick's brother, George, operated in Harvard Square," continued Basil. "Now and then, Nick and I would meet on a Saturday afternoon and we would take a walk by the Charles River. On our way back we used to stop for a cup of coffee at that little hole-in-the-wall and we'd find Arthur there looking as handsome as ever in a white duck jacket and a white cap like the khaki ones soldiers wore in the First World War. He is one of those fortunate beings who has retained his good looks and what is no less enviable—that splended crop of hair. He was fortunate, as well, in managing some way or other to complete his education during the Depression, the Great Depression, as the historians refer to it now—a phrase that has little if any meaning for the present generation. Yet, how many young people in those bitter years relinquished their dreams for a higher education in order to support themselves or help support their families."

"For some, these dreams went far astray," said Elly, "but they had a way of returning time and again to haunt those who were forced to abandon them."

"And for others like Nick," observed Basil, "those grim years proved providential or, at least, he made them so. His dearth of clients gave him the time, he used to say, to enjoy the unhurried company of the finest minds in the world, whose timeless wisdom and tireless wit were within reach of his bookcase."

"Nick was a stoic, to begin with," remarked Elly, "besides, he and my sister had no children, so Nick was saved the ordeal of having to provide for a growing family during that grim decade of the thirties. As far as I am concerned, the truly heroic figure during that period was my mother. As I look back on it now, I realize that it was a time of genteel poverty which masked a 'quiet desperation.'

Basil was doubtful that Elly's mother had submitted then, or at any time, to feelings of desperation. To have done so would have been out of character for a woman of her spirit. He shook his head in wonder as he spoke of her courage. "There was a Homeric splendor to it in those dark years when she was caught in the economic chaos of the Depression, and at the same time she was carrying her own sorrows that came 'not single spies but in battalions.' Yet, the door at Palmer Street remained open. When I think of the breadth, the warmth of the *philoxenia*—the hospitality your mother offered to young and old, I am reminded of that lovely line in the Old Testament: 'Be not forgetful to entertain strangers for thereby some have entertained angels unawares.' "

"I don't remember ever seeing any winged creatures at our dinner table," smiled Elly.

"Not all angels necessarily have wings or halos, my dear," replied Basil, "but your mother did entertain an angelic soul, Saint Nektarios, for days at a time in her Arcadian home, and he expressed his affection for her by performing a miracle that saved her life. I daresay that the galaxy of bishops, metropolitans, archbishops and two patriarchs and a future saint, no less, who broke bread in your parents' house surely are equivalent to one or two angels of the highest rank. But angels or not, the Presbytera would have treated anyone who came to her home with her usual graciousness."

Yes, that was true, Elly agreed, but her mother considered it a high honor when the bishops came to dinner, and she went to great lengths to please them as well as their attendants— deacons, priests, archimandrites, secretaries and other various satellites who invariably can be found orbiting around ecclesiastical dignitaries.

"Mother often recalled the visits of these prelates and the pleasure they had given her. Yet, none of them became so dear to her as Archbishop Iakovos. From the time she first met him when he was serving as a parish priest in Boston, she intuitively felt that the dreams she had cherished for Dion would be more than fulfilled by this brilliant young cleric."

"Ah, indeed they were!" exclaimed Basil, "for he has reached a hierarchical pinnacle as Orthodox Primate of North and South America, and is now recognized as one of the outstanding religious leaders of our times. But I must say that the bond between your mother and His Eminence does not surprise me. They had certain qualities in common which drew them together in mutual respect. To begin with, they were endowed with great vitality and immense *charisma*—a word which applies to both of them in its modern, as well as in its original Greek sense— meaning 'a gift of grace.' They shared, as well, a passionate faith in God and a compassionate love for their fellow beings. Neither of them used, or rather misused, their talents in pursuit of self-interest, but for the benefit of others. To my mind, both His Eminence and the Presbytera are, in one way or another, exponents of the Kantian theory that civilization hangs on the principle that human beings are to be treated as ends and not means."

Her mother wouldn't know, remarked Elly, with a smile, what in the world Basil was talking about when it came to philosophical theories. She had only a few years of schooling, and for that she was forced to go to the nearby town of Dimitsana since in the village of Zatouna, where she was born and raised, only males were allowed in those years to attend school. And equating her virtues with those of her revered Archbishop Iakovos would have struck her as absurd, not to say sacrilegious. Compliments embarassed her and she would brush them aside. Yet, she was very generous in her tributes to others, but not to their face, probably because she thought they might feel as uncomfortable as she felt by direct praise. "So, you have no idea, perhaps, how highly she thought of you and Andromache," concluded Elly.

"If your dear mother had a failing," replied her host, "it was seeing people in a far better light than they deserved to be seen. I speak for myself, however. As far as my dear Andromache is concerned, she has earned whatever encomia come her way for marrying a man with a ready-made family and foregoing without a murmur all of those little niceties a loyal wife deserves."

The afternoon was all but spent and Elly made ready to leave, much to Basil's distress. "I haven't even offered you a cup of tea or coffee," he cried.

"Oh, but you have given me a feast," declared Elly, "a marvelous feast of memories and nothing could have satisfied me more than that."

Elly's response pleased him and he beamed at her saying that her visit had been a delight for him. And what a pity Andromache had gone on an errand and had missed seeing her.

"Of course, I'll come soon again and see you both," promised Elly.

"Yes, do come soon again . . . I am, you know, 'The Last of the Mohicans'—the very last one of them." He kissed her good-bye in the customary Greek way, first on one cheek and then the other.

"May God keep you in the palm of His hand" were the last words Elly heard him say. A few weeks later Basil Despotes died taking with him the tender memories of a forgotten world.

Chapter Seven

When Arthur and Elly arrived in Arlington they were on the threshold of that spectacular period of growth which would lead them from childhood to adulthood. From the time they were born, the locus of their lives lay within the family circle. To their young eager eyes yet undimmed by disillusionment, the fresh world that now lay before them seemed "so various, so beautiful, so new." In this respectable, peaceful town, the two children spent their formative years, and they would recall them in time to come with the roseate aura which clings to memories of by-gone days. And among those treasured recollections was the excitement of seeing for the first time the main part of Arlington, called the "Center."

Arthur and Elly were pleased that their older brother had taken it upon himself to act as a guide on their initial tour of the town. Dion now commanded additional respect than that which is automatically accorded to the first-born son in a Greek family, for he was joining a friend of his, Hercules Petrakis, in a venture to import sugar and coffee.

Dion's new status as an up-and-coming businessman was not of significance to Elly, but she was especially happy to be in her older brother's company. The little girl had a lively curiosity and Dion listened patiently to her many questions and answered them to her satisfaction; besides he often smiled at her remarks or nodded approvingly at her observations. Her sisters, on the other hand, seemed more vexed than amused by her chatter. Yet, whatever Arthur had to say was instantly deemed as being "so cute and so clever!"

Angela, of course, was always the exception. For she displayed neither partiality nor preference for any member of the family, but loved them all with an equal love. Nor did she join sides as her sisters were likely to do against one or another of their siblings, for Angela was simply incapable of expressing a harsh word or indulging in a mean thought or action.

But much as Arthur and Elly loved their angelic sister, they agreed that Angela, or, for that matter, none of their sisters could compare to Dion when it came to *knowledge*. He was forever going to the library and always reading books and magazines at home; one of them which Elly recalled her older brother reading with intemittent bursts of hilarity was *The Saturday Evening Post*. It was worth all the nickels he had spent on that "weekly," Dion declared, for introducing him to a young English writer by the name of P. G. Wodehouse. He would read aloud some passage or other which he thought was marvelously funny. Arthur and Elly would giggle—not that they grasped the Wodehouse humor, but because Dion, who still retained some of the accent of his native tongue, would pronounce "Lady Constance" as *Lady Constánz*.

On their first exploration of the town, Elly wanted most of all to see the school she was to attend in the fall and Arthur was anxious to visit the Fire House. Dion assured his little sister that she would see the school which was located in Arlington Center. As for the Fire House, it was nearby on Broadway—the route Dion followed so as to oblige his little brother.

From where the family lived, Arlington Center could be reached in a few minutes by either Massachusetts Avenue on the lower end of Palmer Street or by Broadway, which bordered the upper end of the street. Both routes were practically equi-distant to the Center at which point Broadway converged with Massachusetts Avenue and ended abruptly at the Center.

A short distance beyond the corner of Palmer Street and Broadway, Elly's attention was caught by a large white house. It was set back from the street and commanded the attention it deserved as the sole survivor of its kind in the town. Four stately columns flanked the doorway of the two-story portico, and reached up to the pediment with its singular wooden fan light. Lofty trees surrounded the house and their long graceful branches arched over it as though to soften its severe symmetry.

It reminded Elly of a picture in her father's study called the *Temple of Zeus*; this, too, she thought must be a temple. Dion, however, informed her that it was not a temple, but a house. But how could he tell, she asked. "For one thing," replied Dion, "temples—Greek temples—had no windows." He went on to say that the classical colonnade of the Whittemore dwelling (the name by which it is known) gave it the appearance of a temple. It had been built, no doubt, sometime during the past century when the Greek Revival style was popular in America.

Although Elly could not follow all that her brother said, "the Greek house," as she named it, would remain a lasting memory. Yet, for all its austere beauty, or perhaps because of it, Elly felt that there was something forbidding about it. Years later, when she read *Mourning Becomes Electra*, she had no difficulty envisioning the setting of O'Neill's play. In her mind's eye it was the same as "the Greek house" which she passed on her way back and forth to school. This house was one of the reasons why Elly preferred Broadway to the favored alternative route of Massachusetts Avenue. The other reason was a neighboring dwelling called the Damon house.

It had been built in the Federal style around 1830 for the Reverend David Damon, minister of Arlington's First Parish Church. Unlike its imposing neighbor, the Damon house stood a few feet from the street, and it was separated from the sidewalk by an elegant nineteenth-century wrought iron fence. The charm of the Damon property was enhanced by an orchard of sixty fruit trees which extended from the rear of the house to the end of the large rectangular lot. The trees reached their glory in the springtime when their blossoms came to a full bloom and formed a pale pink cloud filled with fragrance.

But what intrigued Elly most on the Damon property was a post topped by the iron head of a horse with a large heavy ring hanging from its mouth. It stood on the granite curbstone in front of the house, and its purpose, as Dion explained, was for tethering to its ring a carriage horse or a riding horse that was brought to a halt at the Damon place—before the time that trolley cars and automobiles had come into use.

The horse's head became Elly's talisman, and in all the years she walked by it, she made sure to pat its head—a gesture she believed would bring her good luck.

Nothing on Broadway interested Arthur but the Fire House. He no sooner entered it when a jovial fireman picked him up and swung him on to the driver's seat of the hook-and-ladder fire truck. He then plucked a bright red fireman's helmet from a rack and put it on Arthur's head. It was a thrilling moment for the little boy, who was hardly tall enough to reach the rim of the ponderous wheel. In his attempt to grasp it so as to satisfy his juvenile passion for driving a real fire engine, the fireman's helmet slipped down Arthur's head and completely covered it. At the sight of her faceless brother, Elly burst into laughter. The fireman came to the boy's rescue by freeing his head and setting him once again on *terra firma.* "Never mind your sister, young fella," he said, "when you grow up, you'll make a fine member of the fire brigade, and you'll have a helmet that fits you." He turned to Dion and lowering his voice remarked, "This one belongs to the Fire Chief who's got a 'big head'—if you know what I mean."

Arthur was humiliated not so much by his "loss of face" as by his sister's derision. He was not accustomed to being laughed at, but admired by his sisters, and Elly who was his favorite had forgotten, it seems, how often he had proved his devotion to her. Much to his older sisters' annoyance, he would refuse some sweet or other they had saved especially for him, unless it was offered to Elly, as well. And if only one piece could be had, he would share it with her. But he wasn't going to let her get away with treating him so shabbily. He'd put her in her place at the first opportunity, which came a few minutes later when they reached the Russell School.

"Here we are, Elly," said Dion as he stopped in front of a large, square, three-story red brick building.

"Is this a reformatory?" asked Arthur innocent like.

"I thought you had learned to read in the first grade," replied Dion, as he pointed to the lettering RUSSELL SCHOOL above the doorway. Oh, he could read all right, Arthur remarked airily, but he hadn't bothered to look at the name. It was such a dingy old place he really thought it was a reformatory—or maybe a prison, he added somewhat lamely.

Elly suspected that Arthur's remarks were meant to make her angry. They served, however, only to arouse in her an instant loyalty towards the Russell School, which prompted her to exclaim, "Oh, how nice and big it is! It's so much bigger than Arthur's little school in Pittsburgh."

"Nice and big!" he repeated with a jeer. "It's big all right, big and ugly—that's what it is. If you ask me, it can't be a 'nice' school if it's that ugly."

"But who asked you?" retorted Elly.

"Oh, shut up," said Arthur—whereupon he was reprimanded by Dion for using a vulgar term that was especially offensive to the older members of the family, although the younger girls were not above using it when they were at odds with one another.

The bickering between brother and sister gave Dion an opportunity which he seldom overlooked, of making a didactic observation for the benefit of his siblings: "You've heard, I suppose, the old saying, 'Don't judge a book by its cover.' The same can be said about this school or any school; it doesn't matter what it looks like from the outside. What goes on inside is what really counts—that is, whether or not its teachers are good teachers, and their pupils are well-taught and well-behaved or else they'll get what they deserve," said Dion significantly. "They should appreciate the free education that they are lucky to get in this country, and they should respect their teachers who drum knowledge day in and day out into the pupils' heads."

Having finished his brief homily, Dion announced they would walk a short ways up the avenue to see something which he thought they would like. "But before we go," he said, "you two should shake hands and forget your squabbling."

Arthur, whose anger was short-lived, eagerly offered his hand to Elly, who took it with disdain, and only because of Dion's request. She could not forgive her brother for telling her to "shut up." Well, she would do just that . . . she would *never* speak to him again! To make sure, however, she would not be tempted, for Elly was by nature a talkative child, she decided to avoid Arthur by skipping a few steps ahead of him.

She had not gone far when she came to a clearing that stretched between the public library and the Town Hall. At the further end of it she could see what looked like a small grotto framed by a semi-circle of trees and shrubs. In the midst of it was a pool with a figure kneeling by the water's edge. As she gazed at it wondering what it could be, her brothers caught up with her. Elly promptly forgot her vow of silence and exclaimed, "Look, Arthur, look at that beautiful thing—there, by the pool, is it a statue?"

It was, indeed, a statue called the *Menotomy Indian Hunter*, the work of Cyrus Dallin, one of America's foremost sculptors. Dallin, whose home and studio were located in Arlington, considered the town's original name "Menotomy" far more befitting than its present one. He crusaded tirelessly for its return ". . . in the name of poetic association, in the name of historic significance and in the name of a vanished people who loved this beautiful spot."

"I thought you would like it," said Dion, "it's what I had in mind to show you. Let's get nearer to it."

At close range Dallin's statue has the vitality of a living legend rather than the static quality of a figure cast in bronze. In the simple act of quenching his thirst, the Indian hunter reveals his inherent grace and dignity; his one hand is cupped to catch the water while with the other hand he holds his bow and arrows, and the goose he has shot lies lifeless on the ground beside him.

The children were eager to touch the statue. Elly, however, wondered if by doing so they might hurt it. She asked Dion who pondered over the question with deliberate solemnity; no, he did not think it would do any harm. The Indian was cast in bronze—a material that was not easily damaged. It was not proper, though, for people to go about doing as they pleased with "public property" which in this instance, meant that it belonged to every one who lived in Arlington, and everyone should care for it properly. But since they had never seen a statue like this one before, they could go ahead and look it over. "Be careful," he added, "you're more likely to hurt yourselves than the Indian Hunter."

While the children were absorbed with the statue, Dion walked a few steps toward the street from where he could better view the Universalist Church—"one of the area's most notable Victorian buildings which should probably be considered Arlington's finest architectural ornament of any period, in any date, and for any function." The church was built in 1841 and designed in the Greek Revival style. After 1860 it was remodeled in the Italianate Revival style by Rev. Thomas W. Silloway, an eminent Victorian architect.

Most likely Dion was attracted by the Greek architectural principles on which the Universalist Church had been designed and to which it owed its elegance. He seldom went by it without pausing to admire the structure, which is listed in the National Register of Historic Places.

In the many times he had paused to admire this house of worship, it never could have occurred to him that one day it would be known as the Greek Orthodox Church of Saint Athanasius the Great. It serves more or less one thousand families of Greek descent that now live in the town of Arlington, where once only one Greek family had made its home.

As soon as Elly returned home she went directly into the kitchen to share with Eleni her first impressions of Arlington. Elly felt closer to Eleni than to her sisters, and Eleni had greater affection for the little girl than for any of Elly's siblings.

The servant girl's attachment to the youngest of the Douropoulos offspring had taken root in the period following Elly's premature birth. The infant spent the first weeks of its precarious existence in the kitchen, which served as a comparatively crude but practical substitute for the present day incubator. With Cerberean vigilance, Eleni kept the old iron stove burning night and day so as to maintain a steady warmth and a continual flow of steam from the large kettles of boiling water. It was then, perhaps, that a dim consciousness of a constant and caring

71

presence took hold in the infant's inchoate mind and led to a mutual lifelong devotion.

Elly gave Eleni a rapid-fire account of her venture on the world beyond Palmer Street. The speed with which Elly could speak both in Greek and in English was a habit formed by necessity in a large family, and especially so if its members are highly articulate. In such a milieu one learns early on that the slighest opportunity to speak must be seized instantly and utilized to the utmost by saying one's piece as quickly as possible—or run the risk of not saying it all, or worse still losing the chance of saying it at all.

Eleni considered the three storied, red brick grammar school the most significant of Elly's descriptions. She regarded schools as hallowed places where children were taught *letters*—a demotic Greek term for "learning." Eleni did not know how to read or write; all she knew was how to make a cross when her signature was required, and it troubled her that the sacred symbol of her faith was also the humiliating sign of her ignorance. Beyond this distressing coincidence, Eleni did not spend time indulging in self-pity for her lack of education. She had accepted her limitations as the outcome of matters beyond her control. She was a shepherd's daughter born and bred in a rustic Arcadian village that was too small and too poor to support a school for male children, let alone for females. In Eleni's time schools for girls could be found only in a few of the large towns for the daughters of the well-to-do, and not for the likes of those who came from the peasantry.

Elly ended her account with a promise to take Eleni to see all the places she had seen. She was particularly anxious to show Eleni the Russell School—*her school*—which she praised extravagantly since Arthur was not within earshot to mock her. She couldn't wait for school to start so that she could learn how to read and write!

"I thought you could do that already," remarked Eleni.

Yes, she could read, but only little words like *dog* and *cat*. Arthur had taught her the alphabet and he showed her how to write her name—not just her first name but her whole name and she proudly spelled it out loud: E-L-L-Y D-O-U-R-O-P-O-U-L-O-S.

72

"Well, that's more than I can do," said Eleni.

"You can't write?" Elly asked incredulously.

"No, I can't write or read," she replied.

Elly was taken aback; she thought all grown-ups could read and write. Eleni must be joking, and Elly was about to tell her so, yet, the child somehow sensed that this was not a laughing matter. For a few moments she pondered over Eleni's disclosure, then she suddenly cried out, "Eleni, guess what? Oh, you'll never guess, so I'll tell you: I'm going to show you how to write your name! Not right now but as soon as I really learn to write. And guess what else? I'll show you how to write your name in Greek, too! Babá says we'll be starting Greek lessons soon as he finds a good teacher."

"That remains to be seen," replied Eleni noncommittally. She didn't see any sense in talking about it since Elly had not even started school.

"But I'm going to school soon, and I'll learn fast. You just wait and see."

"I don't doubt that," said Eleni, nor did she doubt that this clever chit, God love her, would teach her to write her name with those mysterious signs called *letters*. The thought that in her mid-thirties she would learn to write her name overwhelmed her. Up to now no one had cared whether or not she could do so—no one but this little girl! She had an impulse to hug her, but Eleni had learned early in her simple rustic upbringing to hide the intensity of her feelings. She merely gave Elly a shove towards the door and admonished her to wash her face and hands and to put on a clean frock—company was coming to dinner. "And tell your sisters to come down stairs," she added, "they've been primping up long enough, and you'd better remind them that the doorbell will soon start ringing."

The girls were expected to do their share of the daily chores while Eleni assumed the drudgery of keeping a large household in optimum order. Yet, she would not undertake such simple tasks as answering the doorbell or bringing in the traditional tray of refreshments, which is invariably offered to a visitor in a Greek home. Nor would she wait at the table during a family or company meal. In Eleni's mind these ordinary duties of a servant exposed the stigmata of her servitude. By refusing to perform them she asserted her dignity and affirmed her self-respect without which her humble lot would have been infinitely harder to bear.

Eleni was an ordinary looking person—the kind that one would pass by without as much as a glance. Yet she had certain attributes that were worthy of notice. She managed, despite her labors, not to appear slovenly. She was always nicely groomed and neatly dressed; the luster on her sensible black shoes showed they were vigorously polished each morning, and her aprons, which she wore only when she worked in the kitchen, were clean and crisp. Eleni's facial features had no distinction except for her eyes which were uncommonly round. Eleni wore glasses with circular tortise rims that emphasized the roundness of her eyes, and brought to the fore her thin bird-like nose. The combination of these various shapes and forms reproduced on Eleni's face the look of an omniscient owl.

But what was most peculiar about Eleni's eyes was the change that took place in them when she was aroused to a high pitch of anger. Arthur could recall years later that they seemed like "balls of fire pouring out a formidable spate of sparks," and he confessed he was tempted to goad poor Eleni on just to see that display of oracular fireworks.

In defense of Eleni, Elly would remind her brother that even though he tried to infuriate her, Eleni never held it against him—in fact, Elly could not recall Eleni ever saying an unkind word or using unseemly language even when she was greatly provoked.

Oh, but she had forgotten, Arthur would respond laughingly, that Eleni often used a scatological remark that she addressed directly to Satan. It was never her fault if the bread she baked failed to rise, if a kettle of egg-lemon soup curdled or if a bottle of wine or oil slipped from her grasp. Such minor mishaps and major misfortunes, as well, Eleni attributed to that contemptible fallen angel known as Satan. And the only way she could get even with him was to mutter: "*Skata sta yenia tou*"—or, in other words, "Shit on his beard."

Eleni would have preferred to get hold of the Evil One and battle it out until he was defeated, which Elly and Arthur had no doubt she could do, for despite her average height and weight

74

Eleni had astonishing physical strength. It came to light by chance soon after the young country girl arrived with the Douropoulos family in America.

One morning, while sweeping the front porch, Eleni noticed two Italian laborers on the opposite side of the street trying to dislodge a large boulder that had rolled onto the sidewalk from a nearby excavation. She watched them for a while as they struggled to move it. She finally tired of looking at their clumsy, futile efforts, and putting her broom aside, she went across the street. She walked around the boulder gauging its size and its weight; it was not larger and probably not heavier than the ones she had cleared off from the rocky Arcadian land her father needed for a pasture.

The men were startled by the unexpected appearance of a girl walking slowly around the boulder and scrutinizing it as though she had never seen anything like it before. One of the workmen twirled his forefinger near his temple and the other nodded his head in agreement. They exchanged a few words—the poor thing could get hurt with all the debris that was lying around. They started towards her to tell her so, but stopped short as the girl quickly spat on the palms of her hands and heaved the stone beyond the sidewalk. She started to cross the street, but turned and gave the stupified men a smile—a curious little smile.

Chapter Eight

When school opened Elly came in contact for the first time with a large number of her peers. Despite the dissimilarities in their upbringing, Elly shared with her classmates in the excitement of their new status as neophytes of the Russell School. They shared, as well, an immense curiosity regarding their teacher, Miss Elizabeth Day, their very first teacher, and therefore a singular personage in their young eyes.

Miss Day looked as though she had stepped down from a shelf that housed a collection of exquisite antique dolls—only she would not have stepped down, but jumped down lightly, for Miss Day was a sprightly creature in spite of her immaculate white hair, which was coiffeured in an elegant pompadour.

Short and small, but well-endowed fore and aft, Miss Day achieved, with the aid of a tight corselet, an "hour glass" figure, which was a Victorian prerequisite of fetching femininity. She was obviously proud of whatever anatomical appanage nature had bestowed on her, and refused to lessen its worth by submitting to the ephemeral fashions of the twentieth century.

In the classroom Miss Day's attire consisted of a shapely black or navy blue skirt that reached to the tips of her high-buttoned shoes. Her invariably white shirtwaists were handiworks of art fashioned in fine muslin, embroidery and lace. Their high collars and long sleeves were edged in dainty ruching that softened the aging face and hands, whose fingers were bedecked by a staggering variety of rings. Her one main adornment, however, was a gold brooch with a clear glass surface which covered a strand of silky blond hair.

"I used to wonder and still do," said Elly in her recollections of Miss Day, "if that lock of hair was her own from the days of her golden youth, or was it, perhaps, a cherished memento of some lost but never forgotten suitor?

"But what I have now come to appreciate about Miss Day was her adherence to certain values that have become as unfashionable in the twentieth century as her nineteenth century wardrobe. She was innately a lady, who made a strict order sound like a polite request and gave a smiling thanks for the slightest favor she might have asked of anyone. Yet, she kept a firm hand and eye on us as she marched up and down the aisles in her rustling skirts, leaving behind her a scent of lavender, making sure that we formed our letters properly. Her patience was immense, her criticism gentle and her praise generous, and if a rebuke was in order, it was made in private so that our self-respect was not publicly diminished. . . . Miss Day was a delightful anachronism such as we had never seen before and shall never see again—and more's the pity."

In her eagerness to be on time for the first day of school, Elly had hastily patted the horse's head that stood by the curbstone of the Damon house. On her way home, however, she stopped to give it a series of grateful little pats, for this talisman she had chosen had not failed her. School was as wonderful as she had hoped it would be, and even more so in one unexpected way, for she had made a friend. Well, she really couldn't call her a friend yet, since they barely had time to tell each other their names.

Elly liked the flowered print dress the little girl was wearing, and she admired the bright blue hair ribbon that matched her bright blue eyes. Her hair was an odd, coppery color with a burnished sheen to it that reminded Elly of butterscotch candy. She was petite in size but perfectly proportioned so that she seemed more lithe and graceful than the average child of her age; but behind that elfin-like appearance, a lively mind was taking form which Elly would in time come to admire and respect.

During recess time, she approached Elly and simply announced

77

"I am Barbara Winn." Elly, in turn, responded with her name. A dignified silence fell between them as they looked at one another in the grave manner of children when they first meet—a manner based, perhaps, on some instinctive sense of propriety by which the young observe and appraise each other.

The ringing of a bell signified the end of recess and their brief meeting. It was, nevertheless, the beginning of a life-long friendship between a child whose Puritan forebears were among the earliest settlers of Menotomy in the 1600s—and a child of Hellenic descent who had but recently arrived in the town now known as Arlington.

A bad cold kept Elly at home for more than a week. When she returned to school she met Barbara Winn in the cloakroom. After saying she was glad to see Elly again, Barbara lowered her voice and whispered, "You mustn't ever talk to Gertrude Wells—you know who I mean—the one who lives near you and wears the heavily starched dresses you said you don't like."

Yes, Elly knew her—and, yes, she didn't like dresses that were stiff as a board from too much starch but, still, why shouldn't she talk to her, Elly asked Barbara.

"She's not your friend," answered Barbara.

Elly was nonplussed by this laconic reply. She really didn't care if Gertrude was her friend or not; she had already made friends with most of her classmates, but that was no reason for not talking to Gertrude if she felt like it, so Elly asked again, "Why shouldn't I?"

"Oh, I'll tell you later . . . some other time," said Barbara.

"No, you won't," retorted Elly, "you'll tell me right now! You started it, and you're my best friend and you have to tell me *now*."

Barbara found herself in a quandry. She had not intended to tell Elly what Gertrude Wells had said, for she feared it would hurt her badly. Besides, that would make Barbara a tattletale which went against her innate sense of decency and her proper upbringing. But Elly's insistence and Barbara's loyalty towards her friend broke down her resolve.

Miss Day, it seems, was concerned by Elly's protracted

absence from school. She asked Gertrude, who lived around the corner from Palmer Street, if she would find out why her classmate had not been in school for more than a week.

Oh, no! Gertrude had declared, she couldn't do *that*. She wasn't allowed to go to Elly's house, or to play with her either.

The sudden silence that fell over the room was broken only by Gertrude's nervous giggle that preceded and followed whatever she had to say. Miss Day waited patiently until the giggling had subsided before she spoke again. Her usual polite tone of voice had a frosty edge to it as she inquired: "May I ask why not?"

"Because," she replied, "they're *Greeks*!"

Gertrude's words aroused in Elly's mind the sudden awareness that she was different—different in a way that at first puzzled her. Up to this epiphanic moment, she was not conscious that her Greek blood placed her in a peculiar status. She began to wonder if outside of her loyal friend, Barbara Winn, others regarded her and her family as inferiors that should be shunned. Slowly she became aware that she lived in two separate spheres— one was the American world, to which she was bound by accident of birth which claimed her loyalty and her love; the other was the land of her ancestors, which aroused in Elly a passionate pride for her Hellenic heritage; each of these worlds moved in its own orbit, and throughout Elly's life, they would time and again collide, and merge, separate and re-unite. Yet, they could never be in complete concord.

Soon after school began, the children started taking Greek lessons. Their teacher, Cleonike Apostolou, was an eccentric spinster known as *Kyria* Cleonike. The Greek prefix for "Mrs." which preceded her first name was given to her gratuitously as a mark of respect for her profession; it was also meant as a consolatory gesture to mitigate the sorrow of her spinsterhood.

Cleonike accepted the title as simply due her since she would have acquired it except for a tragic accident which befell her fiancé, Orestes, less than twenty-four hours before their marriage was to take place. He had arrived by boat in Constantinople (Istanbul) where the nuptials were to be held the following day. He had recently graduated from the Theological School and was

79

still wearing the seminarian garb.

In his eagerness to see his betrothed, Orestes rushed down the pier, and in his haste he stumbled and fell headlong into the water. "Those long sweeping robes," Cleonike would say, "those robes he wore with such grace and dignity were his undoing." They became waterlogged and dragged her beloved Orestes to a watery death. And never was she to lay eyes on him again. Cleonike recited this sad story without a tear but with a macabre relish that made the *cosmos* question its veracity as well as Cleonike's sanity.

Arthur and Elly had no doubts, however, about their teacher's mental condition. Who else but a mad woman would act as she did as soon as she reached the corner of Palmer Street? To the mortification of her pupils and to the neighbors' amusement, Kyria Cleonike would march up the street brandishing her perennial umbrella and shouting in Greek with a shrill voice, "Come Elly, come, Arthur . . . come, come, my little birds . . . Kyria Cleonike has arrived . . . it's time for your lesson." On and on she went until she reached her destination.

It was taken for granted that the teacher would stay for dinner whenever she came to Palmer Street. But one miserable cold winter night, Mrs. Douropoulos suggested that Kyria Cleonike stay overnight. One night led to another, and another, as several weeks—or it may have been several months—went by with Kyria Cleonike ensconed indefinitely in the Douropoulos household.

This was a catastrophic development for the children as the Greek teacher's daily presence meant daily Greek lessons. Kyria Cleonike sensed their resentment and complimented them lavishly, but only when their parents were present since she deemed it more politic to be in their good grace than that of their children. . . . Ah! she would gush, such manners, such felicity in speaking Greek, and the way the little dears used the "plural" in addressing her and their elders; all these were proofs of the superior milieu in which the children were raised, and in which she felt completely at home.

Arthur and Elly began to fear she would stay forever, but an unfortunate episode caused Kyria Cleonike to replace her gross flattery with hysterical outrage. Her protracted visit ended in disaster when Arthur, in helping her to be seated at the dinner table one night, pulled her chair away rather than towards her. He apologized profusely and insisted that it was an accident, a miscalculation of timing. Father Douropoulos ordered his young son to leave the dining room at once, and Elly was told to do likewise. She had disgraced herself by clapping her hands in glee when she saw Kyria Cleonike sprawled indecently on the floor.

Banishment from the table was a mild form of punishment for the children since they could depend on Eleni to bring them goodies and milk. In this instance she was especially generous in the way of choice edibles. Eleni had no use for Kyria Cleonike, who was in the habit of refering to her as a "servant." Eleni knew her place well enough, and she didn't need anyone to make it clear, least of all that old leech of a spinster.

The Greek teacher that followed in Cleonike's wake was an amiable, rather shy, personable young man in his mid-twenties named Christos Pappas. He had studied at the Divinity School of Athens University, and after fulfilling his military obligations had come to the United States. *Kyrios* (Mister) Pappas, as the children called him, first came to Arlington soon after his arrival from Greece. Arthur and Elly liked him from the start, and they often spoke of him with affection when they recalled their youth in Arlington.

In one of those sessions of revived recollections Elly asked, "Do you remember what a glorious relief it was to get rid of poor old Cleonike—thanks to you—and have the good luck to get Kyrios Pappas as our teacher? I used to call him 'our Greek tutor' when I wanted to impress people."

"That shows what a snob you were, but I must admit the term you used was correct since a tutor usually means someone who gives private lessons which is what Christos Pappas did in our case.

"Yes, we were lucky. He had a gift for teaching, although he had not been trained for it. Father recognized him as a born pedagogue and hired him to teach in the Greek Parochial School in Boston. But 'our Greek tutor' went well beyond teaching in various Greek communities. He eventually became director of the Greek Archdiocese Department of Education and Overseer of the Parochial Schools—and finally achieved his noble ambition—to be ordained a priest.''

"I have forgotten," said Elly, "for how long a time he gave us lessons in Greek. Do you remember?"

"Not more than a year and a half or two at the most, I'd say, before he left Boston for greener pastures. But in that length of time he taught us to read and write in Greek and he drilled us mercilessly on those endless Greek declensions. He'd say he was doing us a favor because if we mastered the elements of Greek grammar, we wouldn't have to learn English grammar . . . that was true, of course, but we were too young to appreciate what he said."

"I suppose he was a little hard on us," remarked Elly, "but we were hard on him, too . . . remember when one of us would drop a pencil and then both of us would scurry under the table to find it? We'd make silly faces and giggle as quietly as we could at those weird high-buttoned Greek shoes that Kyrios Pappas wore; of course he could hear us and—"

"And when we re-surfaced," Arthur recalled with laughter, "the poor fellow would lift his eyes upwards and intone in a sorrowful voice: 'Kyrie, eleison'—Lord, have mercy. I never could make out whether he was imploring the Lord to have mercy towards him or towards us."

"Fortunately, mother made up for our remissions," said Elly, "by finding that sweet girl that our teacher married. He had confided in mother his desire to become a priest, and with that in mind she saw to it that his bride would be worthy of her future role as a 'presbytera.' What I liked the most about our Greek lessons," continued Elly, "was the respite Kyrios Pappas gave us about fifteen minutes before the two-hour session was over. It was heralded by Eleni's arrival, and this was no small concession on Eleni's part. But she had taken Kyrios Pappas with 'a good eye' as we say in Greek. Besides he was a *male* teacher and not some daffy female like poor Cleonike. So, she would come bearing mother's lovely old silver tray with the usual small cup of Greek coffee, a glistening glass of cold water, some sweet or other, and a hand-embroidered tea napkin."

"All I remember about that tray," confessed Arthur, "was the way Eleni would tuck a two-dollar bill for our two-hour lesson under one side of the saucer and folded inside of it were two nickels for car fare. Eleni had instructed us not to watch Kyrios Pappas as he pocketed the money. That, she would say, would be rude of us and embarrassing for him."

"As though," Elly remarked, "the poor man had to stealthily take what he had painfully earned. But such politesse no more exists today than the two-dollar bill or the nickel car fare that would take us the whole length and breadth of Boston and all its suburbs, besides."

For a while neither of them spoke as their minds wandered in the endless maze of memories until Elly asked, "What are you thinking of, Arthur?"

"Of mother . . . what Christos Pappas said about her," he replied, "I used to see him now and then by chance; he always expressed his deep respect for father, but it was mother who had aroused his greatest admiration. The last time I saw him I told him that mother, who was then in her early nineties, had gone again to Greece for a short visit. He was delighted to learn that she was still vigorous enough to travel. 'But I am not surprised,' he said, 'I consider your mother a remarkable woman . . . a woman of regal presence . . . she had the makings of a queen.' "

When the house on Palmer Street was but a distant memory, the two youngest Douropoulos offspring would often recall the early days in Arlington as the happiest ones of their childhood. The family, yet untouched by sorrow, glowed with a resplendent flame that Arthur and Elly would in time realize was too lovely to last. . . . During that period of their life, Arthur and Elly, like children the world over, had no thought of the past nor concern for the future but lived in a carefree present that is the prerogative of the young. It was a time when the two children became aware of the exciting world of learning; they adjusted readily to it and functioned successfully in it judging from the report cards they proudly brought home from school. They were, to begin with, precocious children, for they were reared in an essentially adult environment, and thanks to their older siblings, by the time they entered the first grade they could speak English as fluently as Greek.

Throughout their school years, English was their favorite subject. It was not surprising, therefore, that Arthur became in his senior year editor-in-chief of the *Clarion*, the Arlington High School literary magazine. The next year Elly followed in her brother's footsteps with the additional distinction of being the first girl to be chosen as editor-in-chief of the *Clarion*.

As native-born citizens, Arthur and Elly represented the first American generation of Greek parentage. Their adjustment to school and its peripheral activities was relatively less difficult for them than for their Greek-born sisters, for the climate in the first decade of the twentieth century when the greatest number of Europeans entered the United States was, in general, inimical towards the immigrants. The attitude of hostility was in a way ironic since many of those who displayed it were aliens themselves, who had preceded the newcomers by a generation or so. As for the long-entrenched American establishment, it tended on the whole to ignore the foreigners or at best to tolerate them since they were useful in developing the vast resources of the New World.

The two older Douropoulos girls, Angela and Sophia, were fortunate not to have experienced any unpleasant episodes in going to or coming home from school, for the Notre Dame Academy which they attended while the family lived in Baltimore was close to their home. Demetra, the third daughter, was the tomboy in the family and often chose to go her own way. The idea of going to a religious school which was run by Catholic Sisters did not appeal to her. She preferred the public grammar school, which she entered soon after the family had settled in Baltimore.

The rowdy youths who roamed the city streets for the special enjoyment of taunting the "greenhorns," as the immigrants were often called, spotted the little girl coming home from school. They stopped her and demanded that she tell them her name. Demetra was not easily intimidated, but sensing that this was a band of "inquisitors" she decided to comply with their demands. They laughed uproariously when they heard her name . . . so, it was "Demetra," was it? Who ever heard of a name like that? Oh, so she was a foreigner? And where did she come from they wanted to know as the crowded menacingly around her. But before they could lay a hand on her, Demetra bolted from their midst and dashed for the nearest corner and disappeared from sight by entering a narrow side street. She continued running as fast as she could when suddenly she found herself in a little park. She looked over her shoulder . . . no one was following her . . . the bullies had apparently decided not to bother with her . . . perhaps they had found some other hapless foreigner to harass.

Her sense of relief gave way to bewilderment and then to anger. Why had no one told her she would be jeered and laughed at because she had come from another country? Everybody kept saying how lucky they were that the Church was sending their father to America, and how lucky they were that they could afford to be sailing on a fine boat in first class cabins! How excited they all were when they arrived in New York. They never imagined that a city could be so big . . . and their brother was already there to meet them. They were all so happy to see him after almost a whole year since Uncle Nicholas, Babá's brother, had come from America and had taken Dion back with him for a visit. He was about to come home and go back to school in Athens, but instead *they* had all come to the New World!

It was all so strange and wonderful when they left the pier, and Dion bought some funny-looking yellow fruit from a man who had a cartful of them. They were called "bananas," Dion said, and he showed them how they should be peeled before you tried to eat them. They were really delicious and before long the whole bunch was gone. But Dion bought some more so they could eat them on the train that was taking the family to Baltimore; They could hardly wait to see their new home in America, and now here she was wishing they had *never* left Greece.

Demetra sat down on a bench to catch her breath. Despite her gloomy thoughts, she had to admit that the little park was a pretty spot. It was shaded by tall trees and surrounded by small rose-red brick row houses with white marble steps. They were the kind built in the Georgian style that once lined most of Baltimore's quiet streets, but in time were replaced by housing that was more efficient by modern standards, but sadly deficient

85

in the aesthetic values of old. . . . Her eyes wandered from these charming little houses to the opposite side from where she sat, and she caught sight of a somewhat small frail elderly man with a kind, gentle face. He seemed to have been waiting for the little girl to look in his direction, for he had laid aside the book he had apparently been reading. As soon as she glanced at him, he smiled and waved his hand at her in the cordial manner of an old friend.

"I had the feeling," recalled Demetra, "from the moment I saw him that he had been waiting for me . . . that he had somehow guessed—or rather he *knew*—what had happened, and he was trying to show that he cared for me—cared for a homesick child in a strange world. Perhaps it was only my imagination, but whatever it was, that sweet smile, that gesture was so comforting that my misery dissolved. I felt happy again that we had come to America, and I was tempted to tell him so. Yet, I hesitated to speak to him, not that I had been told never to talk to a stranger—as children are warned today—but because we had been taught to wait for our elders to speak first to us." Instead, she smiled shyly as she waved back to him, and with a light heart she found her way home.

At suppertime Demetra gave an account of what began as a misadventure but had ended happily because a kind gentleman had given her a smile and a friendly wave of his hand, as though he had been an old friend. She thought he might be a priest, for he was wearing a long black robe—like the kind Babá wore at home, and the same kind of collar except that just beneath it there was a splash of bright red color in a kind of velvety material.

He was, indeed, a churchman—no other than the unforgettable brilliant and beloved American hierarch, Cardinal James Gibbons of Baltimore.

Chapter Nine

The dichotomous existence which would continue throughout the life of the two American-born offspring in the Douropoulos family began when they entered school. Their appearance, their speech and their manner gave no indication, however, that they were raised in an environment which varied significantly from that of their schoolmates. And, indeed, in many respects the two children did not differ from their contemporaries in Arlington. They often joined the neighboring children in playing the age-old games such as hide-and-seek, tag, blind-man's-buff and scores of others which are a universal legacy to all children.

When Arthur and Elly were young, children continued as in eons past to create games which often were determined or inspired by their surroundings and limited only by their own ingenuity. Those who, like the Douropoulos siblings, happened to live nearby trolley-car lines, enjoyed a particular kind of entertainment. It involved the laying of a penny on a trolley track, and then waiting until a "street car" came along. The end result was the metamorphosis of a humble piece of copper into an artifact smooth and slim and glowing with burnished beauty.

The one day of the week when Arthur and his little sister met their peers on common ground was Saturday afternoon at 2 P.M. Only an act of God, such as an earthquake or a cyclone, would have possibly kept the children of Arlington from converging *en masse* at the Regent Theater. After pushing and shoving their way beyond its portals, they felt a rising excitement that reached its peak when the "piano lady" walked down the aisle. Homage to this personage, who was considered indispensible for the fullest enjoyment of the "silent movies," was expressed by ecstatic shrieks and whistles accompanied by thunderous clapping of hands and stomping of feet.

This cacophony came to an abrupt end with the first tinny notes from the old up right piano that stood with pathetic grandeur in a pool of light by the corner of the stage. As the huge brocade curtain that covered the screen slowly parted, a reverential hush fell over the wave of childish heads.

"We became positively catatonic," Arthur would recall laughingly, "as we watched Tom Mix, William S. Hart and those mad Mack Sennett comedies, or the antics of Fatty Arbuckle, or those of Harold Lloyd and Buster Keaton. They were all marvelous in their own way, so I can't say which one or which ones I liked the most."

"Well, I can tell you," said Elly, "which were my favorites: Mary Pickford, without question, headed the list, and I was mesmerized by Theda Bara with those smouldering eyes. And Pearl White—she used to play in one of those *ad infinitum* serials—something called, I think, *The Perils of Pauline*. It should have been called that if it wasn't. She was forever in some dreadful plight, but always saved in the nick of time. As for that darling little fellow, Jackie Coogan, all the little girls simply adored him."

"Not only little girls or little boys but grown-ups, as well, fell under the spell of those early actors and actresses. But they were more than spellbinders; they were truly the legendary giants of those years who made Hollywood the legend it was and still is today."

"But you haven't mentioned the greatest of them all," remarked Elly.

"Ah, I've left him for the last—that frail, pitiful little man was not a 'giant' but a genius. For who else in that relatively crude period of film making reached—or could reach even now with the spectacular improvements in motion pictures—the exquisite artistry, the humor and pathos he achieved by a mere shrug of the shoulder or the bemused lift of an eyebrow? And who else could make the young and the old laugh one moment and cry the next without his saying a word or uttering a sound?"

"Who else?" echoed Elly, "who else but that forlorn little tramp, Charlie Chaplin."

Dolly Endicott and Mabel Davis were close neighbors and close friends. They often met in the afternoon for a cup of tea that usually followed a séance with the "ouija board." One of these sessions took place soon after the Douropoulos family had moved to their new home which was next door to the Davis house.

Mabel, known as "Mabe," was especially pleased that afternoon. The small wooden planchette which ran on little wheels with the slightest touch of the hand, had spelled out on the ouija board's alphabet a most satisfactory message for Mabe from her late sister-in-law, Mrs. William F. Davis.

Dolly Endicott, who was more amused than impressed by the ouija's supernatural powers, commented drily that Mabe didn't need any spiritual assurances to verify the care she was giving her now motherless little nephew, Billy, and his older sister, Ruth.

"But it's such a comfort," said Mabe, "that dear Ada isn't worrying about the children. I'm not worried either," she added, "about Billy any longer. Now that he's made friends with that adorable little boy next door, he's happy again, happy as a lark."

Mabe was in her early thirties, a short, buxom, charming woman who had spurned several offers of marriage for one reason or another. However, a few months before her sister-in-law's sudden death from an infected tooth, she became engaged to Llewellyn "Mac" Evans, a debonair Scotsman, who swept her off her feet. Still, Mabe's loyalty to her family was such that when Ada died she informed "Mac" she would not marry him unless he agreed to become a member of her brother-in-law's household. "Mac" accepted his finaceé's ultimatum and a few months later Mabel Davis became Mrs. Llewellyn Evans in a quiet family wedding.

Among the presents the newlyweds received was a handsome cloisonné vase from Dion Douropoulos. Mabe was delighted and touched, as well as surprised, by Dion's kindly gesture.

During one of those "feasts of memories" which Elly and

her brother often indulged in, Arthur mentioned the gift Dion had sent to Mabe Evans.

"Oh, I figured that out a long time ago," said Elly with a superior air.

"Did you really?" asked Arthur with a straight face.

"Of course I did. It wasn't hard to see why. Dion's room, you remember, faced Mabe's bedroom; well, Mabe had the habit of prancing around her room before and after her bath 'in the buff' as kids say today, and had the habit besides of not pulling down the shades."

"Ah, so that's it, is it?" replied Arthur innocently, "well, I must say it was quite decent of Dion to repay Mabe in such a gentlemanly way for the entertainment she had offered him gratis."

Bill and Arthur were handsome boys with the kind of rare good looks that are not diminished by time. Bill had straight blond hair, blue eyes and a ruddy complexion. He was tall for his age with a large frame that presaged a mature height of over six feet. Arthur had curly light brown hair, brown eyes and a clear fair skin. He was moderately tall and relatively slim. Both boys enjoyed sports and spent a good deal of time at the Spy Pond playground—an area equipped with tennis courts, a baseball and football field and other athletic facilities which the town provided and maintained for the Arlington school children.

Arthur was a better athlete than Bill despite his friend's larger physique. As he grew older, Arthur took part in a number of athletic activities including the high school track team, the hockey team, skating and tennis. Of all the sports, tennis was the one he enjoyed the most and the one in which he excelled. His proficiency in it led to his being appointed coach of the Harvard tennis team during the time he taught there.

Mrs. Douropoulos was uneasy about the friendship between her young son and the boy next door. Billy was, she admitted, a winsome child, but he obviously lacked discipline. He came and went as he pleased, and thought nothing of interrupting Arthur when he was studying his Greek lesson or doing his homework. Her uneasiness turned into distress when she learned

90

that Mrs. Eagleston, a nearby neighbor, had complained that the boys came into her yard and helped themselves to the pears from her fruit tree. The Presbytera brought the matter to her husband's attention by remarking, "My father—God rest his soul—used to say, 'Bad company destroys golden virtues.' "

"Now, what's this all about?" asked Father Douropoulos obviously irked that his wife had interrupted him while he was looking over the morning mail.

"I can see you're busy," retorted Mrs. Douropoulos, "but what I have to tell you is, I believe, more important than the mail." She went on to say that she was upset because she feared "Beelee" (as she pronounced Billy's name) was a bad influence on their young son. Mrs. Eagleston who lived near the corner in the large gray house with that lovely Seckel pear tree in her yard, saw the boys from her window filling a bag with pears, and when she knocked on the window they dropped the bag and ran away like a pair of thieves.

"At least they were smart enough not to take the 'evidence' with them," her husband remarked, with a flicker of amusement in his eyes. "Now if that lady had been smart, she would have given them as many bags as she could lay her hands on—or better still, gotten hold of a cart and had the boys remove those pears lying on the ground like a rotting carpet with a miasma of flies, wasps and hornets hanging over it. The wonder is how the boys escaped getting stung to death. I must say they were lucky."

"I don't understand how you can joke about it," cried Mrs. Douropoulos, "joke about stealing as though you condoned it!"

"I condone nothing of the sort, as you well know, and so will our son know as soon as I talk with him. But let's keep matters in their proper proportion and not equate childish mischief with the destruction of 'golden virtues.'

"You should examine, I believe, your own views and feelings at this point," Father Douropoulos continued, speaking no longer as a parent but as the teacher he had been a large part of his life. "What, for instance, makes you think that it was not your son but the 'bad influence' of his friend that brought about the problem at hand? I suspect the trouble lies in your belief and that of Arthur's sisters, as well, that he is an angel—which I hope

91

he isn't, since angels belong in heaven and not on earth. His mother and his sisters would do him more good by showing him some benevolent neglect rather than doting on him and seeing him as a model child. What the boy needs is to try his wings, to make his mistakes and learn from them—and the freedom to make, if he wishes, a friend of the boy next door, who as far as I can see is a fine little fellow.

"And who knows if this early comradery of theirs might not blossom into a 'Damon and Pythias' friendship? You will never know if you cut it in the bud."

The Presbytera overcame her uneasiness about the boy next door, and before long her approval gave way to affection. For Billy Davis had won her heart by his effortless charm. And as the years went by, no one rejoiced more than Arthur's mother in the friendship between the two boys.

When Bill went to college and then on to law school, he no longer lived in Arlington, but he returned to Palmer Street whenever he could find the time to accept Mrs. Douropoulos' standing invitation for dinner. After Bill graduated from law school, he was soon on his way to a spectacularly successful career that would take him far afield. Yet Arlington would remain the source of his fondest memories among which were the meals he had during his student days at his friend's house.

"At that time," Bill recalled, "Elly and Arthur were the only two children in the family who had not yet left Palmer Street. I suppose it should have seemed strange that so few were now seated around that large oak dining table, but I wasn't really aware of those empty spaces, for 'Mother D' (as Bill called Mrs. Douropoulos) gave the room a fullness by her mere presence. But even when she left the room the force of her 'permanent magnetism' was such that her presence could still be felt.

"She was a most solicitous hostess who went out of her way to please her guests. She never forgot my passion for Greek olives, and I would always find by my place a bowl of those black beauties glistening in a marinade of olive oil and vinegar with a delicate hint of *rigani*."

Bill's introduction to Greek olives came at an early age when

Arthur had first taken him into the Douropoulos' well-stocked larder. As they were rummaging for food, Bill spied a large earthenware crock filled with olives; Arthur disliked them and advised his friend not to eat them. "They're awful—awful bitter," he warned. Bill, nevertheless, put one in his mouth, and the result was "love at first taste." He proceeded to eat one after the other until footsteps were heard. . . . Arthur grabbed his friend by the arm and whispered, "Eleni's coming—let's beat it." They fled from the pantry, but not before Bill had hastily stuffed as many olives as his pocket could hold.

Despite Mabe's rubbing and scrubbing the olive oil stains on Billy's pants refused to budge, and driven to despair, Mabe gave strict orders: her nephew was not to have any more olives.

Mrs. Douropoulos had long since made up for Mabe's heartless ruling by those omnipresent olives that awaited Bill each time he came to dinner at Palmer Street.

Among the experiences the two boys had shared was one that Elly often asked her brother to repeat, for like a favorite old record played over and over again, its repetition increased rather than lessened its charm. This little episode took place during a hot summer afternoon when Bill and Arthur were playing checkers on the shady side of the Douropoulos porch. A car came wobbling up the street and stopped in front of the house.

"Oh, boy! look at that flat tire," exclaimed Arthur.

"It's a 'beaut' all right," said Bill, as they ran down the porch steps to get a closer look.

The driver, a somewhat lumpish, middle-aged matron, came out of the car in a state of confusion. "What happened? Oh, what happened to my car?" she cried.

"Your tire, Ma'am . . . it's flat as a pancake," Bill informed her.

She began wringing her hands and wailing, "How dreadful! What shall I ever do now?"

"Don't worry—we can fix it for you," said Bill.

The woman looked skeptical, but Bill assured her that he had often changed tires on his father's car. Mr. William F. Davis, Sr., owned a bright red Reo. Its color was startling—at a time

93

when most cars were black—and its size was extraordinary. For it had been built to accommodate "Big Bill," a man of prodigious girth, who weighed over 350 pounds.

Bill appointed his friend as his helper and set to work as he barked orders like a drill sergeant to Arthur, who followed them more out of loyalty to his friend, rather than any desire to toil and sweat on a hot day for the benefit of a silly lady driver who didn't even know she had a flat tire.

When they finished their work, the woman was all smiles; she dipped into her purse and brought out two crisp one-dollar bills and waved them gayly. "You dear, beautiful boys! You're angels, both of you. I don't believe in spoiling young folk, but you deserve a generous *pourboire* for doing such a fine job for little old me."

Arthur was stunned by this unexpected bonanza, but he did not forget his manners. He began to murmur his thanks when Bill gave him a sharp kick in the ankle, and to his dismay, he heard Bill say, "No, thank you, Ma'am, we can't accept any money."

"Don't be silly, you deserve it, you've worked so hard, both of you—here, take it."

"Thanks just the same, but it's out of the question," said Bill firmly.

"But why not?" she persisted.

"Because," replied Bill, "our motto is: 'To Serve,' and our slogan is: 'Do a good turn each day' . . . you see, Ma'am, we're Boy Scouts."

Years later, when reviewing this episode, Arthur remarked to Elly, "Of course I was furious at Bill; a dollar for each of us was a fortune in those days. Later I realized it was not priggishness, but Bill's innate decency that prompted him to refuse that money, and that reminds me of a remark of William Johnson Cory. He was, you know, considered the most brilliant tutor at Eton in his time—a writer and a fine poet, as well, though he's hardly remembered now."

"You certainly remember him. You've quoted so often his poem on *Heraclitus* that I can recite it by heart."

"Ah, yes, that's a splendid thing of his . . . as to his remark, he said: 'There's a little touch of vulgarity in the thought of any reward—for anything, ever.' Bill didn't have the slightest touch of the vulgar in him even though he was anything but prissy. What he did have in abundance was an elegance of spirit. You and I, however, failed to see it because we had assumed a cynical attitude toward the 'Anglo-Saxon' world.''

''But, we couldn't have been cynical; why, we were too young then to know even the meaning of that word,'' protested Elly.

''Well, then let's say we felt a little superior rather than cynical in judging Bill as a prig. That, you see, was only a cover for our uneasiness about the 'Anglo-Saxon' world to which he and your friends, and mine, no less, belonged. We greatly admired that world, but we didn't feel we were a part of it despite our apparent acceptance in it.''

''I doubt if it's ever possible to align two such disparate worlds,'' said Elly.

Arthur was no longer listening to Elly, but was talking more to himself than to his sister. ''Bill,'' he murmured, ''was a prince only we didn't realize it until he died.''

Chapter Ten

Arthur was more fortunate than his little sister in finding a friend of the same age who lived next door. The little girls in the neighborhood were two or three years younger or older than Elly. Despite this chronological disparity, which is inconsequential in later years, Elly played with them occasionally, for they were nice little girls, although she would have preferred the company of the friends she had made at school, especially her favorite friend, Barbara. But none of them lived close by; the exchange of visits was, therefore, postponed until the children were older and could manage the considerable distances between their homes.

But the lack of compatible playmates did not disturb Elly; for from the time she had started school she began to feel "grown-up" and found more enjoyment in exploring her new surroundings than playing with dolls or engaging in other childish pastimes.

One of the significant discoveries for Elly, and for Arthur as well, was Arlington's public library. It is known as the Robbins Library and was built in the Italian renaissance style with buff-colored sandstone and with a green slate roof. Besides its distinguished architecture, the Robbins Library had the distinction of being the direct descendant of the first free library in Massachusetts, and the first children's library in the nation.

For Arthur and Elly the most intriguing part of this handsome building was the children's library with its inviting small round tables and child-sized chairs. During their initial visit they each received a library card entitling them to take whatever books they desired for two weeks, and went home with as many books as they could carry. A few days later they returned the books, and chose another batch to take home with them—a routine they faithfully followed during the years they lived in Arlington.

The interest that Arthur and Elly had in books was not surprising since all the members of the family were readers except for the Presbytera. She was well versed, however, in the Old and New Testament, and in a thick volume entitled *The Lives of the Saints*. She had also read *Les Misérables*, which her husband had described to her as a great classic that dealt with the forces of good and evil. When she had asked him which of the two prevailed, he had answered, "If you read the book, you will find out for yourself."

Mrs. Douropoulos was greatly impressed with Victor Hugo's masterpiece and deeply moved by the compassion the Bishop of Digne had shown towards Jean Valjean, an ex-convict who stole the bishop's silverware after the saintly man had befriended him. When the thief was caught, the bishop not only refused to condemn him, but returned to him the silver he had stolen as well as a pair of silver candlesticks Jean Valjean had apparently overlooked. The bishop made only one request of the ex-convict—that he use the silverware as a means to begin a new and honest life. Jean Valjean fought valiantly to fulfill the bishop's request in spite of the misfortunes that beset him, to the end of his life.

The Presbytera never regretted the time she had spent in reading "that wonderful story which proves," she would declare triumphantly, "that goodness has the power to destroy evil!"

When Father Douropoulos spoke about his wife's lack of interest in reading, he would say to his children, "Your mother is wiser than the rest of us; she has chosen to *live* life rather than to *read* about it.

Alexandra had, indeed, chosen to live life in its fullest measure. But her zest for living was not simply a matter of choice; she was "a force of nature" as the French say; moreover, she possessed a natural ability that Walter Pater describes as the art of "getting as many pulsations as possible into a given time."

She lived each hour of each day with intensity . . . with "high passions . . . which give a quickened sense of life, of ecstasy and the sorrow of love" . . . and which yield "a quickened, multiplied consciousness. . . ."

She had, as well, the capacity to accept with grace whatever life had to offer—an attitude which is expressed by Saint Paul: "I have learned in whatever state I am in, herewith to be content." Although Alexandra appeared to be profligate in the use of her enormous vitality, she conserved much of it, nevertheless, by accepting her lot in life. She did not dissipate her time or her energy on futile longings, regrets, and anxieties. Nor did she delve into her psyche in order to "discover herself," or what today is called finding "one's identity," which has become a fashionable preoccupation much to the advantage of the psychiatric community. The Priest's wife did not feel the need to find out who she was; she simply accepted herself as God had seen fit to make her.

The Presbytera was the first one in the family to get up in the morning, and the last to go to bed at night. Before she went to sleep she would say her prayers in front of the *iconostasion*—the icon stand which was an integral part of a Greek home in Alexandra's time. This little "indoor" shrine need be nothing more than a small table, a shelf, a mantle or any suitable place that could hold the family icons, as well as a censer, a cross, and a bottle of holy water. It is readily seen to be a hallowed place by the presence of a votive vessel called the *candili* which burns night and day as a symbol of Christ's Eternal Light.

In the Douropoulos home this miniature "shrine" could be found in the master bedroom, and it was adorned with several old icons and a picture of Saint Nektarios, the first Greek Orthodox saint to have been photographed. This picture and an icon of a thirteenth century Byzantine madonna were especially treasured by Alexandra Douropoulos. The icon had been handed down in Alexandra's paternal family from generation to generation. The other was the picture of the future Saint Nektarios (then known as the Metropolitan of Pentapolis) which was in an ordinary dark frame. It contrasted sharply with the rich mellow colors of the icons, some of which were partially covered with an opulent overlay of gold. Nektarios had given the picture to Father Douropoulos and the Presbytera before they left Greece— "so that you will not forget me," he told them—as if they could ever forget this saintly soul, who had honored them with his friendship, who had performed a miracle during his visit to their home in Arcadia, who had ignited the flame of Constantine Douropoulos' latent desire to enter the priesthood, and who had ordained him with his own hand.

Every night Alexandra ended her prayers with one she had learned as a little girl which begins:

Now I lay me down to sleep,
I pray the Lord my soul to keep . . .

The Greek version of this child's prayer is, however, an appeal to one's guardian angel rather than to the Lord. Consigning thus her eternal soul to a reliable celestial being, Alexandra would quickly fall asleep. . . . The next morning, revitalized by a few hours of serene slumber, she would begin the day well-dressed and well-groomed. She had not succumbed to the habit of slipping into a bathrobe or a house dress or whatever attire involved less work than getting into full "panoply" early in the morning. She considered anything less in the way of dressing as a form of *sloth* which in her view was as pernicious as any of the other "deadly sins." Each new day was for Alexandra a re-affirmation of life. And life was a priceless gift from God that should not be desecrated by indolence.

Soon after the Greek family had settled in Palmer Street, some of the neighbors began to express the view that the foreign element in their midst did not prove to be, after all, a catastrophe. Indeed, some of the residents conceded that the newcomers gave a fresh, colorful ambiance to the staid, not to say, prosaic atmosphere of their neighborhood. The priest and his wife, however, were as unaware of this favorable turn of opinion as they were regarding the distress their arrival had caused to most of the residents of Palmer Street.

Mrs. Douropoulos greeted her neighbors with her usual cordiality, and if some of their responses were hardly civil she attributed their curtness to a natural reticence, for she had been told that the "Yankees" were a people of few words. They were certainly less voluble than the Americans she had met before coming to live in New England. The contrast, however, which she experienced most sharply was that between her present environment and the one in which she had been born and raised. She found none of the gregariousness which prevailed among her people, and which was expressed in the conviviality of Sunday visits among relatives and friends—in the exuberant celebrations of engagements, and weddings which in due time were normally followed by joyous baptisms. The profusion of food and wine at these events would no doubt strike the New Englanders with a strong puritanical strain in their veins as absurdly extravagant and possibly hedonistic.

Even funerals, though decorously subdued, had a social significance depending upon the status of the deceased, and a didactic value, as well, by emphasizing the wisdom of enjoying life before it was too late to do so. The modern Greeks still adhere to the Aristotelian precept that "man exists for the betterment of his mortal rather than his immortal improvement."

Regardless of how the neighborhood felt towards the newcomers, Alexandra found much that was praiseworthy in her New England neighbors. She considered them sensible, quiet, unassuming people who were close to their families and to their Church, and who went about their activities without fuss or fanfare. What impressed her the most, however, was their industriousness which was exemplified by Mr. Ernest Morrison, a neighbor, who lived at the corner of Palmer Street.

The Morrisons were evidently well-to-do, for their house was large, and besides had a two-car garage; it was well-built and undistinguished—the kind of dwelling that appealed to most of the prosperous Arlingtonians in the first quarter of the century. Mr. Morrison was apparently not socially ambitious or he would have settled in the section of the town known as the area "above the tracks," whereas the bourgois and heterogeneous elements were, in the main, established "below the tracks." These two terms originally referred to the geographic demarcation created by the Boston and Maine railroad that ran across the middle of

Arlington Center. Eventually these terms acquired a sensitive socio-economic connotation that was tacitly understood though not openly acknowledged.

Mr. Ernest Morrison was a tall, spare man with an angular weather-worn face. His neighborliness amounted to a curt greeting and a stiff smile, that is, if he smiled at all. . . . In talking with Elly about the old Palmer Street days, Arthur recalled him as a laconic, self-contained New Englander addicted to the Anglo-Saxon "work ethic." "I still remember," said Arthur, "the infernal racket of his old Hudson car from spring to fall as he drove past our house at the crack of dawn on his way to work. He acted as his own overseer of the large tracts of farmland he owned. Some of them stretched south and west of Palmer Street, clear down to Massachusetts Avenue—only a few blocks away from Palmer Street. It was one of his truck garden farms that Dion saw on his first trip to Arlington; and it gave a rural atmosphere to the area which made Dion decide then and there to find a house close by."

"I don't remember him too well," said Elly, "I only saw him if I happened to be playing outside when he returned home from work. But I do recall what mother would invariably say if she happened to see him driving past our house late in the afternoon. 'Po, po, po!' she would exclaim, 'how hard he works, that poor man!' "

"That poor man," repeated Arthur with a laugh, "was already wealthy by the time we arrived in Arlington, thanks to the income he derived from the valuable farmlands he had inherited from his father; in fact, soon after we came to Palmer Street, he began selling his land. Before long, row after row of streets and houses were sprouting on that large expanse of fertile soil just a few blocks from where we used to live."

"I don't know," remarked Elly, "when or where I heard that 'Farmer Morrison'—as mother used to call him—left a tremendous estate. I believe whoever told me about it said that it amounted to somewhere between fifteen and twenty million dollars!"

"Well, people do exaggerate; still it's not unlikely," replied Arthur. "After all, he owned some of the most valuable land in

Arlington, that was expanding at a rapid rate. Besides, he was one of those shrewd Yankees where money was concerned—the more they have, the less they show it. I wonder what mother would have said if she had known that 'Farmer Morrison' was a millionaire or even a multi-millionaire, according to the local gossip.''

''Oh, she probably would have said: 'Po, po, po! that poor man working so hard when he doesn't have to!' ''

''I think she would have said more than that,'' said Arthur, ''mother, you know, wouldn't miss the chance of making some kind of an analogy for the benefit of her compatriots, so she might very well have added: ' Ah, the Greeks . . . *they* know how to enjoy life with money or without it. In Greece, she'd say, they work in order to live, but in America, they live in order to work. 'And if you tried to tell her that she might be mistaken—since she didn't really understand the Anglo-Saxon, or specifically the Yankee mentality, she'd reply, 'But I do know the Greeks, and they have a nicer feeling for life.' ''

When Liberty Bonds were issued in the First World War, Mrs. Douropoulos applied her energies in behalf of the Government's efforts to raise money. She began her activities by going first to various Greek enterprises; for a trial run she decided to visit a *kaffenio*—a ''coffeehouse,'' called the ''Odysseus''—in the north end of Boston. This institution of long standing in Greece, which caters exclusively to a male clientele, was re-established in America by the early Greek immigrants.

In the congenial atmosphere of their compatriots—without the distracting presence of womenfolk—the men relaxed; they drank their rich black coffee or sipped the potent, anise-flavored *ouzo*, played cards or backgammon, and smoked to their heart's content. Their greatest enjoyment, however, came from indulging in what is an obsessive preoccupation of the Greeks: the subject of local, national and international politics which begins with a semblance of restraint and invariably ends in a storm of invectives.

The proprietor of the ''Odysseus'' was Mr. Plato Pantos who, in private, was referred to as ''Mr. P. P.'' (his initials afforded an irresistible pun since they sound the same in Greek as the word "pipi" which is the expression little Greek children use for "urine").

Mr. Pantos was in his usual place behind the cash register when he saw a woman entering his establishment. He was surprised, and at the same time, dismayed at this irregularity. With a formidible frown he started to approach her when he had a sudden flash of recognition—why, it was the Presbytera! He had seen her a while back in church, and she had impressed him as an elegant lady. He had inquired about her and was told she was the priest's wife. Well, the last place he expected to see a Presbytera was in *his kaffenio*—or in any kaffenio, for that matter.

With a smile instead of a frown, Mr. Pantos greeted her, and then hurriedly pulled a chair next to a nearby table.

"Please, sit down, Presbytera . . . do sit down," he repeated, since at the moment he could think of nothing more to say or to do.

The Presbytera sat down, looked around her and remarked, "You have a nice place, and a busy place, Mr. Pantos."

He felt a surge of pleasure that she had gone to the trouble of finding out his name. What a charming woman!

"It's Saturday, and that's why the place is more crowded than usual. But to tell the truth, we do well every day in the week— with God's help," he added, more for the sake of the priest's wife than his personal belief that the Almighty had enough to do than to be concerned with Plato Pantos' *kaffenio*.

"With God's help, of course, and with America's help, too," said the Presbytera. "Now America needs *your* help—*everyone's help*—bleeding as she is in this terrible world war!"

A stillness fell over the room as soon as the customers of the "Odysseus" became aware that a woman had appeared in their midst; the only sound that could be heard was her husky voice to which she added a dramatic overtone for the benefit of her audience.

"And I have come here today, Mr. Pantos," continued the Presbytera, "to sell Liberty Bonds that the United States has issued to help America preserve her liberty."

103

At the word "liberty" Mr. Pantos sprang to his feet—"*Liberty*!" he cried, "Liberty! That great legacy from our ancient forefathers which we have treasured through the centuries and which we have shared with the civilized world. Let us all give what we can to help preserve it for the country we have adopted for ourselves and for our children."

His words were immediately acclaimed by a unison of cheers: Long live *Eleutheria*! Long live *Ameriki*!—Long live Liberty! Long live America!

Mrs. Douropoulos left the Odysseus more than pleased with the results of her first endeavor to sell Liberty Bonds, and a good part of her success she attributed to that lovely word *Eleutheria*.

By the time Alexandra reached Palmer Street, it was already dark and her house was brightly lit. This was an indication that her husband's homecoming had preceded hers. If his wife was delayed beyond sundown, Father Constantine would invariably announce to his children, "Your mother will be coming home any moment now, so turn on the lights."

"I still remember after all these years," remarked Elly, during an exchange of early memories with Arthur, "the glee we felt, or at least I felt, at fulfilling Babá's orders to flood the house with light when mother was late coming home, as if she were a queen returning to her castle after dark and finding it all aglow."

"That's quite a romantic notion you had," smiled Arthur, "one that I suspect father shared with you, for mother was a queen, in *his* eyes. But what intrigues me about this sacrifice of lights for mother's sake was that it contradicted father's concern about wasting electricity. He would roam about the house turning off electric bulbs that were burning needlessly, and all the while muttering about the folly of spending money which only served to make the Edison Electric Light Company richer than it was—or should be."

"It was a different story, of course, when it came to mother; you know Babá adored her—and since she loved light, he was willing to go to the expense of pleasing her.

"I don't remember if I told you," Elly went on to say, "that I once asked mother why she had such an aversion to any dark room or place. She replied that Hades was fearfully dark, and so she wanted as much light as she could possibly have while she was in *this* world. Can you imagine mother, a devout Christian woman, saying that!''

"I'm not surprised, not in the least," said her brother, "mother, you see, was a Christian in spirit, but a pagan at heart.

If, according to Arthur's view, his mother possessed a duality in her nature, she possessed, no less, a singlemindedness in pursuing what she considered her duty; she was, therefore, determined to continue doing her share in behalf of the war effort. After she had exhausted all the available Greek sources—by selling bonds to her compatriots, she looked about for a wider area in which to further her mission.

She noted that some of those who were volunteers for the sale of Liberty Bonds did their work from open booths that were light enough to be readily moved from one spot to another at the discretion of those who manned them. Her request to the proper authorities for one of these "kiosks" was granted, as well as her request to begin her mission at the corner of Boylston and Tremont Street, one of the most active intersections in Boston.

If the Presbytera decided to try her luck at another strategic spot—say, in the Boston Common or the Boston Public Gardens, she had no trouble enlisting the help of a couple of passersby, who never failed to oblige her. But her choice of location did not matter, it seems, for wherever Mrs. Douropoulos happened to be, she ended the day with record sales. She did not, however, give herself any credit for her successes—for she was truly unconscious of the magnetic force of her personality—but attributed them to the passionate patriotism that had swept across the nation. Indeed, it was a time that united both natives and newcomers in contributing with unprecedented generosity for the preservation of liberty against a foe hell-bent to destroy it.

Soon after the four Liberty Bond drives ended, Calvin Coolidge became Governor of Massachusetts. During the early part of his administration the volunteers with the highest records in bond sales were invited to the State House. Alexandra Douropoulos was among these honored with citations and medals and given a German helmet as a memento of the war;

105

it was made of heavy metal which came to a peak in the form of a lethal spike—the kind worn by Kaiser Wilhelm and the members of his elite corps. This grim souvenir of the First World War would become an ironic reminder of the promise of lasting peace—a promise that, within a quarter of a century, would be buried under the rubble of the Second World War.

At dinnertime the Presbytera described the day's events. She was proud, so proud, she said, to be among the honored volunteers. They were mostly "Yankees," and Mr. Coolidge, (the future thirtieth President of the United States) was, she surmised, one of their kind, "a nice, quiet sort of man"—yet so unassuming considering that he was the Governor ensconced in that elegant golden-domed building; and he, himself, the Governor, if you please, escorted them on a tour of the capitol. "We saw only a part of it—such a vast place," explained Mrs. Douropoulos, "with all kinds of paintings, sculptures, tablets and beautiful flags. It's a treasure house, let me tell you." It was a day, she concluded, that would remain a memorable one of her life in America.

An infinitely more memorable day was in store for the Hellenic world a decade after Alexandra Douropoulos' long life came to an end. One can only imagine the exultation she would have shared with her compatriots when Michael S. Dukakis became Governor of Massachusetts on the second day of January in 1975.

The "Duke" as he is affectionately called, was the first American born of Greek parentage to become head of the state. He was also the only Governor of Massachusetts thus far to serve for three terms—a unique tribute to his honorable and humane leadership. And in 1988 he achieved the additional distinction of being the first Greek-American chosen by the Democratic Party as candidate for the President of the United States of America.

Chapter Eleven

The first year of Elly's life in Arlington remained in her memory as the *annus mirabilis* of her childhood—the year which marked the beginning of her adventure in the realm of learning, and her venture into the world of her American peers.

One of her first discoveries in that first year of school was the manner in which American children's birthdays were celebrated. They were apparently gala occasions marked by gifts from relatives and friends, and by parties at which guests were served mounds of ice cream along with huge pieces of cake. This was no ordinary cake, mind you. It was called a "birthday cake." Every bit of it was frosted and gorgeously decorated with swirls and flowers bordering the words: HAPPY BIRTHDAY. And this magnificent creation was brought to the table all lit up with tiny candles!

Such affairs had never taken place at Elly's house; only name days—the "feast day" of the saint after whom one is named— were celebrated, especially the head of the family's name day, which in the Douropoulos household was Saint Constantine's Day. The house on Palmer Street then overflowed with people coming and going, but not before they had partaken a tidbit or two—and often a good many more—from the staggering array of delectables along with the indispensible libations with which they could offer the standard toast: *chronia polla*—"many years" to Father Douropoulos.

Whenever Elly heard her schoolmates describing a birthday party (and with each repetition the presents became larger in number and the cake larger in size) Elly tried to convince herself that name days were more exciting. Yet, Elly would have by far preferred birthdays to be celebrated just with ice cream and a birthday cake glowing with candles.

At some time or other during her grammar school days, Elly confided in her best friend, Barbara Winn, about her family's indifference towards birthdays. Only silly old namedays, which she described as well as she could, were celebrated at her house. Barbara filed this bit of interesting information in her young but already well-organized mind.

When the two girls were in their early adolescence and thus old enough to visit each other freely, Elly was invited on her birthday to dinner at Barbara's house. "I accepted her invitation gladly," recalled Elly, "it was so nice of her to ask me (and for many more after that first one) since she, of course, knew that birthdays were of no consequence in our family. Besides, going to the Winns' lovely old house that was built in 1680 was infinitely more intriguing than visiting the homes of my other Arlington friends."

The first time Elly ever saw a tomahawk was one that served as a doorstop in the front entrance of the Winn house. It was part of an enormous collection of Indian arrowheads, birdheads (for killing birds) and stones used for some purpose or other, all of which were found when the Winn farmlands were plowed. These artifacts were probably made and used by the Wampanoag Indians, a tribe that once inhabited the territory that is now Massachusetts.

From top to bottom the house was an antiquarian's dream come true, but for Elly the attic was the most exciting part. Although all kinds of fascinating memorabilia from centuries past must have been stored in it, Elly only had eyes for the astonishing collection of clothes that were worn in years long past by members of the Winn family. The men's clothing, including the wedding outfit of Barbara's great grandfather, and the tall hats of the day were of less interest to Elly than the dresses hanging from the rafters. They were made in a variety of materials and colors and adorned with a variety of trimmings—some were worn with pantaloons and with hoops which hung from the rafters. One of the dresses that Elly especially admired was an elegant turquoise-blue taffeta gown* that had been made with a bustle. "I can still remember it vividly," said Elly, "whenever my mind goes back to those magical hours I spent in the attic of Barbara's house more than half a century ago."

When Elly was invited on her birthday for dinner at Barbara's house, it did not cross her mind that she was to have her own— her first birthday cake. Her childish days were over and so were her childish longings, or so Elly thought until she caught sight of the tall tender angel cake decorated simply with small slim white candles. She was suddenly overwhelmed by the thought that it was *her* birthday cake and that it had been made just for her by Barbara's mother—a dear, bustling little lady who reminded Elly of her own mother. For Mrs. Winn was another of those selfless women that had a genuine concern for the welfare of others.

This first birthday cake of Elly's belied the time and trouble required to prepare it, especially without the help of today's electric egg beaters. As she stared at it, touched and pleased by all it conveyed, she did not realize that it would become for her a small but significant symbol of an era that would vanish along with those who gave meaning and depth to life in her young years. They were people impervious to the burgeoning twentieth century "cultus of the personality," the kind of people who adhered to the old-fashioned yet timeless verities such as kindness and thoughtfulness. They would remain in Elly's mind ever after as the truly "beautiful people."

The revelation which startled Elly more than any other during her first year at school was that the "Greek" Easter and the "American" Easter were not celebrated at the same time. She had heard her schoolmates chattering excitedly about the new clothes they would be wearing on Easter Day. But the nearness

*This dress and other garments of historical interest and value have been donated to the Smithsonian Institute in Washington by Mrs. Scott Adams (the former Barbara Winn), whose late husband was the ninth great-grandson of William Bradford, the first Governor of the Plymouth Colony, and one of the party that sailed on the "Mayflower."

of it did not strike her until one of the girls solemnly announced that she was praying "awful hard" for good weather *this* Sunday because her new "Easter bonnet" would be ruined if it rained. "It's very pretty," she said, "and very expensive. It's got yellow daisies on it and long black velvet streamers on the back that come right down to my shoulders."

Elly was puzzled. Easter was around the corner, so to speak, yet at home she had seen no signs heralding the arrival of the most radiant celebration in the Greek Orthodox calendar. In the Douropoulos household, indeed, in every Greek household, the preparations for Easter were marked by a manic activity. No nook, no cranny escaped a fervid cleaning; curtains were washed and starched, and the lace ones were painstakenly pinned on the curtain stretchers; rugs were thrown over the clothes lines and attacked with the metal carpet beaters until they no longer harbored a particle of dust.

For Elly, however, the infallible proof that Easter was close at hand came when a luscious aroma permeated the house. At the first whiff of it she knew her mother was in the kitchen preparing the *lambropsomo*—the Easter bread that would serve as a spectacular centerpiece at the traditional Paschal meal of roast lamb. No one, Elly was sure, no one but her mother could make so wonderful an Easter bread. Elly loved to watch her mix the dough, adding as she went along a "pinch," as her mother called it, of cinnamon, nutmeg, anise and clove powder, and a jigger or two of ouzo. As the finishing touch she would shape a piece of the dough in the form of a cross and encircle it with a crown studded with ruby-red Easter eggs.

On her way back from school, Elly walked slowly as she brooded at the lack of any preparations at home for Easter. She couldn't make sense of it. After all, her father was a priest, and priests should know all about such things. She could only come to one conclusion: For some reason or other her family wasn't going to celebrate Easter. But why, she wondered, why? She started running home as fast as she could to find out what had gone awry.

Eleni was in the kitchen ironing when Elly burst into the room, and without waiting to get her breath she asked, "Tell me, Eleni, why aren't we going to celebrate Easter?''

Eleni put down the iron and looked askance at Elly. "Where did you ever get such a notion! Of course, we're going to have Easter. We're Christians, not heathens, and all Christians alive—and the dead ones, too, I wouldn't be surprised—celebrate the Holy Day of Resurrection.''

"But we haven't done anything about it, and Easter is coming *this* Sunday; everybody said so at school, and all the girls were talking about their new clothes, and Miss Day showed us how to make Easter baskets from strips of colored paper, and —''

"Oh, that's the *American* Easter . . . well, if the *Amerikanoi* want to celebrate it next Sunday, that's their business. Our Easter comes three weeks from Sunday—plenty of time to get ready for it, and time enough for you to get a new frock, so don't you fret.''

"But how can there be *two* Easters?'' cried Elly, more perplexed than ever.

"There you go again—asking why this and why that! Don't you see I'm busy? I haven't got the time to keep answering all those questions of yours.''

"Then I'll ask Babá as soon as he comes home.'' Her father, Eleni informed her, was in his study upstairs busy working, and she had better not disturb him now.

"I don't think he'll mind, even if he *is* busy,'' said Elly pointedly, and started to leave the kitchen when Eleni reminded her to knock on the door "like all decent people should do'' before barging into a room.

"I always do that,'' retorted Elly, and making a little moue at Eleni she ran up the stairs.

Eleni returned to her work, but her mind was on Father Douropoulos. She wondered if his children realized how hard he worked—carrying single-handed the burden of a large family, and a large parish. Yet, he was always thoughtful and kind towards his family, and no less to her. Why he, the patriarch of the family, would come to the kitchen *himself* for a glass of water rather than trouble her for it; but what especially showed his concern for her took place every day at the family dinner table. After Father Douropoulos said grace, and before anyone was

111

served, he would fill a plate for Eleni and have it taken to the kitchen for her. When one of his children asked him why he served Eleni first, he replied, "Because no one sitting at this table deserves more consideration than Eleni who serves all of us faithfully day in and day out."

The sound of Elly's chatter floated down to the kitchen from the priest's study. That kindly "pater familias," thought Eleni, had interrupted his work to listen to Elly's silly questions about Easter. As far as Eleni was concerned there was only *one* Easter—the Greek Easter, and she could not quite understand what Elly was fussing about.

"And Eleni couldn't tell me," reported Elly to her father, "why we aren't having Easter this Sunday; she said she was too busy to tell me because she was ironing." Elly paused a moment and then added, "She really wasn't *that* busy."

But the child's oblique inference of Eleni's ignorance was not fair. For the complicated computations which determine the date of Easter can disconcert both scholarly laymen and learned church men. Although the Western and Eastern Church basically agree that Easter should be observed on the first Sunday after the full moon following the vernal equinox, the Greek Church takes into account other variables, as well as historical factors. Besides, it bases its calculations in regard to Easter on the Julian rather than the present day Gregorian calendar and therefore, must establish the date of the Greek Orthodox Easter accordingly.

Father Douropoulos simplified his reply to Elly's questions by saying that for hundreds of years the Greek Church had decided the date of Easter's arrival. Every now and then the "two" Easters, as Elly called them, happened to fall on the same Sunday (for reasons, said her father, that were too difficult for her to understand). That, however, was not the case this year. "But it really does not matter," he went on to say, "if our Easter comes a week or more later, for whenever it comes it is a glorious event. You will enjoy it especially when you are old enough to go to church for the beautiful Easter midnight service."

"Why can't I go *this* Easter?" cried Elly, for if she could look forward to that "beautiful Easter midnight service" she might feel less unhappy about its delay.

"It's a long service that ends well past midnight, and that's too late for a little girl," replied her father.

"But I'm not a little girl any more. If I'm old enough to go to school, why can't I go to church on Easter night?"

Father Douropoulos began rearranging the papers on his desk. "That's enough of arguing. Run along, now, and be a little patient; our Easter will be here before you know it."

"I'm sorry I bothered you, Babá," said Elly in a small voice.

As she turned to leave, her father caught sight of the dejection on her face. "Why don't we let Mother decide about your coming to church this Easter," he remarked casually.

As Elly skipped out of the room, her father smiled. He had no doubt she would be at church on Easter by her mother's side, for Elly would have little trouble getting maternal permission. Of all his daughters, this youngest one had won her mother's deepest affection.

In a relatively short time after arriving in Arlington, the Greek family was no longer considered a threat to Palmer Street. This benevolent change of attitude was largely due to Dolly Endicott's crusade in behalf of the priest's family. Despite her unfortunate marriage to a charming but parasitical Frenchman, Dolly's views carried weight. For she could boast—though she was too well bred to do so—of her descent from one of the preeminent families in New England. Dolly made a point of saying time and again that she considered the Greek family an asset to the neighborhood; they had given Palmer Street a certain *élan*, a *joie de vivre*, if you will, which was most refreshing. Although some of the neighbors could make no sense of those silly sounding foreign words that Dolly was in the habit of using, her approval of the Greek family was obvious as well as contagious; and before long the new neighbors were looked upon if not as an asset, at least, as an "interesting" addition to Palmer Street.

The status of the children also underwent a change during the time they attended the Russell School. In the elementary grades they were known as the "Greek children," a term which, intentionally or not, set them apart from the rest of their class-

113

mates. But by the time they merged with the pupils from the rest of the Arlington grammar schools into a single student body in the junior and senior high school, their ethnic designation was practically forgotten.

When they entered junior high school Arthur and Elly came in contact with Arlington's youth of "undiluted Anglo-Saxon blood," who lived above the tracks, and the two children soon established friendships that were destined to span a lifetime. Even though the future would find friends scattered far and wide, they nevertheless kept in touch with each other; and when they had the good fortune to meet now and then, they would recall the distant memories of school days—memories that were poignant reminders of irrevocable youth.

Much as they enjoyed recalling their school days with old friends, Arthur and Elly found more pleasure when just the two of them had a chance to review their early years in Arlington. They had shared most of their youthful experiences from the same vantage point, for they were closer in age and in outlook than the rest of their siblings.

An unforgettable memory in Arthur's and Elly's first year in Arlington was a New England ice storm which combined dazzling beauty and stark tragedy. It had silently come and gone during the night, and when day came, the sun rose on a world encased in crystal. The boughs of the maple trees that lined Palmer Street were curved and interlaced like sprays from a myriad of fountains that had frozen in mid-air. Each branch and stem and twig was enclosed in a glittering sheath of ice. The rays of the sun caught their refracted light in a million sparkles that changed with the slightest shift of the eye into a rainbow of colors.

The schools in Arlington were closed that day, and two young teachers who boarded in a house nearby Palmer Street went outdoors to enjoy their unexpected holiday. They slipped and fell more than once on the ice-clad sidewalk, yet each time they scrambled unscathed to their feet amidst gales of laughter.

As they looked about them at a world transformed overnight into a fairyland, they spied a branch dangling from a nearby tree. With girlish exuberance they tried to reach it. The first girl ailed in her attempt; the other jumped high enough to grasp hold of

114

it only to fall lifeless to the ground, for that innocuous looking branch was a lethal live wire.

Up to the time of the young teacher's death, Elly had the vague notion that only old people who were ailing died. The realization that anybody could die, and die suddenly, bewildered and frightened her. Arthur was troubled by her obvious distress; but even though his knowledge about death was almost as elementary as his little sister's, he tried to soothe her as best he could.

"Everybody dies, sooner or later," he remarked in a casual tone. "It's like Eleni says, 'If your number comes up that means it's your turn to die' and so you die—you see, that's all there is to it."

"But who chooses them, I mean the people who've got to die?" asked Elly.

Arthur replied that it was somebody called *Charos* (in ancient Greek mythology, he is known as Charon, a grisly old man who represents Death). "When Eleni heard about the teacher," explained Arthur, "she kept crossing herself and muttering, 'Po, po, po! The poor girl, young as she was, her time had come, and Charos snatched her away. Po, po, po!' "

"Does he come for *everybody*?" asked Elly.

"Yes, that's his job, and he's got to do it."

For a few moments Elly was silent then she suddenly cried, "Oh, Arthur, you know what? That horrid old man—I mean Charos—he's going to make a mistake some day. Everyone makes mistakes, don't they? Well, he can't remember everybody's number—there's so many of them, and do you know whose number he'll forget?"

"I suppose it will be yours," said Arthur with a sarcastic grin which Elly overlooked in her excitement.

"It's *mother* he's going to forget—forget all about her, so mother won't die—no, she'll never, never die!"

She's afraid, terribly afraid that mother might die, thought Arthur, and what could he say or do to dispel his little sister's fear of losing her mother that she loved—with a love akin to adoration?

But to Arthur's surprise and relief Elly resolved his dilemma. Her vivid imagination had, it seems, overwhelmed her to the extent that she could no longer endure her self-inflicted anguish; she, therefore, sought to escape her morbid fancies by suddenly exclaiming, "Let's play dominoes. And let's forget all that silly stuff about dying."

Eleni, as usual, was in the kitchen and could hear the children as they played in the dining room on the large, heavy, mission oak table. They were chatting and laughing and bickering now and then which indicated that everything was going along normally. Eleni, however, was still brooding over the young teacher's death. Ah, the poor girl, her body was still warm, and already forgotten, it seemed. Not that she expected little children to grieve; they lived only in the immediate present. One moment they were drowning in tears, and the next moment engulfed in waves of laughter. Let them be . . . time would bring them their share of sorrows.

Eleni remembered when her father died—she was no more than eight years old—and from that black day on she had never dared to laugh in front of her stony-faced, dried-eyed mother who had no time for the luxury of tears, what with four young children to raise. Eleni, who was the oldest, helped her mother tend to the livestock and the land so that they might have enough to eat, though it was never enough however hard they worked.

Shortly after her father—a gruff, yet kindly, devout man— had died from a heart attack, Eleni ventured to ask her mother why God had taken him away from then. He must have known how much they loved him and needed him.

"The Lord," replied her mother, "takes first those he loves most."

"How can He be so cruel!" cried Eleni, as she began to sob.

"Bite your tongue, my girl. It's blasphemy to question God's will. And keep your tears. You will need them to ease your sorrows when they come. . . . They'll come," she repeated grimly, "they'll surely come."

The Douropoulos offspring, thought Eleni, were lucky so far; they had yet to know the grief that Charos leaves behind, especially if the first loss in the family is the death of a father, the pillar of the household. They were lucky, indeed, to have their father— and what a father they had! A man of the cloth, a priest who

116

practiced what he preached; surely God must love this worthy man and grant him a long life for the sake of his children and for the good of his parish. Suddenly her mother's words came unbidden to Eleni's mind: *"The Lord takes first those He loves the most."* She felt a chill run through her and her round owlish eyes filled with fear for Father Douropoulos.

As Arthur and Elly grew older their perspective grew clearer. Eventually they came to realize that during the years between early childhood and the onset of adolescence, the family had been at its strongest and their parents in the splendor of their prime. They would later recall that time of life with poignancy, for when the inevitable changes within the family began, "the magic circle" was broken—and what had been would never be again.

During their youthful years the two children considered their parents as the dominating figures in their life. The Presbytera's compelling personality exerted a powerful influence on her household, but Father Constantine in his quiet way was the sustaining force in the family. He exacted neither respect nor affection but, nevertheless, he was accorded both, as well as unsolicited gratitude for the judicious way he exercised his patriarchal powers as head of the family.

He believed that children's minds could be stimulated and developed—the sooner the better—by exposure to surroundings other than their usual ones. During the summer when his pastoral duties were somewhat less demanding, he undertook to acquaint his two youngest children with some of the famous institutions in or nearby the city of Boston. He took them to the Museum of Fine Arts, to the Boston Public Library in Copley Square and to Harvard University's Botanical Museum, which houses the inimitable collection of glass flowers made in Dresden by Leopold Blaschka and his son, Rudolph, both renowned as artists and botanists.

"We were intrigued by those marvelous flowers—all handmade in colored glass; they were exact duplicates of American flora," said Elly as she reminisced with Arthur about those early sight-seeing ventures with their father. "But Babá was disappointed, I think, because we apparently didn't show much enthusiasm about anything else we saw."

117

"The trouble was," remarked her brother, "that he gave us more credit than we deserved in assuming we'd appreciate in our young years the treasures he had taken the time and trouble to show us."

"Yet, we really were more excited than Babá realized—not by what we saw, but simply because we were with him. We felt so proud of Babá. People kept looking at him; they couldn't help it, he was so handsome, and the elegant way he wore his clothes, and the way he walked . . . and the ebony gold-knobbed cane he always carried. You were lucky—you and Sophia," added Elly "to have inherited his rare good looks, at least."

"I don't see where the rest of you were short-changed in that respect," he retorted.

Elly smiled at Arthur with affectionate amusement. He was still inordinately modest, still as incapable of accepting with grace a deserving compliment as when he was a bashful little boy. Elly's smile grew broader as an incident that had taken place long ago came to her mind.

"What are you smiling about—like a Chesire cat?" Arthur asked somewhat warily.

"Oh, just something that came to me all of a sudden—nothing of any great moment—just a little episode on our way to church with mother. We were about ten or eleven years old at the time. You've probably forgotten all about it, so I'll remind you of it. We had just come up from the subway station to the street when a woman coming from the opposite direction spied mother and stopped to talk with her. She was wearing a khaki-colored out-fit, heavy walking shoes and carrying a knapsack on her back. I remember thinking it was a strange way to dress, especially on a Sunday morning. After greeting mother she said something like 'how nice to see you again, Mrs. Douropoulos.'

"Mother looked puzzled. She was obviously at a loss to place her. Then the lady—you could tell she was a lady by the way she spoke, in a cultivated voice with a decidedly Bostonian accent—reminded mother 'how much everybody enjoyed that lovely tea party at your house a few months ago,' She went on to say that all the members of the Cosmopolitan Club were delighted with the wonderful Greek pastries mother had prepared.

That club—in case you don't remember—was formed by a group of Boston ladies from the Brahmin caste to further relations between American and foreign women.''

"I don't remember anything about it," said Arthur, "but the whole thing sounds patronizing to me."

Elly ignored his interjection. "And the lady with the knapsack said that she particularly liked those simply delectable cookies smothered in powdered sugar, but for the life of her couldn't pronounce their long name that began with the letter 'k.' Mother beamed with pleasure. 'Ah, the kourambiethes—yes, long name—best Greek pastry, I think, too.' She also expressed her pleasure at having had the Cosmpolitan Club ladies for tea. And all the while mother was talking, I could have died from embarrassment at her English. It sounded like some kind of *lingua Franca.*"

"We were overly sensitive in our early years about our parents being so obviously foreign," remarked Arthur, but, actually mother managed very well with whatever English she knew when none of us were around. She sensed our uneasiness and it made her feel uneasy as well. At any rate, the way she spoke English was not in the least detrimental to her capacity for making friends—American friends—who were devoted to her. In fact, she entertained them often when she lived alone in Boston—after we had all gone our way and the house in Arlington had gone, too—the way of countless homes during those rough years of the Depression."

"It was only natural when we were young," said Elly, "that we wanted to conform—to be like the other children, not to stand out as being different because of our foreign background. . . . And now to go on with my story." That lady who had met them on the street was a Miss Eleanora Sears, related Elly, a socialite whose picture had appeared in the newspaper, a day or two after they had seen her. She was a well-known figure in Boston as a hiker who had broken many records hiking from Boston to various places within and beyond Massachusetts.

"Bully for Eleanora, but what has she got to do with father's attempts to arouse our interest in the historic and artistic gems

119

of Boston? Just what, may I ask, is the point of your long digression?''

"I'll get to it if only you wouldn't interrupt me. Well, when Miss Eleanora Sears was about to leave, she noticed us, or rather *you*, I should say; she apparently couldn't resist tousling your lovely curly hair, and exclaimed, 'What an Apollo he is!' ''

Arthur broke into a raucous laugh. "That woman was simply asinine, and no doubt a spinster, to boot. No one who knows anything about boys would tousle their hair and say they looked like Apollo! The whole story is ridiculous, and I don't believe a word of it; even if it were true, how could you possibly remember all those silly details about an episode which supposedly took place ages ago?''

"But it's true, it really is; Mother wouldn't have mentioned it again and again if it weren't. She loved to repeat that you were considered an Apollo by one of Boston's 'grandes dames,' and one of the bigwigs in the Cosmopolitan Club, no less . . . at least, mother had the good sense not to mention that remark in your presence. As a matter of fact, with the exception of this particular instance, I don't recall our parents showering any one of us with praise, though there must have been times when we deserved a compliment or two.''

"Ah, but when it came to you, Elly, mother wasn't exactly restrained in enumerating her favorite daughter's virtues to her older sisters. Without meaning to, mother increased their resentment toward you, which, if for no other reason, was based on the accidental fact of your being much younger than they were.''

"What I think really bothered them," said Elly, "was having another female in the family. Fortunately, your arrival preceded mine by thirteen months and fulfilled their longing for a little brother. So, I am beholden to you for making my appearance less painful for them, and for me than if, God forbid, I had shown up first. Besides, since we were close in age, I received, at least, some of the overflow from the attention that was showered on you—which reminds me of one of Eleni's sayings: When the basil gets watered so does the pot.

120

"But now that all of us are no longer young, I don't think those old feelings of resentment still exist."

"I wouldn't be so sure of that," replied her brother with a mischievous grin.

Chapter Twelve

As far back as she could remember, Elly had been aware of her sisters' partiality for their little brother. She did not, however, resent this blatant favoritism, for Elly, herself, was devoted to him. She was content that he, in turn, was devoted to her and had chosen her as his companion and confidante. Even when Arthur began to spend a good deal of time playing with Billy Davis, she did not mind her brother's preoccupation with his new-found friend.

Elly was thrilled with the thought of going to school, which, she felt, would not only give her entrance into the world of knowledge but mark her debut, as well, into the "American scene." To be sure, she had moments of uneasiness about this *terra incognita* where she would not feel as protected as she did in the secure atmosphere of home and family. But to her relief, she adapted to the new atmosphere with the facility of a chameleon.

The daily routine of entering the American world of school in the morning was reversed in the afternoon when the children returned to the house on Palmer Street. They did not come back like the "latchkey kids"—a species of recent development—to a silent, empty house. Some member or other of the family was bound to be at home. In any case, the faithful Eleni would be waiting for them with a glass of milk and some cookies.

When one of the children—and usually it was Elly—appeared with a bruised knee, Eleni would utter a series of "po, po, po's" followed by a scolding. Elly wasn't a little tot, Eleni would remind her, but a schoolgirl now, and it was time she learned to walk in a lady-like way instead of tearing around like a tomboy. Whereupon Elly retorted, "Everybody says that mother walks faster than anybody else, but she's still a lady, isn't she?"

Eleni overlooked Elly's question and proceeded to clean her knee. After she had removed the dirt and bits of gravel she took a small knife and saucer and headed for the wine keg in the cellar. She began to scrape onto the saucer as much as she could of the small amount of greenish gray mold that had formed around the upper rim of the wine keg. She applied the mold directly to the bruise of Elly's knee, tied around it a clean strip of sheeting as a bandage and declared, "There now . . . it's a nasty scraping you got for yourself. But in a day or two, it'll be all healed, without any more trouble either."

"We didn't realize," said Elly in talking with Arthur about their youthful past, "that Eleni's rustic remedy of using mold from wine kegs was a crude but effective form of penicillin."

"As a matter of fact, mold from various sources, such as certain kinds of molded bread, were used to clear infections well before Eleni's time," said Arthur, "I remember mother saying that her mother—our grandmother—warded off infections by finding a large spider web then carefully removing it and putting it on a deep cut or wound; the result was a complete healing of the injury. Incidentally, speaking of those wine kegs that were regularly delivered to our house, Bill's Aunt Mabe once asked me what was in them. When I told her it was wine, she raised her eyebrows and said, 'Oh, really!' I gathered she didn't think well of wine. This confused me as I used to think that all grown-ups drank wine and that therefore they all liked it. So, I asked Dion, our most reliable source of information, and our private oracle, as well."

"What a nuisance we must have been to poor Dion, always pestering him with our childish problems and questions," said Elly, whereupon her brother reminded his sister that she was the one who asked the most questions. Elly admitted as much, yet,

Dion never seemed to mind; he was always so kind and patient. Yes, he was all of that, Arthur agreed—and much more than that. But they were not old enough then to appreciate Dion's brilliance, or that wonderful, whacky humor of his which, at times, was subtle and also served as a means to cover his sensitivity. For he carried the painful burden of having failed to live up to the expectations of his family and his teachers who had recognized early on his exceptional mind. Arthur wondered what other Greek of Dion's time could have relished as much as Dion had, P. G. Wodehouse's hilarious caricatures of certain types in English society. Surely few if any of Dion's compatriots in America would have been as steeped as his brother was in literature of an immense variety.

When Arthur told Dion about Mabe's obvious disapproval of wine, his older brother had listened to him with that curious little half-smile of his that gave him an expression of sardonic amusement.

"So, you don't think Mrs. Evans (he was too courtly to call her 'Mabe') is well-disposed towards that ancient potion extolled in the Holy Scriptures as '. . . wine that maketh glad the heart of man.' " But what should he tell Mabe, asked Arthur, if she wanted to know more about the wine? She might question him again because Bill said that she was always pumping him about what was going on at our house.

"Tell her it's needed for Communion," Dion replied.

"But it isn't all used for that, is it?" asked Arthur in a tone of surprise.

"No, not all of it," admitted Dion. He hadn't kept track, he added, how much of it was for home consumption . . . still a good deal of wine was needed at each liturgy for those who desire Communion on Sunday or on Holy Days, or certain feast days—"that is, the name days of certain important saints, and so on; therefore a priest who is wise makes sure he always has enough of it at hand."

Elly shook her head laughingly. She doubted if Mabe would be taken in by Dion's flippant, not to say, specious explanation. Arthur thought it more likely that Bill's aunt would have been offended since the Unitarian Church to which she belonged offered Communion in the form of bread and wine and that these sacred elements of the Eucharist should not be talked about in a frivolous fashion. Although the Unitarians, continued Arthur, represent a liberal denomination, the Protestants, as a whole, are not given to jokes about religious matters. The Greeks, however, seem to relish them, including jokes about their clergy, who often are the target of Hellenic humor, the kind of humor that has become more or less a part of Greek folklore, which would not be the case if it were either offensive or irreverent. It usually involves simple village folk whose lack of urbanity serves to emphasize an innate shrewdness which their sophisticated city brethern might well envy. Unfortunately this provincial folk humor, which is expressed orally in "demotic" Greek, loses its unique flavor in translation since idiomatic words and phrases have no equivalent in English.

"We must have heard most of these stories," added Elly, "from many of the people who came to call at Palmer Street, and especially from those visiting priests who never failed, it seems, to have one or two up their sleeve." But come to think of it, Elly had no recollection of her father telling them any of these comical ancedotes.

"Neither do I," said Arthur, "but perhaps he had repeated them so often before our time that he had no desire to say them again when we had reached an age to appreciate them. Besides, father was innately serious-minded, not given to banter or light talk, yet he had wit, and humor with an ironic edge to it. Do you remember the time when mother kept praising Mrs. So and So?—what a devout woman she was, a true Christian, faithfully attending church services come rain or snow or ice; and more often than not, even before the priest had arrived to begin the long Orthodox liturgy; even before the sexton had time to light the candles in the church, she would make the rounds of the ikons stopping at each one to say a tearful prayer."

Father Douropoulos had made no comment when his wife first mentioned this stirring example of ecclesiolatry, but after she had repeated it more than once, he remarked, "It is not her devotion to the church which prompts that woman to arrive at God's House every single Sunday at the crack of day. It's simply a guilty conscience that compels her to beg forgiveness of the Almighty and His retinue of Saints for the same sins she commits week in and week out.''

Of all the memories that crowded in Arthur's and Elly's mind whenever their thoughts returned to the house on Palmer Street, none were more memorable than the ones of their father as he sat at the head of the table during dinner time. At home he wore the clerical robe, called a *rason*, which in his native land is the only permissible attire for the Greek clergy. Father Constantine was particular about the quality and the workmanship of his clothes. He, therefore, ordered this type of robe from England where tailors are adept in sewing such attire since some of the Anglican priests wear similar habiliments. His rason was made of a fine black wool cloth which the Presbytera called "tibet." Elly had been intrigued by the name of this material but was unable to find anyone who had heard of it, until by chance she asked an elderly salesman of woolen goods who told her there was, indeed, such a material, made from Himalayan lamb's wool which was no longer exported, and most likely no longer made. But whatever its material may have been, the robe had a special elegance to it which added to the impression the priest made as a dignified, elegantly attired *pater familias*.

The family dinner—an institution which by now is all but doomed to extinction—was a daily ritual for those who grew up in the earlier part of the twentieth century. For the Douropoulos family it was a pleasant interlude when arguing, bickering, criticisms or complaints were not tolerated. Neither Father Constantine, whose concerns encompassed Boston's Greek community, nor Alexandra, whose interests spread across her husband's parish, discussed at the table the problems that beset them in their respective activities.

According to Sophia—whose keen memory often shed light on many of Arthur's and Elly's vague recollections of times long past—what gave the family dinner its special ambience was the lack of any tension or friction between their parents. "They had a relationship of extraordinary harmony which was strange when you considered, if nothing else, the dissimilarity of their

126

temperaments. Yet, they had no apparent conflicts regarding the problems and difficulties that surely are unavoidable in any family, especially one the size of ours.

"Of course, you don't remember mother as I do," said Sophia "since the two of you weren't even born when she was relatively young. She didn't have then the mild disposition and the patience she developed as the years came along with those terrible blows that were her sad fate to bear. They softened her, but they would have embittered any woman with a lesser spirit. In the old days she could get irritable and easily exasperated with us, and at times we thought of her as a 'tartar.' Well, I suppose it was only natural that she would feel harassed with so many females under one roof.

"As for Babá, mother would remind us that he had a bad but, fortunately, a short-lived temper; yet, from what we could see it wasn't ever directed towards her. I don't remember him being really angry. Perhaps he, too, had grown milder with time." Sophia stopped talking and a look of perplexity came over her face. "Oh, my!" she declared, "I've digressed so, I just can't remember the point I was trying to make."

"That happens to everybody," said Elly reassuringly. "Memories have a way of coming helter-skelter to our mind, and that's why it's so easy to lose your train of thought."

Arthur grinned at Elly. "Speak for yourself, Scheherazada. I'm not in your league when it comes to endless stories with endless digressions."

"Ah, yes," said Sophia brightly, "I remember now what I wanted to say: We used to think that mother and father settled whatever differences they had between them in private, well beyond our hearing. But since I've had children of my own, I realize they don't need to hear their parents arguing in order to see how things are between them. Children intuitively know how their parents feel towards each other."

Arthur nodded his head as though in accord with Sophia's views; Elly doubted if he had really listened to what their older sister had said. For while she was talking, Arthur kept running his fingers through his hair, a gesture that indicated he was absorbed with some matter other than the one at hand.

His thoughts had strayed back to the family dinner, back to

the time when familial bonds were strengthened by breaking bread together; and when the main part of the meal was finished, and the table cleared of all its clutter, the usual simple, "en famille" dessert, a large bowl of fruit, made its appearance. Apples were Father Constantine's favorite fruit, particularly the kind called "Delicious" which have a lustrous deep red skin, a delicate fragrance and a distinctive shape that slopes downwards to form an inverted crown at the base.

He would peel and slice the apples, and with a fork dip the pieces into a goblet filled with *Mavrodaphne*—a fine sweet dark Greek wine. He would then pass them along so that everyone might savor what he declared was a combination of ambrosia and nectar fit for royalty.

"I loved to watch Babá," reminisced Sophia, "peeling an apple. I admired the deftness of his long graceful fingers that were always meticulously clean, which made us think twice about coming to the table without first washing our hands."

Dinner came to an end when their father gave thanks to the Lord for the food they had shared through His benificent grace. No one, however, left the table, for there was more to come— not in the way of usual nourishment, but what Arthur called in retrospect "the postprandial period" which offered food for thought. "Father didn't take advantage of his status as head of the family to monopolize the conversation," remarked Arthur, "but encouraged us to talk about anything of interest that had happened to us during the day."

"But we weren't anxious," said Elly, "to talk about ourselves. We preferred to hear what Babá had to tell us about his adventures during his day."

Her brother took exception to Elly's calling them "adventures." He thought of them more as episodes, vignettes or observations that would have been rather uninteresting if someone other than their father had recounted them. "But Babá presented them in a way that left an impression on our minds by making us aware of the humor and the pathos—I mean the element of drama that often lies beneath the banality of ordinary life."

Only later, admitted Arthur, he realized his father's wisdom in not succumbing to the temptation of many parents to moralize and to lecture their offspring, or to indulge like most Greek fathers in praising the glory and grandeur of the Hellenic race.

"Much as we respected Babá," commented Elly, "if he had done that, we wouldn't have lingered so willingly around the dining room table. As it was, we sat there so long that the neighbors must have wondered just what was going on at our house every night."

Indeed, this was a source of wonderment in the neighborhood. For Mrs. Bertha Belcher, who lived on the upper part of Palmer Street, it was also a matter of concern. She decided to talk it over with Mrs. Potter, her good friend and a fellow parishioner of the Congregational Church. She could trust Bessie Potter not to repeat whatever she said about her neighbors—not that Bertha Belcher was a gossip, you understand; still what she had to say about those bizzare nightly sessions going on across the street from her friend's house wouldn't make things easier for those poor, misguided foreigners.

Sipping slowly the cup of delicious S. S. Pierce coffee dear Bessie had brewed for her, Mrs. Belcher aired her thoughts about "those odd goings-on" at the priest's house. "You can't help it, you know, seeing right into their brightly lit dining room, the way they keep their window shades half-way up. And would you believe it, Bess, on my way back from our weekly evening meeting of the Ladies Guild at the church, I always find them still sitting—I should say glued—still glued to their chairs around the table. Now, what do you suppose is going on?" The question was purely rhetorical since Mrs. Belcher did not wait for an answer, but lowered her voice and pointed a finger across the street. "What goes on 'over there' every night is a *séance*, yes, a séance, and you know as well as I do, Bess, what our Reverend says about such things—they are the evil work of the devil."

Mrs. Potter gave a little laugh which upset Mrs. Belcher. "Apparently, you don't agree with my views—in fact, you find them amusing; well, since you spend so much time keeping track of that foreign family, why don't *you* tell *me* what you think goes on 'over there' night after night."

"If you want my opinion, Bertha, I believe they're talking— just talking."

"Talking—just talking?" asked Mrs. Belcher incredulously. "Why, that's absurd! But what could they be possibly talking about all that time?" she asked suspiciously.

"I have no idea. Maybe they just enjoy conversation."

"Well, that's one for the books all right! You'd think they would have something better to do with their time. Imagine that! talking, just talking, night after night for hours on end."

The typically Greek family enjoyed the now practically obsolete practice of sitting around the dinner table long after the evening meal was finished. This custom was not overlooked when guests were present. To do so would have denied them the opportunity to engage in *kouventa*—conversation, an ancient predilection of the Greeks. Even in the more formal atmosphere which prevailed in the Douropoulos home during the visits of ecclesiastical dignitaries, the usual interval following dinner was not curtailed but, in fact, prolonged. These churchmen gave a fresh dimension to the conversation or the discussion at hand, which they dominated, not only because of their hosts' consideration of them as guests, but by virtue of their status as religious leaders, and by the very strength of their personalities.

Their names and their titles were similar to those that resounded from the roll calls of the hierarchy during the theocratic millenium of the Byzantine era to this day. Their regal liturgical robes and daily habiliments were no different than the ones worn for hundreds of years by their ancient brethren . . . nor was their loyalty towards the doctrines and dogmas of Orthodoxy less passionate than those of the early guardians of the Faith. These prelates who visited the priest's house on Palmer Street differed, however, from their predecessors in one main respect: They were urbane men who felt very much at home in the secular world of the twentieth century.

"When the bishops* came to dinner" was a phrase that aroused a treasury of memories, especially, for the Presbytera, who considered their visits, and rightly so, a great honor.

On one occasion three of the highest ranking hierarchs of the

---

*Bishops, metropolitans, archbishops, and patriarchs—are, in effect, bishops.

Greek Church were gathered at the house on Palmer Street: Archbishop Meletios, Head of the Church of Greece, who in a few years was enthroned as His Holiness, Ecumenical Patriarch of World Orthodoxy; Bishop Alexander of Rodostolou who would remain in New York as the first Archbishop of North and South America; and the Right Reverend Chrysostomos, destined to be the next Head of the Church of Greece. He is described by Archbishop Michael in his book, *The Orthodox Church*, as "The most learned and erudite man in all the Orthodox Church." The fourth member in Archbishop Meletios' entourage was Hamilcar Alevizatos, a distinguished professor at the Divinity School of the University of Athens and a pre-eminent authority on ecclesiastical law.

This was, indeed, an occasion which would remain in the annals of the Douropoulos family. For the Greeks of Boston, the arrival of these dignitaries was a historic event. Archbishop Meletios' mission in the United States was to unite the Greek Orthodox parishes—now fragmented more than ever due to the political dissension in their motherland—by establishing a desperately needed Archdiocese in America. During his trip to Boston, the Greek priests in New England were summoned to present their credentials, and to make known to His Eminence whatever problems or difficulties they faced in their respective parishes. The day after his arrival His Eminence celebrated the Divine Liturgy with the solemnity and grandeur of his high office. In the evening he attended a reception at Symphony Hall as guest of Bishop Lawrence. This highly respected and most gracious Episcopal prelate introduced the Head of the Greek Church as "The Most Reverend Meletios, Lord Archbishop of Athens, Primate and President of the Holy Synod of Greece." (A detailed account of Archbishop Meletios' purpose in coming to the United States, and his activities during his visit to Boston, can be found in *The Nicholas C. Culolias Papers*, Houghton Library, Harvard University, Cambridge Massachusetts.)

The Greek Orthodox Archdiocese that was established under Meletios' direction proved ineffectual in bringing about unification of the Greek churches and communities in America. The hope for a lasting solution of the political schism that had be-

131

deviled the Greeks would not materialize for more than a dozen years until the administration of Archbishop Athenagoras, the second Primate of the Greek Church in North and South America. His tenure began in 1931 and came to a glorious end when His Eminence was enthroned as Ecumenical Patriarch, Head of World Orthodoxy, in Constantinople (Istanbul), the legendary Byzantine capital and the earliest center of Orthodoxy. This historic ecclesiarch of majestic physical and spiritual stature unified through his personal "credo of love" the shattered Greek churches and communities in a lasting concord throughout the land.

It remained for Archbishop Iakovos, the present Primate of the Greek Church in the Americas, to bring to its finest "anthesis"—the flowering of Orthodoxy—whose new roots are now firmly expanding in America's soil. Archbishop Iakovos, a worthy successor of the great Athenagoras, is an ecclesiarch of profound spirituality and worldly wisdom whose view on catholicity and ecumenism has placed him among the foremost religious leaders of our time. And thanks to His Eminence's dynamic leadership, Orthodoxy is now recognized as one of the major Christian Faiths in the United States.

The adherents of the Greek Orthodox Church believe that their faith is worthy of this recognition. For since the time of Orthodox Christianity was founded in 33 A.D., it endured and triumphed over seismic upheavals; bloody wars were fought in its name, and countless men and women, and children, no less, gave their lives through the ages for its perpetuation; and not a few of them faced a torturous death for their irrevocable belief in the new Faith. For nearly two thousand years the Greek Orthodox Church not only survived, but retained, with hardly an iota of change, the ancient form of its majestic and mystical liturgy to this very day.

Chapter Thirteen

As soon as the priest entered his small office in the church basement, he saw the letter propped up against the inkwell on his desk. It contained a brief notice, signed with a flourish by the president of the Executive Council, notifying the Reverend Constantine Douropoulos that his services as pastor of the Greek Orthodox Church of the Annunciation in Boston, Massachusetts, were no longer required.

His dismissal, sudden and curt as it was, did not take the priest by surprise. He was not the first, nor would he be the last, casualty of the political storm between the Church and State that had now reached the Hellenic communities in the New World.

The demoralization which resulted was such that the Greek Orthodox Archdiocese of America was unable to bring a semblance of order to the chaotic conditions in the Greek churches. Indeed, more than a decade would elapse before order was restored. In the meantime, the churches were controlled by members of an Executive Council or a Board of Trustees. These laymen had arrogated to themselves the power to do as they pleased; they could discharge a priest with impunity for whatever reason they deemed valid, with complete disregard of his canonical rights. And during this political debacle, if his views differed from theirs, the priest had no choice but to stagger from pillar to post in hope of finding a place where he could perform his sacramental duties. In more than one instance, these pioneer

133

churchmen were ousted from the very churches they had established and maintained.

Many of Father Douropoulos' parishioners did not accept his ouster as valid since the Executive Council refused to hold a meeting at large. The church membership, therefore, had not legitimately voiced an opinion about the priest, who occupied a post by the authority of the Holy Synod of Greece—a priest whose loyalty to the Church and to the congregation was beyond reproach. The members of the Executive Council, however, considered his dismissal as a *fait accompli* and ignored any attempts to reverse their decision.

In a letter to Archbishop Alexander dated October 2, 1920, Father Douropoulos apprises the Archdiocese of his anomalous position in the Boston parish. In it he expresses his deep gratitude for the devotion, concern and affection his supporters have shown to him. They are sentiments he feels no less for them. But he fears that the longer his faithful followers press for a meeting, legitimate as it may be, to resolve the impasse caused by his dismissal, the greater will be the divisiveness within the parish. He, therefore, respectfully submits his resignation. The Archdiocese had no choice but to accept the priest's resignation since it was powerless at the time to cope with—let alone control— the virulence of the political plague that had infected the Greek Church.

This shameless treatment of the pioneer priests caused them and their families irreparable harm, and this has remained a stigma in the otherwise heroic struggle of the Greek immigrants in establishing the foundation of their ancient Faith in the New World.

When Father Douropoulos resigned as pastor of the Greek Church in Boston, life at the house on Palmer Street did not change perceptively, at least, not on the surface. As always, the door was open to a variety of visitors, including those who came to pay a call as an expression of continued loyalty and affection for their former clergyman. Some of these visitors were "displaced" priests who came to commiserate with Father Constantine on their mutual plight, and to vent their anger at the heartless treatment to which they had been subjected. Even though it was a painful period for Father Constantine, he did not allow himself to become embittered or to indulge in self-pity. He had kept himself as busy as he possibly could, and whenever he had the opportunity he acted as a *locum tenens* for a priest who, for one reason or another, was unable to officiate at his respective church. He also offered to celebrate the liturgy and to perform whatever sacramental services were needed in a small community—within reasonable distance—that could not afford a permanent priest.

In spite of his efforts to keep himself occupied, Father Constantine discovered as time went by that he often had "time to spare." It struck him as ironic that now when he had reached the sixth decade of his life he would come to know the meaning of that commonplace phrase. How he would have relished a few free hours in his youth to lie on a grassy slope and gaze idly at the sky and dream the grandiose dreams of the young! And what did it matter if those lofty flights of youthful fancy would fade away in the harsh reality of future years? What mattered was the dream, not its realization. "Time to spare" had little, if any, meaning for Father Constantine in the past. His early days were not long enough to do what was expected of him or of any youth whose family depended on the land for a living. The once fertile soil of Arcadia had sustained not only it inhabitants from time immemorial, but the barbarous hordes with their droves of cattle that had swept across it time and again through the centuries. However arid its soil has become, this mountain region in the heart of Peloponnesos has been the historic homeland of the Arcadians for thousands of years, and to which they are passionately attached. Arcadia was the birthplace of Constantine Douropoulos where the roots of his Hellenic ancestors were so deeply imbedded that invaders were unable to deracinate them, even during the more than four hundred years of Greek subjugation by the Ottoman rulers.

During his boyhood, it did not occur to Constantine to resent the little, if any, time he had for himself. Those who, like Constantine, were born before the twentieth century, did not expect, let alone demand, the considerations, entitlements or concessions which are extended in the present era to the young as a matter of course. In Constantine's time the stage of development from childhood to adulthood was not treated as a special period but as a natural and normal process of growth.

The poverty of the Greek soil, which is less than a third arable, requires the united efforts of the entire family to insure survival. As soon as Constantine was old enough to help, he was given tasks to perform that were commensurate with his physical strength. That he could be of help to his parents gave him a sense of being a responsible member of the family. And in later years he would attribute his vigorous health to the exercising of his body in the bracing mountain air of Arcadia.

The hard work required of the able-bodied in a rural environment does not diminish the zest for life which the Greeks possess. It finds an outlet in the fullest enjoyment by young and old in any pleasurable occasion that comes their way. When the Sabbath arrives, the villagers put aside their cares for the day. Life, they say, is inescapably sad, so you might as well enjoy it. . . . In the morning, the women along with their children fulfilled their religious obligations by going to church. But the men, on the whole, were more noticeable by their absence than by their presence in God's house. Yet, no Greek male, in all conscience, would fail to be present at church on Good Friday to mourn Christ's death on the Cross; or worse still, fail to join his fellowmen at the Easter midnight service in the glorious moment of the Resurrection when one and all Christians cry out in exaltation: Christos Anesti! Christ Is Risen!

Of all the village festivities—bethrothals, weddings, christenings and name days traditionally celebrated on Sunday—the most exciting for Constantine was his father's name day. It was truly a feast day when platters were heaped high with food, when wine flowed as freely as water and dancing was an indispensible part of the merrymaking. Athanasios Douropoulos (called Thanasi, a common shorter form of his first name), as befitted a host celebrating his name day, was the first to lead a typical Greek dance formed by a semi-circle of men and women each holding the hand of the other above shoulder level. Although Thanasi was somewhat stocky, he danced well, for he had the self-assurance of a man who was respected for his honesty and his decency and for his valor as a guerilla fighter in the Greek Revolution of 1821.

His wife, Christina, followed her husband as the leader of the next round of dancing. She was a spirited young woman who had blue eyes, light brown hair with a reddish cast and a fair complexion. Christina's coloring indicated a strain of foreign blood in her veins. She had inherited it most likely from one of the many red-headed Frankish crusaders who invaded and occupied Peloponnesos for approximately two hundred years during the Middle Ages. The Franks were benevolent rulers; besides, they were crusaders willing to die for the Cross, so that marriages between the Franks and the Greeks were probably not uncommon.

The annual celebration for his father's name day that took place when Constantine was about eleven years old, would be one that the first-born son of Thanasi Douropoulos would remember the rest of his life. For at that particular occasion Constantine first saw his mother with a detachment that usually comes—if it comes at all—to an offspring at a more mature age. Up to that time, he had taken his mother and the special affection she had for him as a matter of course. The young boy had heard it said more than once that his mother was a pretty woman. And now when he looked at her he realized that she was indeed, pretty, and she was graceful, as well, as she led the line of dancers with a lively step—yet with a certain dignity befitting the wife of a respected member of the community and the mother of three sons and a daughter.

The Greeks admire a good dancer, for since the days of ancient Greece, dancing has been a life-enriching Hellenic tradition. Indeed, Plato considered the art of ''dancing'' an essential part of a good education. It was obvious to Constantine that his mother was the center of interest as she danced, and that she was conscious of the admiration she aroused and was excited by it. For he had never seen before such a high color on his mother's cheeks.

But that ''high color'' led people to say later that it was not a sign of excitement, but an ominous indication that Christina's blood was too rich for her veins. This was the simple way that the shocked villagers tried to explain Christina's sudden death.

For in the week following Thanasi's name day celebration, the poor woman died from a massive stroke.

Constantine was close to adolescence when his mother died. Devastated as he was by this sudden loss, he soon suffered another unexpected blow. Thanasi was shattered by his young wife's death and distraught at the prospect of raising three sons and a daughter without her help. Added to his misery was the precarious condition of his finances. Although Constantine was a great help to his father in taking care of the land and the livestock, Thanasi, nevertheless, decided to take his son to the ancient Arcadian Monastery of Saint John, the Forerunner, and place him in the service of the venerable Abbot Joachim. He was known as a deeply devout, kindly old man, and Constantine's father had no doubt that the boy would be well-treated. Besides, he believed that Constantine would get a superior education, at no cost, under the tutelage of the scholarly monks at the monastery than he would receive in the one room village school. Moreover, Thanasi was a proud man who did not want to send his son to school shabbily dressed and shod, thus exposing—at the boy's expense—his father's present financial difficulties. In the cloister, young and old wore at all times a simple black *rason*, or cassock, and sturdy leather sandals made by the industrious brothers.

But the father's most compelling reason for deciding to place Constantine in the monastery was to give the boy a head start in his education, hoping thereby, to fulfill his late wife's ardent wish—and his own wish, no less—that their first-born son would become a "lettered" man, as the Greeks say.

Thanasi expected his son to work hard for his keep at Saint John's Monastery. "The Prodromos," as the Arcadians call it, was organized like all Greek Orthodox monasteries according to a cenobitic or communal type of monasticism. As a self-sustaining organization its survival was dependent not only on spiritual zeal, but on the unremitting toil of the entire brotherhood save for those enfeebled by old age or illness.

Constantine's labors at "The Prodromos," however arduous they might prove, would be well-rewarded according to his father's understanding. Beyond his daily nourishment, he would

138

receive sustenance as well for his mind and spirit that would fortify him in his quest for "learning." Without an education Constantine or any one of his peers who came from a rural background would be tied to the earth like his father and his forefathers. His survival, like theirs, would depend on daily toil and daily supplication to the Almighty to grant a beneficent proportion of sunshine and rain.

Thanasi Douropoulos and his contemporaries earned their living by a husbandry that hardly differed from that of their Homeric ancestors. In similar fashion they tended their flocks of sheep and goats on the slopes of the immutable mountains and likewise followed the age old practice of transhumance, moving their herds in the winter to the more clement climate of the valleys and plains. They plowed their fields and planted seed and celebrated the harvest with festive rites and paeans of gratitude as myriads of Greeks had done before them. Their vital supply of oil came from the same hardy species of silver-leafed olive trees that outlast by scores of generations those who plant them. And the wine which has lessened the sorrows and increased the joys of Hellenic life throughout the long centuries was and still is commonly resinated. The pine tree balsam which is used to flavor the popular "retsina" wines gives them a peculiar acerbic taste that holds an inexplicable appeal for the Greek palate.

Constantine's father had no dreams for his own life. His bucolic existence close to God and nature was enough to satisfy him. His greatest source of satisfaction stemmed from the fact that he was born a Greek and from the awareness that his ancient heritage of civilization was shared with the rest of Western mankind.

The "Hellene," as the Greek is called in his own language, considers his country as a vital part of the cosmic schema. And in extreme but not uncommon instances of blind latria, he conceives it as an exclusive planet with a magnificent sun uniquely incandescent and a glorious azure sky singularly luminescent. As for the light—to describe it is to desecrate it. He can only murmur in reverent ecstasy, "The light . . . ah, the light of Greece . . . it is a *thauma*—a miracle!"

The Greeks' characteristic way of saying, "our sun, our sky, our light" gives rise to the suspicion that they may consider these natural phenomena to be other than those operating universally.

A man of resolute action, Thanasi lost no time investigating the possibilities for Constantine to enter "The Prodromos." By a stroke of good fortune, which he attributed to Divine Providence as a sanction of his plans, he was informed that his son could go at once to the Monastery as the youth who had been serving as an acolyte had been called for required military service.

For the first time since his wife died he felt a sense of relief. He was doing all he could for their son's education and he had no doubt that his wife's spirit was rejoicing. He had never forgotten what she said to him one day when Constantine was a little boy and she was helping him wash his hands.

"Look, Thanasi," she exclaimed, "look how fine, how beautiful his fingers are even though he plays in the dirt the whole day long . . . these hands are not meant to hold an axe or a hoe, but a pen and a book!"

The euphoria Thanasi felt was short-lived, however, as he began to consider his present financial status. The past three months were the worst he had experienced in his lifetime. They had brought not only the unbearable anguish of his young wife's sudden death, but cataclysmic rains that damaged the crops and destroyed the raisins which were spread on the ground to dry under the autumn sun. Of all his produce, the golden raisins were the easiest to sell and the most profitable; And now a whole year's labor was a total loss!

To pay for his son's keep was not obligatory on Thanasi's part. Constantine was expected to earn his way—and that he would more than do, for the boy was both able and conscientious. He would have preferred to pledge a respectable sum in his son's name and especially to make a sizable donation in his wife's memory. He would take, of course, as much as could possibly be carried by horse and donkey to the Monastery. He would not spare the best of his wine and oil, nor would he begrudge the good Brothers his finest cheese, the choicest of grapes, nuts and raisins, as well as some of his plumpest chickens. This generosity might seem quixotic from a rational point of view since the Monastery had a brimming larder of foodstuffs thanks to the monks' industriousness. Irreverent cynics often claimed that so large a larder was motivated mainly by their reputed proclivities for "the pleasures of the table." But the issue was not whether the monks used the common offerings of food to satisfy their suspected gluttony. Travel was difficult and dangerous through Arcadia's steep mountain roads—often nothing more than footpaths—so that those who came to "The Prodromos" usually remained overnight and were lodged and fed at the expense of the Monastery.

What motivated Constantine's father was simply a matter of *philotimo*—that quintessentially Greek trait—the zealous guarding of *honor*, one's own honor and the honor of one's family, at all times and at all cost. In its more specific meaning it refers to the individual's self-image and that which is projected to others. This image in both its subjective and objective manifestation is tolerable only if it reflects self-respect, a sense of personal dignity and worth that comes from upholding the ethnic traditions of decency, generosity, hospitality towards relatives and friends, and no less to strangers. To say that a Greek is lacking in *philotimo* is to condemn him as one who has demeaned himself and his country.

Chapter Fourteen

A few days before Constantine was expected at the Monastery of Saint John the Prodromos, Thanasi, in his usual laconic manner told his son that he was placing him "in the hands of those who were close to God." Constantine's upbringing, which was based on filial respect for the patriarchal rule exercised in the Greek family, prohibited him from questioning or protesting in any way his father's decree.

The day that Constantine was to leave home, he followed his usual routine of getting up early to do his chores. He worked with a deliberate briskness that belied the numbness of his spirits. But when he started to milk Zeppa, the goat, his hands were neither quick, nor steady. Of all the livestock on the farm, Zeppa was his favorite. As far back as he could recall she had been his responsibility. Zeppa repaid his affectionate care with an endless stream of warm rich milk. This unfailing gift of hers was transformed into fine feta cheese and creamy yogurt which, along with her milk in its elemental form, was the basic sustenance of the family's simple fare.

For a while, Constantine patted Zeppa gently, then all of a sudden he began to whisper fiercely in her ear. "Don't you dare go away, Zeppa, don't you ever dare. You must stay right here, right here, until I come back!" When would that be, he wondered, when? He gave her a sharp slap on the rump. "Silly goat," he muttered, "I really don't care if I never see her again!" and he ran in anger toward the kitchen.

His sister, Theone, was standing on a wooden stool that made it possible for the eight-year-old girl to reach the primitive stone sink in order to do the dishes or to bend over the tub while scrubbing the clothes. Theone was now the only female in the family and after her mother's death, she assumed, as a matter of course, the household duties undaunted by the limitations of her size and her age.

Then and there Constantine's fragile mask of manliness fell apart. He took her hands in his. For the first time he noticed how red and blistered the small fingers were. He wanted desperately to say something to comfort her, but he did not know what to say or how to say it. Silently he kissed her goodbye and fled in tears. For the rest of his life Constantine Douropoulos could not think or speak of his sister without emotion.

The day before his son would leave for the monastery, Thanasi Douropoulos worked like a man possessed. At night he fell into bed longing for the surcease of his misery in the deep slumber that follows utter exhaustion, but much as his body and mind craved for rest, he could not sleep. He stared vacantly at the white-washed walls that were softly lit by the *candili*, the votive light on the icon stand in the corner of the room. By the flame's pale glow he could dimly discern the shadowy figures and faces of the ancient icons. These were the "lares and penates" of his household handed down from generation to generation by his pious Christian forebears.

In the center of this array of saints, Thanasi's wife had placed the icon of the *Panagia*, the All-Holy One, as the Greeks call the Virgin Mary. It was to her, Queen of the Heavens, with the Christ Child cradled in her arms, that Christina addressed her prayers each morning and each night.

From the time she had entered her husband's home, she had assumed the duty of filling each day the *candili* with the purest olive oil, placing a new wick in its tri-cornered metal holder. With child-like delight she watched the fresh, strong flame leap up and soften with its golden glow the somber beauty of the Byzantine Madonna.

143

Since his wife's death, Thanasi had faithfully cared for the *candili*. It was only after he had gone to bed that he realized he had forgotten to perform the daily ritual which would keep the it burning; and as though to chide him for his negligence, the flame sputtered pitifully a few times then quietly expired.

Thanasi felt uneasy in the total darkness that now enveloped him. For a moment he struggled with the impulse to get up and attend to the matter; but the intense weariness he felt overcame his uneasy conscience. May the Virgin grant him forgiveness— and a few hours of restful sleep. Tomorrow, the first thing in the morning, he could take care of the *candili*.

Thanasi was never certain thereafter whether he had fallen asleep or was still awake, when he heard a voice barely audible calling to him from afar.

"Thanasi"—the name reached him in a gentle whisper, and instantly he knew it was Christina's voice coming from the grave. No one else could have uttered his name in so tender a way. He strained every nerve in his body to catch the faint disembodied words that followed.

"Tomorrow, when you go to 'The Prodromos' take with you my diamond cross. Place it on the Panagia's icon that adorns the bare stone wall in the chapel of the Monastery and pray to Her Grace to guard and guide our son." The voice faded away. A fearful silence filled the room. Trembling, Thanasi rose and groped his way to the icon stand. He found the *candili* and lit it. By the light of the newborn flame, he reached Christina's dowry chest and gently opened it.

After the tearful farewell to his sister, Constantine went back to the courtyard where he found his father loading the provisions that his horse and donkey would carry to the Monastery. The boy hurriedly wiped his eyes on his sleeve. His pride did not permit him to be seen crying, especially by his father—a man with a heart of stone, thought Constantine bitterly—who could banish his child from home without a sign of regret! If his mother were alive *she* would never have allowed so cruel a sentence. Since her death, Constantine tried to obliterate her from his thoughts. If he could forget her he might be able to get rid of that strange, frightening, hollow feeling that had not left him from the time his mother was lowered into the darkness of the grave. But it was of no use . . . he could not escape her . . . time and again she came unbidden to his mind . . . and he would see her as he had seen her last . . . in the narrow wooden coffin . . . cold and silent and white . . . like a piece of marble.

At these thoughts of his mother, the lad surrendered to a torrent of tears. But lest his father witness this new outburst of grief, he turned abruptly on his heel and went towards Zeppa, who was tethered to a nearby tree.

Despite Constantine's attempt to hide his misery, his father had caught sight of the grief-twisted face, and it went to his heart. He gave no indication, however, that he was aware of his son's despair but continued working at a slower pace to give the boy time to collect himself. Finally there was nothing more to be done. Thanasi looked up at the sun and surmised the morning was half spent. "Come my boy, it's getting late," he cried.

The boy deliberately ignored his father. Thanasi was not a man to waste time or words. He strode up to his son.

"Didn't you hear me, Costa? I said it's getting late and we must be on our way."

The boy was taken aback. He expected, indeed, he wanted his father to get angry so that he could justify even more his feelings of hostility. But Constantine caught the harsh tenderness hidden in the gruffness of his father's voice. He had called him "Costa"—the nickname his mother used whenever she spoke to him. The boy did not trust himself to reply for fear he would break into tears once again.

His father went directly to the tree to which Zeppa was tethered and untied her knot. Constantine was bewildered but managed to find his tongue. "Oh, don't let her loose," he pleaded, "she'll only follow us!"

"That's what I want her to do," his father remarked casually, "to follow us to the monastery. I've an idea the Brothers will be glad to have a goat like Zeppa around."

At first, Constantine did not grasp the meaning of his father's words but when he realized that Zeppa was going along with him to The Prodromos, an incredulous smile lit up his tear-stained face. What a good, kind, wonderful father he had—a father with a heart of gold! If only he dared tell him how much he loved him! (Greek fathers, although greatly attached to their offspring, consider it undignified to subject their children or be subjected by them to expressions of endearment or manifestations of affection.)

But in the midst of these unexpressed filial sentiments, his sister brought the two younger boys, Nicholas and John, to the courtyard so they could say goodbye to their brother before he left home. At the sight of his siblings, Constantine was suddenly filled with uneasiness.

What would they do without Zeppa's milk? Oh, no, he couldn't take her away from them. He must tell his father not to leave her behind, but before he had a chance to speak, he heard his father say, "Don't expect me home until late tonight. I'm going to stop at Pappá Pavlos' house. He has a nanny goat to spare."

"Is she expensive?" Constantine asked anxiously.

"She's worth a good sum—a healthy little animal she is, with plenty of milk, but it's not a matter of money. Pappá Pavlos prefers my wine to my drachmas."

Thanasi had one of the best vineyards in the area. That explained why, people said, the priest visited the Douropoulos house more often than he did any other in his parish. It will be a fair exchange, thought Thanasi; Pappá Pavlos can enjoy my fine wine at *his* house and we can enjoy his goat's fine milk at *our* house.

Before mounting his horse, Thanasi felt his pocket and assured himself that the black velvet box which contained Christina's cross was safe and sound. The little caravan started off but stopped when it came to the stone archway that led out of the courtyard. Here, before leaving his territory, Thanasi made the sign of the cross and asked the Lord to guide and protect them. And then he went on his way.

They had little to say as they traveled the long lonely road to the Monastery. But even if Thanasi and his son were not by nature reserved in speech and manner, the relationship between a Greek parent and his offspring precludes the camaraderie that is often found among their Anglo-Saxon counterparts. The paternal role of the Greek is uniquivocally patriarchal. The father acts not only as a dependable provider for his family but as an advisor and mentor to his children even at the risk of incurring their overt resentment or hidden hostility. This attitude is based on the fact that the innate differences which exist in the relative age and status of parent and child cannot be bridged or equalized and any attempt to do so appears to the Greek patently incongruous.

At the start of their journey the father glanced now and then at his son. He could see no signs of the grief that so recently had darkened the boy's face. "Youth," reflected Thanasi philosophically, "lives in the joy and the sorrow of the moment." He had been moved by the boy's obvious misery, but it had caused him no regret as far as his decision was concerned to send Constantine away from home. That his son did not appreciate his motives did not trouble him. He was not out to win the love or the goodwill of his child, but to do his duty as a conscientious parent, even though it was to his own disadvantage.

Thanasi remembered his father's sage words: "Understanding comes only with the years." And the time would come when Constantine would be grateful for the chance to get an education and be thankful he was born well after those black years of tyranny when education was forbidden to the Greeks. For a race that considered its heritage of cultural riches as a sacred trust, the outlawing of its schools was an insupportable barbarism. Plato's words still echo in the Greek mind: "Education is the fairest thing that the best of men can have."

To counteract all possible extent the evils of enforced obscurantism, the Greeks resorted at great peril to the so-called "secret schools." Classes were held at night in dark hideouts when a teacher could be found, possibly some aged village priest no longer able to fight for "The Cause."

There is hardly a Greek at home or abroad who does not know by heart the demotic poem attributed to the children born in bondage during the Ottoman rule who ventured forth in the dark of night seeking their ancient legacy of learning:

Shine, my little moon, so bright,
Light my way to school at night,

147

Where I learn to read and write,
Learn of God's good works and might.

This touching little ode to the moon came to Thanasi's mind
as he contrasted his offspring's good fortune with the tragic lot
his forefathers had to bear in their time. God only knows how
many of them had lived and died in misery during those bitter
years of servitude, which began on that fatal last Tuesday on May
29th of 1453—the day when Constantinople, the magnificent
jewel of the Byzantine Empire, fell into the hands of the infidel—
the day that remains ineffaceably carved on the memory of the
Greeks as the most infamous day in their history.

Thanasi would be ever grateful that his children from the moment of their birth had breathed the air of freedom, which for
the Greek is the very breath of life itself. And he would be ever
thankful they were born to the sound of church and school bells
ringing freely in a liberated land, for Greece had risen like the
immortal phoenix—the emblem of the Greek Revolution—from
the ashes of devastation; and mountain-wreathed Athens, which
had been reduced to the pitiful status of a sordid village, was
once again the glorious capital of Greece, and once again would
become "The School of Hellas," as Pericles proudly called her
more than two thousand years ago. Even while the country was
still in the throes of the vicious aftermath of the bloody War of
1821, facing political dissension and economic chaos, the Greeks
nevertheless achieved a cherished desideratum—an institution for
higher education—the present University of Athens, which was
established in 1837. Within a decade another vital institution was
founded, the Rizarios Theological Seminary for the education
of those who would dedicate their lives to the Church.

Thanasi possessed the love of learning and the great respect
for knowledge which is deeply ingrained in the Greek. He was,
therefore, willing to face the likelihood that his children in acquiring an education would reject the Spartan existence to which
he was committed. But now it was no longer only the search for
knowledge or its acquisition that caused the young to leave home.
Mere lads all over Greece—whether educated or not—were for-
saking the villages for the thriving urban areas where they could

148

earn a less precarious livelihood than the impoverished one to which their elders had long been inured. As far as Thanasi was concerned, he had expected no more from life than a man's fair share of happiness and sorrow; he had been content to live quietly and die peacefully and like his countless progenitors become in time part of the sacred soil of his motherland.

The world was changing and Thanasi was prepared to see his sons leave home and to give them his paternal blessing. But he could not envision by the utmost play of his fancy that one day they would venture far from the towns and cities of Greece, beyond her golden shores, her sapphire skies and crystal waters to reach an ultramontane land where they would live and die and be laid to rest forevermore in alien earth.

Thanasi Douropoulos died at the start of the great exodus to America which attracted more male population from Peloponnesos than from any other part of Greece. As he had anticipated, his three sons left Vancon, the Arcadian village of their birth and had gone to various parts of Greece to earn their living. Several years after their father's death, the three brothers, Nicholas, John and Constantine, emigrated, one by one, to the United States during the first decade of the twentieth century. Thanasi had felt sorry for parents who were separated from their children by a vast ocean. He was fortunate that his sons had stayed in the Peloponnesos. For when his time came to die they could reach home within a few hours to give their father the "last kiss" before his coffin was closed. And then Charon would take charge of him, leading him on that dark, lonely journey to Hades, the land of the dead. What more could a man ask for at his death bed but to be surrounded by his children before his eyes were closed forever? Yes, he was a fortunate man who loved his three sons and his daughter and loved them each with an equal share of love. On that point he would quote an old proverb: "Whichever finger hurts, it will pain the same as any finger on your hand."

His assurances notwithstanding, whenever Thanasi used to speak of his first-born son his voice carried a tone of obvious pride, for Constantine was a *morphomenos anthropos*—an

149

educated man—a seminary graduate and a school teacher, no less. As for Constantine's filial attitude, it was typical of the kind expected of an offspring born in a forgotten era when the foremost obligation towards one's parents was expressed in the simple biblical commandment: Honor thy father and thy mother.

Even though his mother had died when Constantine was a young boy, he honored and cherished her memory throughout his life. For she had been the center of his world—the only world he had known as a child—the small pretty village of Vancon nestled against the gentle slope of an Arcadian mountain. His roots had been nourished in its soil, and beneath its sod his forefathers were laid to rest in their rough-hewn wooden coffins; and his mother had been buried beside them in the full tide of her youth.

Her untimely death had not only intensified the inalienable bond which exists between mother and child, but had assumed in Constantine's mind a mystical significance. Because of her death, his father had placed him in the Monastery of Saint John—a step which eventually would alter the course of his life. The boy's initial reaction to this brusque change from his familiar surroundings was one of despair. But as the weeks and months went by, Constantine's misery slowly dissolved in the quietude of the cloister; and as he became increasingly aware of the spiritual aura that permeated the monastic atmosphere, he felt the first stirrings of love for the Church which ultimately led him to embrace the priesthood.

He wished he had known more about his mother—the woman who had governed his destiny by her absence rather than by her presence. When Constantine or his siblings asked their father about their mother, he would respond in his usual taciturn way, "She was a good Christian woman from a respectable, God-fearing family." If they pressed for more information he would simply say, "Let her lie in peace."

Chapter Fifteen

Through the years, Constantine had managed to reconstruct the significant parts of his mother's life. She had, indeed, come from "a respectable, God-fearing family" that was typical of the parochial Greek world in the nineteenth century. Christina, however, had contributed on her own account a certain luster—an unexpected touch of glamor, so to speak, to the family name by having as her godfather *Capetan* Dimitri Hadjichristos. The Captain had fought with distinction in the Greek Revolution of 1821 which finally terminated more than four hundred years of Turkish tyranny. He epitomized a true *pallikari*, the laudatory epithet reserved for those who are bold in action and brave in spirit.

The Captain had promised Nikos Karanicholas, a comrade-in-arms and a fellow Arcadian from the village of Vancon, that he would be his *koumparos*, the sponsor or best man, at his friend's wedding. According to Greek custom, the *koumparos* is also expected to christen the first child of the couple whose marriage he sponsors. A year or so after the wedding, his friend's wife, Katerina, gave birth to a daughter and the Captain became her godfather.

A man who lived up to his reputation for bravura in time of war and in time of peace, *Capetan* Hadjichristos arrived one fine spring day in Vancon to do the honors with a sizeable cavalcade of men who had formerly served under his leadership during the war.

People poured out from the towns, villages and hamlets to witness the long line of horsemen led by their former Captain as they rode by in single file on the narrow mountain passes. They were wearing the *foustanella*—the white pleated skirt-like kilt whose voluminous folds swayed to and fro with the rhythmic rise and fall of the horses' hoofs. Their shoulder-length hair and the long black tassels hanging from their crimson caps swung back and forth with the steady beat of a metronome. The golden braid on their velvet jackets and the silver-handled pistols in their cummerbunds glittered in the sunlight. These weapons would be fired in the air as a salute of honor as soon as the riders reached their destination.

All along the way the cavalcade was greeted by smiling faces and tear-filled eyes. Women dressed in black from head to foot silently wept as they made the sign of the cross in memory of loving sons and husbands, of good fathers and kind brothers and sweet young lovers who had died in the battle for freedom. But at the sight of a handsome boy about seven or eight years old, the mourners wiped away their tears and joined in applause for this Lilliputian version of a mighty warrior.

"*Yia sou, pallikaraki*! Health to you, brave little fellow! May you rejoice in the days of your youth, may you live a hundred years, may the mother be blessed that bore you!"

The boy was Thanasi Douropoulos riding with his father to the christening of an infant girl, who sixteen years later would become his wife and the mother of his three sons—Constantine, Nicholas and John, and an only daughter, Theone.

Constantine, the first born, was destined to come to America as one of the pioneer Greek Orthodox priests in the first decade of the twentieth century.

At a christening, the Greeks reveal their primordial zest for life. Relatives and friends, acquaintances and chance visitors gather in high spirits to celebrate the result of a fruitful union, to honor the continuation of a family name and to offer blessings in behalf of an infant whose birth reaffirms the indispensable guarantee for the survival of their ancient race.

Beyond its social and biological ramifications, the *baptisma* is recognized from a religious point of view as a primary mystical sacrament for only by the grace of baptism can an individual be confirmed as a true member of Orthodoxy. According to the Church, after the baptismal rites have been properly performed, one may then rightfully wear a cross—the universally acknowledged emblem of a Christian. This ancient tenet and, similarily, the one which places on a godparent responsibility for the spiritual welfare of a godchild have lost their original significance. A simple gold cross with a chain, nevertheless, still remains the traditional gift that is given to a godchild by the godfather or godmother at the time of christening. But the cross which Captain Hadjichristos gave to his goddaughter was not the usual kind. It was, in fact, so unusual as to raise Christina's christening from the level of a spectacle to that of a legend.

The village church was filled dangerously close to the point of disaster. No one was so foolhardy or courageous as to hazard life or limb by attempting further entry save for a well-known local character who had travelled a distance of several kilometers to be present at what promised to be the social event of all seasons. This small but rugged old lady was called Kyra Nicoletta—in the provincial style of nomenclature which prefaces a matron's given name by *Kyra*, the colloquial form of "Mrs." She was also known simply as "the Widow." Her husband had been murdered shortly after they were married and she had held that grievous title with pride and dignity for more than half a century.

Nicoletta's husband, Markos Leontaris (his patronym was originally a sobriquet derived directly from the Greek word "lion"), was descended from a long line of *kleftes*—freedom fighters or guerrillas—the precursors of the Greek Revolutionary heroes of 1821, who had shed their blood during the long bitter centuries of enslavement so that one day Greece might again be free. The exploits of these fearless men had become legends for the Greeks and anathemas to the Turks.

The newlywed chieftain had inherited a prepotent measure of his forefathers' ardor for the "Cause" and his timely capture before he had spawned more of his pernicious breed delighted the beys and satraps who governed the Peloponnese from their comfortable headquarters in the Arcadian town of Tripolis. They

153

reported to the sublime Porte that they would see to it personally that the rebel received an appropriate mode of punishment and a befitting style of liquidation. This would indicate to the Sultan in Constantinople that his firmans regarding the proper treatment of the rayahs, the non-Moslem subjects under Ottoman rule, were being carried out to the letter. Indeed, the Sultan's deputies improved on his orders. In their free time between visits to the seraglios of their harems and in the intervals of prescribed prayers and obeisances to Allah, they put their talents to good use by devising a variety of methods for torture that would put Procrustes to shame.

After Markos Leontaris had received his appropriate punishment and befitting liquidation, the officials responsible for this accomplishment felt they were entitled to some sort of entertaining finale to the whole business. A parade, it was decided, would serve a dual purpose—a divertissement for them and a reminder to the Greeks of what was in store for those who dared to defy Authority.

The Turks in colorful array, their portly waists encircled by chabouks—the long, thin snakelike whips which were handy for keeping the "Christian dogs" at bay, marched through the villages of Arcadia. They carried on a tall spike Markos' head neatly severed by the scimitar, that favorite and efficient weapon of the Musselmans.

This particular little episode (for there were many other of greater moment) served only to further the Greeks' passion to replace the crescent of Islam by the Cross of Christianity.

Although Kyra Nicoletta was a great-grandaunt of Christina, she had not been invited to the christening. To do so was quite unnecessary, for she kept a close watch on all the various functions taking place in the vicinity and well beyond it—and held a record of perfect attendance at all of them. Her ubiquitous presence was not resented, however. As the widow of a martyr to "The Cause" she had automatically acquired a certain prestige, and her advanced age somewhere in the mid-eighties, commanded, as well, the respect which is accorded to the venerable members of a Greek community. But beyond the respect and honor due her, she was highly esteemed for her matchmaking prowess and was practically worshipped by the beneficiaries of it.

As a matchmaker, Kyra Nicoletta shunned the practices of callous "marriage brokers" who were more inspired by the worth of their fees than the worthiness of their mission. The good widow would not accept even one drachma for her accomplishments, nor was she so insensitive as to insult the *philotimo* of her clients (my children, she called them) by refusing their kind expressions of gratitude in the form of donatives which kept her cupboard and her wine cellar royally supplied.

The praises from those who, due to her good offices, were enjoying connubial bliss and the blandishments of those who longed to be in a similar state, did not turn Nicoletta's head. Her success in the art of matchmaking was so well established, she could afford to be modest about it. In fact she tried to minimize the importance attributed to her role by saying rather vaguely that "marriage is a *mysterion*" an ambiguous word in Greek which can mean either "sacrament" or "mystery." Following this oracular utterance she would point to the sky and say, "Marriages are made *up there*, my children, not by *me*!"

These remarks were expressed with a conspiratorial gleam in her eye as though she had something up her sleeve, possibly a direct line some suspected to a celestial "Matrimonial Bureau" from where she obtained vital statistics on every male and female within the scope of her operations.

Statistics were essential to Kyra Nicoletta since they could be construed to her advantage, as they often were particularly in handling "difficult or critical" cases which were considered the good widow's specialty. These were instances involving maidens hovering close to the age of twenty-five—a fearful age in those bygone days—for beyond it unmarried females were doomed to bear the stigma of spinsterhood, a sign no less shameful than a "scarlet letter" but for quite the opposite reasons. These unfortunate creatures were on the verge of disgrace not as a result of their own iniquities but simply because their families could not provide them with a decent dowry, which at the time was a prime requisite for matrimony. But a meager dowry or even none for that matter, was not necessarily fatal as Kyra Nicoletta had proven more than once. There were indeed certain assets such as intoxicating beauty of face and form which were powerful enough to anesthesize a man's sensibilities as to the worth of a dowry.

Pluchritude was a highly dangerous bait, however, whose use required the skill of a talented matchmaker like Kyra Nicoletta to avoid an unspeakable disaster. For it could attract a male whose lust was exceeded only by his baseness. And a lovely, innocent, poor girl, haunted by the spectre of spinsterhood, could be led by convincing but utterly false promises of honorable intentions to desecrate the consummation of love outside the sanctity of the nuptial bed.

The "critical cases," (fortunately few at any given time) were those in which the insufficiency of a dowry was compounded by a deficiency in feminine charm. Such instances, cruel or absurd as they may appear today, were, in the past regarded from a matrimonial point of view as "basket cases."

These forlorn, forgotten beings who had lost hope of hearing the jubilant peal of their wedding bells, aroused the Widow's deepest sympathies and greatest efforts. It was duty not dishonesty which made her alter or rather interpret a statistic or two in their favor as well as bringing to light a treasure trove of merits which neither these good virgins nor anyone else suspected they possessed. In achieving what was considered nothing less than miracles in a number of these all but hopeless cases, Kyra Nicoletta had knowingly followed the dictates of compassion—and unknowingly abided by the dictum of Sophocles, her ancient compatriot, who said, "Truly, to tell lies is not honorable; but when truth entails tremendous ruin, to speak dishonorably is pardonable."

But the Widow did not view her work as miraculous but rather as a *psychiko*—a mission of pure charity—a true act of supererogation performed for the salvation of one's own "psyche" as the Greeks call the soul; and it is looked upon as one of the efficacious means of guaranteeing in due time a state

156

of sempiternal bliss. Everyone agreed that Heaven was Kyra Nicoletta's final destination, and that she would have no difficulty whatsoever in reaching it. Her path to Paradise would be brightly illumined by the beneficent light of many a *psychiko* she had performed in her lengthy lifetime.

Chapter Sixteen

The gentle but persistent rains of early spring had steadily nourished the earth and revitalized the ancient soil of the mountains. On cliffs and crags, in gullies and ravines an exotic new world was coming to life impatiently waiting for the sun to release it according to the laws of nature which govern its annual rebirth. With an unfailing sense of duty the sun took command of the heavens and by the time of Christina's christening, the countryside echoed and re-echoed with the Song of Songs: "For lo, the winter is past, the rain is over and gone. The flowers appear on the earth; the time of the singing of birds is come. . . ."

In the morning when Kyra Nicoletta opened the shutters she noted with delight that the sky was a flawless porcelain dome of royal blue that presaged a glorious day worthy of a glorious occasion. But her joy turned to sorrow as she thought of her sister, Phrosene, who had died at the age of ninety a few months before her great-granddaughter Christina was born.

"My poor Phrosene, my beloved sister," she cried out in anguish, "today you should be on this earth and not beneath it—if only you had not been snatched away from us so soon, so heartlessly by Charon." (The Greeks often refer to death as "Charon," the mythological ferryman of ancient popular belief, who transported the departed souls over the River Styx to the chthonic realm of Hades.)

But the pain the Widow felt at her sister's absence from the

living world was unconsciously mitigated by the inadmissible
pleasure she felt at her own presence in it. "Never mind, my good
Phrosene," she added consolingly, "your little sister Nicoletta
will represent you today at your great-granddaughter's *baptisma*,"
and crossing herself she added, "blessed be His name for grant-
ing me the time to perform this happy duty."

In order not to miss a moment of the baptismal ceremonies,
the Widow started early on her hour-long journey and scampered
up the winding road as lively as a nanny goat. Had she continued
at this pace, she might have reached her destination in ample time
to secure for herself a strategic spot inside the church where the
christening would take place. (In past years seats or pews were
not available in the Orthodox churches. The men occupied the
right section of the church and the women the left. The worshipers
remained standing throughout the long liturgical service that extended to two or more hours.)

Instead of keeping steadily on her way, Kyra Nicoletta stopped now and them to exult in the vistas that each twist and turn
of the road exposed to her view. The lifelong love affair the
Greeks have with their country reaches orgiastic proportions in
the springtime. The spectacular metamorphosis that then takes
place, especially on the innumerable hills and mountains, over-
powers the senses by its voluptuous beauty and overwhelms the
spirit by the eternal mystery of Nature's regenerative force.

When the old woman arrived at a sharp hairpin turn, she realized she had come to the last lap of her journey and within a
quarter of an hour or so she would reach her destination. She
knew the terrain intimately as only those can know it who are
born and bred and destined to remain their entire lifetime within
the confines of their native environs. She scurried around the
deep, semicircular bend with a sense of keen anticipation, for
at the end of it she would be on the southern flank of the mountain which was exposed to the full light and warmth of the sun. As
she made the turn, Nicoletta found what she had fervently hoped
to find—the mountain flora in a dazzling state of efflorescence.

A multi-colored mantua spread over a world that was wrapped but a few days before by the dismal shroud of winter. The
sombre face of the mountain was softened by the bloom of

countless shrubs and bushes; creepers and vines bravely climbed the ponderous bluffs and the steepest cliffs to hide their barren surfaces beneath layers of leaves and blossoms. In the crevices of rocks, under scrub and brushwood, between the stones and shards that lie on the ground, the mountain flora finds sufficient nourishment to produce inexhaustable variations of form and color.

There are literally thousands of these enchanting plants that have adorned the Greek landscape each springtide, eons before they were systematically classified by the philosopher Theophrastos, the devoted friend and follower of Aristotle. Many of them are still known by their ancient names—and a number of them are still used for medicinal purposes as cited in "The Greek Herbal," by Dioscrides, the eminent physician and botanist who served in Nero's army. The scholarly works of these two ancient Greeks were the only authorative sources for botanical study up to the sixteenth century.

In all the years the Widow had come to this particular spot, she had never seen it glowing with such vernal splendor . . . no, never had she felt so moved by its beauty, so awed by its grandeur! Instinctively she crossed herself. The roadside was lined with wild flowers and herbs. Pink rock-roses, mauve mallows, golden broom, red valerians, blue campanulas. Flowers beyond measure intermingled with thyme, basil, oregano, marjoram, lavender and a host of other aromatic herbs. Each according to its nature fought gallantly or ruthlessly to capture the vital rays of the sun.

The poppies that are the glory of the Greek countryside followed their own course. They had seized the lower slopes and triumphantly announced their conquest with their crimson banners. Some of the more elegant species preferred to make their habitat apart from their commonplace kin in isolated splendor beneath the filtered shade of tall bushes and shrubs. Here the startling red dragon flower with its long rippled-edged spathe grew beside the strangely beautiful *ophrys*—the rose and chartreuse orchid whose dark velvety lips are stamped with the metallic outline of a horseshoe.

It was not fatigue but emotion that prompted Kyra Nicoletta to find a spot where she might rest for a while. She felt a need to sit quietly, to drink in slowly the loveliness around her, to carry it forever with her lest in afterlife she failed to find anything better or equal to it. She spied a large, oblong stone half-hidden among a mass of handsome plants with sword-like leaves and long, slim stems whose spikes were full of blossoms. She pushed them aside to reach the stone and ran her finger across its surface. Finding no dust or dirt that would soil her best black skirt, the old lady sat down and gazed at the panorama that spread before her. She had seen it countless times yet it always moved her to behold the mountains stretched like a motionless sea of granite waves carved everlastingly against the sky. Their eternal magnitude made her feel more poignantly than ever the frailty of mortality. How many more springtides were in store for her, she wondered. If, God grant, she should live as long as her sister Phrosene there would be a few more yet to come. But did another year or two really matter after all?

The primal fear of death crept over her, but she subdued it by dwelling on her good fortune to have lived the full length of her vigorous years on these Arcadian mountains that were crowned with eagles' nests, these noble mountains that had nurtured generations of heroic men and stoic women whose transcendent passion was the rebirth of Freedom. Her Markos was among the best of this breed. She sighed the long deep sigh of sorrow. For beneath her pride in him lay the shadows of his cruel untimely death and the gentle shades of children that had never seen the light of day. She was painfully aware that only those who leave their progeny behind them can hope to be remembered for a generation or two. Her own name and the worthy name of her husband, which she had retained by virtue of her long and honorable widowhood, would be all but forgotten as soon as she died.

The mountain air, usually crisp and light, was languid with the rich aroma of springtime. Kyra Nicoletta's head began to nod but at the sudden pealing of a bell she became aware that the hour of the christening had come. She was not disturbed, however, by the fact that she had a quarter of an hour's walk still ahead of her. In view of her compatriots' notorious disregard for punctuality, she no doubt would reach the church with time

161

to spare before the *baptisma* would actually begin. As she started towards the road, she cut off a few branches from the heavy growth of flowers that stood partially in her way. For the first time she noticed that the dainty white blossoms were shaped like little stars marked with delicate veins of rosy red. Kyra Nicoletta had no trouble recognizing them as asphodels, one of the most common and most delightful wild flowers of Greece.

Yet, lovely as they were, the old lady gazed at them uneasily, for she suddenly recalled a long forgotten memory—her father's deep aversion toward the asphodel. Our wise progenitors, the ancient Greeks, he would say, considered it "the symbol of death." It was, he admitted, a beautiful flower but one of fearful omen. He admonished his children to play far from where it grew and never to touch it, or else, God help them.

The Widow groped her way to the roadside and turned to glance once more at the asphodels. In perspective they appeared to her like a solid bank of funeral flowers surrounding the bier-shaped slab of stone—the very stone where she had rested but a few moments ago and wondered how many more springtides were in store for her. She knew the answer now.

It was getting late, but Kyra Nicoletta went her way unmindful of the passing time. Now and again she dallied to gaze at the mountains, to look in the heart of a flower or to pluck and smell some fragrant herb; she paused to hear the wind softly stir among the newborn leaves. And suddenly she stopped to listen as her ears caught the distant sound of bleating lambs.

Above their gentle cries she heard the lamentations of a flute whose melancholy notes revealed a shepherd's sorrow at his lonely lot. "Poor, lonesome creature," thought the Widow, "he needs a loving wife."

The shepherd's threnody grew faint and finally faded from the air. Kyra Nicoletta began to walk again with a firm step and a firm resolve to savor to the fullest every moment of this last resplendent Spring.

The first person to greet the Widow when she arrived at the Church was an elderly kinsman of hers known as "Barba" (Uncle) Georgis. He embraced her warmly in the usual Greek fashion

162

by kissing her on one cheek and then the other.

"My dear Nicoletta," he whimpered close to tears, *"Krima, krima,* what a pity, what a pity, to come all this distance and yet not be able to witness the *baptisma* of our dearly beloved Phrosene's great-granddaughter!"

Nicoletta could not refrain from smiling. "Barba" Georgis' fat, little body was rippling with exasperation. He was dressed in the style of the period with a foustanella that was all out of proportion to his size, and it hung practically down to his ankles. Poor, ludicrous creature . . . no wonder that for years Kyra Nicoletta had tried in vain to get him a wife.

He was soothed by her smile, fortunately unaware of the reason for it. "Well, I'm glad you're not upset, little cousin. It would have been impossible to get inside the church even if you had come here hours ago. Those women in there," and he pointed a pudgy finger disdainfully towards the left side of the church, "came in droves since the break of day, I swear, from all parts of Arcadia, by God, and took their stand while you and I, blood relatives, are left out in the cold. Not even a mouse could get in there now! But what can you expect from a pack of harebrained females!" "Barba" Gorgis had restrained himself from delivering his usual litany of coarse epithets on the female sex in front of his kinswoman who knew the cause of his bitter misogyny. He normally referred to all women as *putanes*—whores, every single one of them, "Barba" Georgis would declare bitterly, save for his mother, God rest her saintly soul. . . .

"Anyway, my dear, we're far better off here in the open air where we can enjoy the superb fragrance of roasting lamb instead of suffocating with the smell of incense inside that stifling church." He waved his pudgy hand towards a large cloud of smoke as he sniffed the air voluptuously. "I daresay there must be a dozen or more baby lambs being barbecued for the feast." "Barba" Georgis no longer pestered the matchmaker for a bride. Time had exerted an antiorgastic effect on Nicoletta's old kinsman, and he was forced to sublimate his amorous proclivities by an obscene passion for food.

A group of people had gathered around the Widow to pay their respects but Kyra Nicoletta had no time for amenities. "Get out of my way, Georgis, and all the rest of you," she commanded. She stepped back a pace or two and then the wiry, little body shot forth like a small but lethal missile at the phalanx of sturdy backs that lined the doorway. "Let me through, let me through," demanded Kyra Nicoletta, "I am the infant's great-grandaunt!" Her cry resounded through the church and drowned out the voices of the priest and the chanters. The congregation was startled, and every head turned towards the doorway. In the midst of the commotion she aroused, Nicoletta disappeared in a wave of foustanelles. She reappeared in the first row among the "honor guard" of warriors and wedged herself between the boy, Thanasi, and his father. Ignoring the titters that came from the women's side and the scowling face of Pappá Elias, the priest, she patted the boy on the head, greeted his father silently and nodded graciously to Captain Hadjichristos. He gave her a warm reassuring smile. "By God, the widow of Markos Leontaris deserves to be among the men," the Captain thought to himself. "That old lady has as much courage as any one of us!"

Dimitri Hadjichristos was among the few who knew that Kyra Nicoletta had played a far more significant role in her day than that of a successful matchmaker. Time and again she had proved supremely loyal to the "Cause." She had climbed the granite mountains in the vicious winds of winter and under the seething summer sun to bring the freedom fighters vital messages, ammunition, food and medical supplies—whatever she could lay her hands on that would be of use to them. More by instinct than by knowledge, she found the lairs and dens of wild animals which the *kleftes* had pre-empted as their home. Here they lived and slept the fitful sleep of the wary, with the earth as their bed and the stones as a pillow for their heads.

Many of the guerrillas who guarded the wild Arcadian terrain with their life's blood were mere youths who made up in valor what they lacked in years. The Widow looked on them as the sons which had been denied her; and they saw in her the mother they had left behind and might not live to see again.

The Captain noted how touchingly small and fragile Nicoletta seemed surrounded by his men that towered over her protectively. Yet when he considered her years and the reckless indifference

164

she maintained as to her own well-being, he was grateful that she at least had lived to see the War of Emancipation come to a glorious end. But how many women, he wondered, had nurtured through hundreds of years of bitter bondage the seminal spark of freedom?—the spark that became a flaming torch by whose light the great heroines in the "Revolution of 1821" found their way to immortality, while the names and deeds of countless simple, selfless women lie forgotten with their bones in some long-forsaken graveyard.

Chapter Seventeen

Pappá Elias cleared his throat with a significant cough and recommenced the baptismal service which was about to reach its climax. Captain Hadjichristos, the godfather, in behalf of his godchild solemnly rejected "Satan and all his evil," and recited with proper reverence "The *Nicene* Creed." He then cupped his hands in which the verger poured as much olive oil as they could hold and proceeded to rub the oil over the infant's body. The priest now took hold of the baby girl and immersed her three times in a large bronze basin of tepid water, intoning each time: "The servant of God, Christina, is baptized in the name of the Father, the Son and the Holy Spirit." Following the ancient Christian ritual of triune immersion, Pappá Elias performed the final baptismal rite of chrismation by anointing with consecrated oil the baby's forehead, cheeks and chin, the chest and back. Sputtering and gasping with impotent rage, Christina was duly wrapped in a towel and taken away to be dressed in preparation for the traditional ending of the christening ceremony.

From the corner of her eye, the Widow had been watching young Thanasi. She was not surprised that the lad was intensely preoccupied with the proceedings. He was the eldest of three sons and more than likely had never before seen a naked female form. She was greatly attached to this handsome, healthy lad; besides, she felt somewhat responsible for his existence. When his father, one of the Captain's bravest men, decided to marry, he had relied entirely on the Widow's good judgment and she had found him, with God's help, a most worthy wife. (Nicoletta generously attributed successful alliances to Divine Providence and any misalliances to Satan's malevolence.) The success of that particular symbiosis was clearly evident in the boy that stood beside her.

What a *pallikari* he would be some day! If only she could remain here on earth, what a bride she would find for him! The realization that she would miss this opportunity filled the old woman's heart with sorrow. Her tears were about to flow when a thought entered her mind—an inspiration of prevenient grace that could have come only from Heaven! Kyra Nicoletta felt she must disclose at once this divine message to Christina's godfather. She started towards him unmindful that the baptismal rites were not yet finished. She was saved, however, from her impulsive impropriety by the reappearance of Christina's mother carrying her daughter bedecked in all her christening finery. Exhausted beyond the point of tears, the infant was whimpering like a frightened little animal. But no one paid attention to her misery. It was indeed a small price to pay for the glory of becoming a member of Orthodoxy.

Now that Christina was a full-fledged Christian, her godfather placed a chain with a cross around her neck. Those who were near enough to see the Captain's gift stared at it incredulously. Never had they seen a *cross of diamonds*—a cross that glittered like the very stars in Heaven! The dour-faced priest came close to peer at it and his dim eyes lit up. Well, well, our Captain must be a man of wealth as well as valor. If he can afford a jewelled cross for his godchild, he could surely give a poor old priest a gold piece for his services! He beamed at the Captain, who guessed precisely what was passing through the old man's mind. "I'll make it two, it's worth it," thought Hadjichristos, "to keep him smiling."

People began to whisper and the bolder ones started inching their way through the crowd. *Pappá* Elias reproved them with unaccustomed mildness, gently reminding them to be patient for a few minutes more as the holy sacrament of baptism would soon be completed. Christina's mother proudly laid her baby in the crook of the Captain's arm. Christina instantly stopped whimpering and fell soundly asleep. The Captain had a way with women and children. Carrying the infant snugly in his arm and holding a lighted candle in his free hand, the godfather and the priest walked around the font three times, in the name of the Father, the Son and the Holy Spirit. The service came to an end with the reading of a fitting passage from the Holy Bible.

But as far as Pappá Elias was concerned, the ceremony would not be completed until he had delivered a few words of his own. With an expression of unusual benevolence he offered his felicitations to the godfather and the parents with the customary wish "long may she live." He would have considered this much as adequate for the run-of-the-mill *baptisma* but hardly sufficient for so prestigious a one! He therefore proceeded to extol Captain Dimitri's "memorable contributions to Hellas, our beloved motherland," and to laud his many attributes, the most noteworthy of these being "his *generosity* for which this true Christian will ever be blessed!"

As for his fortunate goddaughter who had just been received in the bosom of The Church, the priest exhorted her with pious fervor "to adhere unfailingly to those priceless maidenly virtues of chastity, modesty, humility, meekness and obedience—always to bear God in mind and never succumb to temptation!" The Captain nodded approvingly. Yes, indeed, he agreed that these were most befitting admonitions—for a nun. "But *allimono*! Alas for the world *if* there be one left," he groaned inwardly, "should these saintly attainments be the goal of every full-blooded female in the land!"

Pappá Elias was elated by the Captain's nod. He interpreted it as a sign of approbation not only for his words but his masterful delivery of them. Dimitri Hadjichristos was, the Lord be praised, an *anthropos tou cosmou*, a man of the world, who could recognize and appreciate superior rhetoric that went utterly wasted on such as the local rustics. Yes, our Captain was highly impressed, and would reward him handsomely.

Overcome by his apparent success and good fortune that would surely follow it, Pappá Elias began to cry. "The miserable, old hypocrite" muttered Nicoletta beneath her breath, "when

168

he isn't babbling, he's bawling with those crocodile tears of his!'' Her distrust of Pappá Elias did not stem from personal animosity or disrespect towards Orthodoxy. The Widow was, in fact, devoutly religious but her reverence for God did not extend indiscriminately to His temporal vicegerents. Her scepticism as to their worthiness was especially aroused by a celibate priest whose sanctimony revealed pietism rather than piety.

On the whole, Greeks lack the puritanical fanaticism evident in some of the austere Christian sects and tend towards a realistic view of the clergy. They accept with amused or cynical tolerance the fact that the high ideals of the Church and the base passions of man are not automatically reconciled by the mere wearing of the cloth.

"Come, my boy," whispered Kyra Nicoletta to Thanasi, "let us be the first to offer our wishes to the godfather." Before the lad had a chance to accept or more likely decline this distinction, the Widow shoved him quickly ahead of her. The Captain saw them coming and handed his tall candle to the verger. He took the old lady's hand and kissed it, not as a worldly gesture but as an act of deference accorded to all churchmen and to those considered venerable. The Widow responded by kissing him on both cheeks. She had known Dimitri Hadjichristos since the time he had seen the light of day. His mother and the two sisters, Nicoletta and Phrosene, were born and bred in the same village. Nicoletta was now the lone survivor of that devoted trio.

After an exchange of good wishes, the Widow reverently kissed the cross that adorned the sleeping infant. "It's worthy of a princess!" she exclaimed.

"And no less worthy of her great-grandaunt," responded the Captain gallantly.

Kyra Nicoletta took a step backwards and looked at him in the proprietary manner of an adoring mother. She noted with satisfaction that neither time nor war had aged him perceptibly save for the streaks of silver that gave a gunmetal sheen to his thick, dark hair and to the Mephisthophelean beard, which suited his lean features better than the heavier ones in the mode at the time. Even though he was close to fifty, his tall trim body had

169

lost none of its grace. The local swains who were half his age seemed callow beside him. They envied his inimitable grace especially when he took the lead in the traditional style of circular Greek dancing; and when he joined the men in the boisterous "Butchers' Dance," he displayed a virility that brought shivers of secret delight to the modest village maidens. Their outward blushes and their inner sighs, however, were in vain for the Captain was not the marrying kind.

He no sooner returned from the war when his mother and Aunt Nicoletta—*Theia* Nicoletta, as he called her—urged him to settle down in connubial contentment. He could choose, his mother stated, any one of the fairest and finest of brides to be had in all of Peloponessos—"I daresay in all of Greece," declared Nicoletta in the peremptory tone of authority.

Out of respect for his mother and regard for her dearest friend, Dimitri listened with amused patience to their endless panegyrics on the blissful state of wedlock that awaited him if only he would hurry and make up his mind. As their insistence grew stronger, his resistence grew firmer until he realized the absurdity of this daily combat between a rugged ex-soldier and two sweet elderly ladies (though "sweet" was hardly the word, the Captain reflected grimly, for those who aim to put a man's head in a noose). But the truth was, he admitted sheepishly, that his ego had been flattered by the constant reminders of his unquestionable appeal to "the fairest and finest" in all the land!

He decided to put an end to the whole matter by confessing he had found "the love of his life"—the only one to whom he would be faithful the rest of his days. He had won her after years of tireless wooing, a mistress that he worshiped, and he would rather die than lose her now.

"Tell us, my boy," his mother cried, "tell us, who is she?"

"She is well known, *manoula*, little mother," her son replied, "a supreme seductress who has destroyed countless men in their passion to possess her.

"Her name," he added softly, "is *Eleutheria*, Liberty."

Following Kyra Nicoletta's cue, the crowd ignored Pappá Elias' sobs. People surged forward to pay their respects to the

170

godfather motivated more by their eagerness to see the diamond cross than to display their good manners. But since the Widow had pre-empted the opportunity, they gathered in little groups waiting impatiently until they could satisfy their curiosity.

The Captain had not seen Kyra Nicoletta for several months and it seemed to him that she appeared frail despite the ruddy color on her cheeks. He suspected it was due to some form of inner excitement rather than to a state of well being.

"My *Capetan*," she began, addressing him with his title as she always did in public. "I have a revelation . . . an unexpected glimpse of the future . . . and I believe it was revealed to me by the good Lord in His infinite kindness so that I may be comforted before I die."

She had seen but a few minutes before, a vision of two figures standing before the Holy Gate in this very Church. They were tall and straight, standing proudly like a pair of fine, young cypress trees, and their heads were adorned with wedding wreathes. In the Greek Orthodox Faith crowns are worn by the bride and groom during part of the marriage service. They were made originally of olive leaves, the ancient emblem of fruitfulness or of laurel leaves, the age-old symbol of triumph, and intertwined with orange blossoms. The office of the crowning is the culmination of the wedding ceremony. It represents the glory and the honor which unite man and wife in the holy sacrament of marriage. Kyra Nicoletta had an additional interpretation of the *stepsis*, the coronation, as the wedding ceremony is called in Greek. For her it represented, as well, a kind of royal investiture which made the newlyweds sovereigns of the domain they would create through procreation, and which they would rule with benevolent wisdom to the end of their days.

"You understand," continued the Widow, "I couldn't see who they were, these two, since they were facing the altar, but I didn't need to. I *knew* who they were, of course!"

"Of course," echoed the Captain with a knowing smile, "who else but the infant girl, Christina in my arms, grown tall and lovely and who else but the young boy, Thanasi, no longer at *your* side as he is now, but a full-fledged *pallikari* by *her* side."

"Of course," repeated Nicoletta in a flat tone, obviously

171

nettled by the Captain's perspicacity.

Hadjichristos realized he had spoiled the dramatic denoue-
ment of the Widow's recitation. He hastened to make amends
by exclaiming most enthusiastically, "Bravo, *theitsa mou*, bravo,
my little aunt! Your idea is positively brilliant, and may you live
to dance at their wedding."

"Don't talk nonsense, Dimitri," retorted Kyra Nicoletta,
revealing her irritation in using his first name and with the tone
of voice she would have used to reprimand him for some prank
he might have committed in his childhood.

"This future match is not a brilliant idea of *mine* but *a divine
inspiration from heaven above*! As for your saying that I shall
be on this earth, and dancing besides, when this revelation comes
to pass, simply shows that you can't add properly . . . *krima*,
shame, for a man of your age! Or do you ignore my years in
the belief, God forbid, that I will become another Methuselah?"

She looked again at the sleeping child and her face and voice
grew gentle. "No, my *Capetan*," she murmured, "by then I shall
be no more than a handful of dust."

Dimitri felt his throat tighten at Nicoletta's intimation of
death. She had been a surrogate parent to him as long as he could
remember, the only being he considered worthy of a love akin
to that which he felt for his mother. His soldier's heart, hardened
as it was, had lost none of the extraordinary tenderness that a
Greek feels for the maternal image.

When the time came for Nicoletta to leave this world another
piece of his life would disappear. His mother had taken with her
to the grave the memories of his earliest existence—the loss of
one's mother, thought Dimitri, was inevitably the loss of a vital
part of one's self. For buried with his mother was her knowledge
or awareness of his prenatal being that began in the mystical moment of conception through the mysterious process of gestation
to the miracle of his birth. Only his mother could recall more
than any other being, the world in which he existed after his birth
and beyond it up to that time when his powers of perception and
memory had developed sufficiently to make him aware of his own
humanity.

And now *Theia* Nicoletta would take away with her the

memories of his early youth. No one but she remained who had known him intimately in his boyhood, who had rebuked him gently for his childish foibles and had praised him lavishly for his boyish achievements. His mother had nourished his body but Theia Nicoletta had nurtured his soul. There was no exchange between them that he could recall of childish prattle nor had she condescended to fairy tales and fables or moral paradigms and religious injunctions considered the proper diet for a growing mind. Instead she fed his spirit with the thrilling sagas of veritable heroes in their daring quest for liberty.

The truth is whether or not Nicoletta had entered his life, Dimitri, as an able-bodied youth would have served in the Revolution that was destined to explode in his day. And he would have served proudly the historic tradition of Freedom which has obsessed the Hellenic conscience throughout the ages. Yet, if he possessed that extra measure of courage which his fellow fighters attributed to him, the credit for it was due to Nicoletta Leontaris. Her impassioned words had incited him to emulate those simple but selfless men whose noble exploits had impressed themselves ineffaceably on his mind.

Impulsively the Captain put his arm around the old lady and pressed her closely to him.

"Be careful!" she cried, hiding her pleasure at his sudden display of affection under a tone of admonition. "You will crush the little one, if you don't watch out."

"You need not worry, little aunt," the Captain reassured her, "so long as she is in my hands no harm will come to her if I can help it. My responsibilities towards her will end only when your vision comes to pass and she is married, if so be God's will, to Thanasi."

The boy was startled at the sound of his name. He had been absorbed in examining the baby's little finger. He had never seen anything quite so exquisite. How could it possibly be so small, so perfectly formed and with an infinitessimal sliver of a moon clearly showing on the rosy little nail!

"Well, my good fellow, what do you think of her?" the Captain asked, lowering his tall frame so that the boy could have a fuller view of his "prospective bride."

Thanasi studied the infant carefully for a few moments. "Her face is too red," he replied, "and I think she looks silly in all those clothes."

The Captain stroked the point of his neatly groomed beard. "Ah, you mean you prefer her without them." And throwing back his head, he burst into a roar of laughter that showed his splendid teeth to their best advantage.

Thanasi hardly heard the Captain's remark nor was he aware of the levity that followed it. He was still staring at the baby, whose eyelids had begun to flutter. He tugged at the Widow's sleeve. "Look, Kyra Nicoletta, Christina's awake!"

"Well, I'm not surprised. The poor little thing must have been frightened out of her wits by that bellow from her godfather—and in Church, no less," she added, casting the Captain a look of severe reproach.

"But she's not frightened—she's smiling," said the boy.

"A bit of gas, no doubt," thought the Widow, but wisely refrained from saying so.

"Indeed, she is smiling and straight at you, my *pallikari*."

"Why?" asked Thanasi more out of curiosity than interest.

"Because she likes you, that's why," was Nicoletta's prompt reply.

"Well, I don't like *her*," replied the boy, but fearing that he had somehow offended the old lady, he added apologetically, "I don't like girls."

Kyra Nicoletta chuckled. "They all say that at your age, but the time will come, my boy, when you will like Christina. You will like her so much that you will want to marry her."

"It's a good thing, I must say," mused the Captain, "that I'm not *your* godfather, Thanasi, as well as Christina's, or you would not be permitted to wed her, you know." (In the Greek Orthodox Faith godparents are recognized as the spiritual parents of those they have christened. Consequently, individuals who have a common godparent are recognized by the Church as siblings and, therefore, marriage between them is forbidden.)

"But I don't want to be married," Thanasi protested, "and I'm never going to get married. No, never!" he repeated emphatically.

174

The Captain replied in a confidential tone, "My little friend, you speak wisely, but let me tell you: the wisdom of youth turns to folly in man."

In view of her age, the Widow's demise shortly after the christening was not surprising. Nor was the marriage of Christina and Thanasi which took place some sixteen years later. Nicoletta's revelation of this eventual union was more a credit to her logic than to her prescience. The meager population of provincial Greece and the inadequate means of transportation and communication restricted by necessity the choice of a mate within a limited area. Christina and Thanasi lived in adjoining villages. Their fathers were old friends and had fought together in the Revolution under the command of Captain Hadjichristos. Both families were on an equal social footing and from the same simple mountaineer stock, so that a union of their children was, in any event, more than likely.

By the time Thanasi and Christina had married, the Widow's name and her prophecy were all but forgotten. This would not have surprised the old matchmaker. She had lived long enough to have had no illusions about the quick remembering the dead.

Yet, by one of those oddities of fate that defy the laws of probability, her name was not altogether forgotten. It was, in fact, remembered several generations beyond her time and several thousand miles beyond the land where she had lived and died—in the American town of Arlington, Massachusetts, a pleasant suburb of Boston, where the oldest son of Christina and Thanasi, the Reverend Constantine Douropoulos, had settled with his family in the second decade of the twentieth century.

The Presbytera often spoke of life in "the old country," especially for the benefit of Arthur and Elly. She believed that her two American-born offspring whose blood was, nevertheless, wholly Greek should not be ignorant of their Hellenic heritage. In enlightening them about their geneology, in which she was eminently versed, she would elucidate on her family tree. "When my father, Panos Regas, married my mother, Angeliki Thanopoulos—may their memories be ever blessed—all the

175

cosmos declared that two of the finest Arcadian families were befittingly united.''

John Limpert, Sophia's husband, who was born in the same Arcadian village as his mother-in-law, justified the pride Mrs. Douropoulos felt for her parents. ''As a young boy I often went with my mother to visit them. I remember my wife's maternal grandparents as gentlefolk—a kind and gracious elderly couple. We never left their house without a mound of sweets. 'For the children,' Mrs. Regas would say, with her kindly smile; and old Mr. Regas would escort us not just to the door, but as far as the gate of his courtyard before bidding us good-bye. Little did I dream that one day I would marry one of his pretty granddaughters, Sophia—the prettiest of them all.''

After exhausting the exploits of her ancestors in the Greek Revolution of 1821, and the contributions of her contemporary kin to their respective professions, Mrs. Douropoulos would come around to her husband's family. She would describe dramatically the only account she considered worthy of emphasis—the christening of Christina, her children's paternal grandmother.

Her husband considered it regrettable that he knew of no other occasion that could give some additional prestige to his plebian background than this one event, if indeed it was altogether true, rather than a romanticized version of what was more likely an ordinary christening. Alexandra was greatly annoyed when her husband cast doubt on the authenticity of his mother's christening, and in front of his children, too!

''Of course it's true,'' she would remonstrate. ''Why, your own father, God rest his soul, told it to me time and again. The poor man, his memory was like a sieve in his old age. He kept repeating himself over and over again. You know perfectly well it wasn't hearsay. Your father was actually *there* at your blessed mother's christening. And he heard with his own ears Kyra Nicoletta's prophecy that one day he would marry the old lady's great-grandniece. Really, I don't understand your attitude. You should be very proud of this event and you should be telling your children about it instead of denying it. It would show them that you are not just a *horiates*, an ordinary peasant, but descended from superior stock.''

176

The Reverend considered these views on his lineage as quite extraordinary. He had never realized, he would say, that a peasant's red blood could be converted into a patrician's blue blood by means of a christening and a cross, albeit a diamond one.

By the end of Mrs. Douropoulos' explications, her audience had usually dispersed save for Elly. The little girl listened with fervid interest to her mother's words, which brought miraculously to life the strange phantom world of the past. Of all the characters her mother mentioned, none intrigued Elly more than Kyra Nicoletta. She was convinced beyond doubt that the old matchmaker was solely responsible for the marriage of her grandparents. She was awed by the thought of this dim, mysterious creature who was indirectly responsible for her own existence. For if Kyra Nicoletta had not prophesied her grandparents' marriage, she had reasoned carefully, her father would not have been born, and she, Elly, would not be alive! This overwhelming discovery she confided at once to her brother, Arthur, from whom she kept no secrets. "Just think, without that nice old Kyra Nicoletta there would be no you, no me, or anybody else in our family!"

Her brother was not impressed. As far as he was concerned, Nicoletta was a silly old woman who had lived a thousand years ago and he didn't care to hear about her and all this nonsense that they wouldn't be alive if *she* hadn't lived. Elly was momentarily crushed by Arthur's supercilious reaction. She was deeply devoted to this "bright and beautiful boy." But she was considered "cute and clever," and it was this cleverness she used to defend herself. "Even though you are a year older than I am," she retorted with hauteur, "you haven't any idea what I am talking about. And besides Kyra Nicoletta didn't live a thousand years ago . . . she was alive at our Grandmother's christening. So there!"

177

Chapter Eighteen

Nicholas and John Douropoulos had settled in Washington, D. C., in the early part of the century, several years before their oldest brother, Constantine, was sent to America by the Holy Synod of Greece to serve as the first priest of a small Greek community in Baltimore, Maryland. How and why they came to the capital of the United States is among the forgotten lore of the early Greek settlers in the New World. Like typical pioneer immigrants of the early nineteen hundreds, the two brothers worked relentlessly in order to survive. Being bachelors they managed better than their compatriots with responsibilities toward their families. By eliminating all but the absolute necessities of life the two brothers managed in a few years to save some money. They used it as leverage to borrow more money and thus expedited the ambition dear to the heart of every Greek—to be his own "boss." In the course of time they became the proud and envied owners of an ice cream parlor, which in the perfervid chauvinism of the expatriated they named "The Arcadia" in honor of their birthplace.

As soon as "The Arcadia" began to show a profit, the brothers decided it was time to pay a visit to their homeland. Nicholas, as the older brother, was the first to make the pilgrimage. He arrived in Greece in approximately eighteen days on a boat that would return to America with a cargo of four to five hundred immigrants, who would pay forty dollars a piece for the privilege of coming by steerage to "the land of promise."

Nicholas disembarked one early summer day at the port of Pireus glowing with sartorial splendor. His suit was elegantly tailored and the boldly striped shirt had been made to order in a fine quality of silk. A gold watch with an elk's tooth dangling on a heavy gold chain adorned his pearl-buttoned vest. The "blucher type" shoes he wore were styled with " bulldog toes," which he had been assured was the latest fashion in masculine footwear. Nicholas justified the great care and cost expended on his wardrobe as a matter of duty. Since he was among the relatively first successful expatriates to revisit the land of his birth, he felt it was incumbent on him to give his countrymen an accurate rendering of a prosperous and dignified American business man. What impression he made in the eyes of the sophisticated members of Greek society is not known. But there is no doubt that he was a sensation among the little bands of urchins that followed him wherever he went. And when he tossed them bright new pennies or shoved sticks of gum in their wide open mouths, they were converted on the spot to life-long zealots of Capitalism. These little boys must have promised themselves to seek one day the land across the sea and become "millionaires" like the munificent "Amerikanos." Many of them came and some of them made their fortune while others struggled to exist. The great American dream was both a reality and an illusion.

Although Nicholas was enjoying the attention he attracted in Athens as a prosperous "Greek-Amerikanos," he left the city hastily to visit his older brother, Constantine, who lived in the province of Arcadia.

Constantine and his younger brother, Nicholas, had not seen each other for nearly a decade. But even though they had lived worlds apart, literally and figuratively, their reunion was touching. The Greeks hold in high regard the fraternal bond which unites those of identical blood strains in the closest possible biological kinship. This consanguinity is powerful enough to efface any disparities that may exist between siblings in respect to their intelligence and education or their social and financial status.

Nicholas also greeted his sister-in-law with great warmth. He considered Constantine's wife, Alexandra, truly a "lady" who

179

treated her husband's relatives with the same consideration she extended to the members of her own more cultivated family. But what had won her the everlasting devotion and gratitude of her husband's kinfolk was her generosity toward Theone, the only girl in her husband's family. She was but a child when her mother died. Single-handed, Theone undertook the care of the household at eight years old and had known none of the joys of a normal childhood. Alexandra feared that the size and quality of Theone's dowry, despite her brothers' expenditures on it, was insufficient to attract a husband worthy of this fine girl. Without discussing the matter with anyone, Alexandra, in her typically independent spirit, decided to divide her dowry legally (it included several parcels of valuable farmland) with her sister-in-law. As a result, Theone attracted a splendid husband and enjoyed more of life's pleasures in her adulthood than she had missed in her youth. She died of old age—a happy woman having lived long enough to see her youngest son, Elias, achieve the rank of general in the Second World War.

Considering Nicholas' inordinate sentimentality and a tendency toward histrionics, he had done well, as it were, not to have burst into tears at meeting his beloved brother after their protracted separation. This should prove how Americanized he had become not only in his appearance but in the cool, collected manner of the Anglo-Saxons, which he greatly admired. So Nicholas thought, until he saw his nephew on whom thus far depended the continuation of the Douropoulos gens. Whatever "sang-froid" he might have acquired instantly dissolved.

"Pray, tell me," he cried, "who is this tall, fair youth with the face of an angel! Can it possibly be the little cherub I left behind me years ago?" He came close to his nephew and scrutinized him from various angles.

"Yes, yes," he murmured, "it *is* Dionysios, the little boy I carried around in my arms for hours on end—ah, how well I remember those days. . . ." He abruptly stopped his soliloquy apparently overcome by tender memories that no one else in the room could recall. He removed a fine linen handkerchief from his pocket and opened it so that the corner with a large monogram faced outside. Even though his eyes were not noticeably moist, he dabbed them carefully. It was a great comfort to him just to feel against his face the elegant handkerchief Tilly Hinckle had given him, as a "bon voyage" gift. She had embroidered it with her own hands, those pretty delicate hands, soft as little white doves, that belied her one and only talent as a "chocolate dipper." Thanks to this buxom blond Fraulein, the chocolates made at the Arcadia Ice Cream Parlor were among the choicest to be had in the capital of America.

Alexandra interrupted Nicholas' reverie on Tilly Hinckle's multiple charms. "Yes, indeed," he heard his sister-in-law say laughingly, "it is our Dionysios, of course—yet hardly the little boy you last saw ten years ago but a graduate now of the Rizarios Seminary. He received his diploma a few days ago with high honors even though he was the youngest in his class," she added as she beamed with ill-concealed pride at her son, who was no less disconcerted by his mother's blatant praise than by his uncle's maudlin emotions.

"What! Already a graduate of Rizarios Seminary did you say? Impossible! I simply can't believe it, dear sister," exclaimed Nicholas in a tone of utter incredulity that changed instantaneously however to one of absolute certitude. "No, I'm not surprised, not in the least, that my nephew is the youngest and the brightest that set foot in that famous institution. Yes, indeed, I spotted that brilliant mind from the time he was an infant. My only regret," he added wistfully, "is that I must leave shortly and miss his ordination."

Constantine must have caught the look of distress on his son's face, for he hastened to reply to his brother. "I am afraid, Nicholas, that you have been carried away by your good heart which leads you to misapprehend or misinterpret facts in order that they may fit your benevolent view regarding those you love. But let me assure you there have been others as young if not younger than Dionysios who have graduated from Rizarios Seminary and who have earned as high if not higher honors than he has achieved. As for his taking the holy vows shortly as you seem to expect, it would be unusual, indeed, at so early an age save in an instance, perhaps, of some rare youth with a truly saintly soul, which I am inclined to believe your nephew does not

181

possess."

Mrs. Douropoulos was also aware of her son's discomfort and now spoke with what she believed was considerable restraint. "The Director of the Seminary, Bishop Nektarios, has recommended that Dionysios spend a year or so preparing for entrance to the Divinity School at the University of Athens. The Bishop believes that a degree in Theology will help our son achieve a worthy goal."

His sister-in-law's disclosure, modest as she tried to make it appear, aroused in Nicholas another wave of febrile excitement and he was moved to embrace his brother anew. "Like father, like son . . . where else can the apple fall but under the tree that bears it?" he asked sententiously. "You, dear Constantine, brought honor to our family by getting an education at the Seminary in Tripolis and then your diploma as a teacher and superintendent. And now your son is going on to greater heights. With his brains and his learning he may become a Bishop—yes, a Bishop," he declared emphatically.

"Why not an Archbishop while we're at it?" asked Constantine laughingly. It was a waste of time, he realized, to try and talk sense with his brother; the years had not changed him in the least. Nicholas was still as illogical and lovable as ever—an ebullient spirit perennially arrested in a hebetic state from which his heart, however, had managed to escape; and it had developed into what the Greeks call "a heart of gold"—a complimentary phrase of dubious merit since it is usually applied to those whose kindness is their one, and often only, solid virtue.

"An Archbishop, eh?" repeated Nicholas. "Of course! And why not?" he exclaimed exuberantly to cover his blunder in ascribing to his nephew a lesser office than his abilities deserved. "Let me tell you he will be a far better one than some of those bearded dotards the Holy Synod stuffs down our throats willy-nilly.

"I'm sure you agree, Constantine, what that Synod needs is new, clean, young blood to replace those frustrated old bishops who run the Church and go on living forever, feeding like vultures on the wicked hope that the incumbent Archbishop will die. All they do, each and every one of them, is to pray morning, noon and night for nothing else but to be *the one* elected and pompously enthroned as the next Ecclesiarch of Greece! But actually it doesn't really matter, not a whit," he concluded in a tone of indifference, "which one becomes Head of the Church—they're all in their dotage—bishops, metropolitans, archbishops, and all cut from the same cloth."

Constantine could not resist smiling at his brother's inadvertent pun (which exists in Greek and other languages as well)—not a bad one, at that, he thought with amusement. But his wife found nothing whatsoever entertaining in Nicholas' criticism. Why, it was practically blasphemy! She was appalled to see her husband smiling and to hear her son giggling uncontrollably. She gave Constantine a look of severe rebuke and a lesser one to her son. She could hardly blame him when his own father was grinning fatuously like a silly schoolboy at his brother—his younger brother, mind you—who was recklessly reviling the Holy Synod and all its members, those pious men who upheld and protected the Church of Greece!

She would have expected her husband, who was schooled in theology, at least to reprimand Nicholas for indulging in such a shocking diatribe, especially in the presence of his nephew who was still in the impressionable stage of a neophyte seminarian.

Alexandra was not the type of wife to withdraw into aggrieved or sullen silence at her husband's remissions. She would be the first to acknowledge that she had married a man of superior quality—an exceptionally handsome man besides—whom she loved, respected and admired. But it was not in keeping with her unusually independent and forthright nature to accept or assume the traditional role of a passive Greek wife who would acquiesce to her husband's beliefs or opinions if they differed significantly from hers.

The submissive attitude of the Greek woman in Alexandra's era, whether it was maintained out of decorum, expediency or modesty, belied, however, the influence she exerted, and still exerts, both as a wife and mother. Her matriarchal strength is sufficiently powerful to threaten the ego of the male. And it may account, in part, for his need to preserve or appear to assert his masculinity by dominating his spouse so as to attain in his own eyes and in his own domain at least a factitious aura of omnipotence. And since her husband apparently had no intention of reproving his brother, Alexandra felt she must do so herself.

"Oh, Nicholas," she exclaimed reproachfully, "you must not say such things; they simply are not true. Archbishop Theoclitos, Head of the Church, is an honorable ecclesiarch and so are the hierarchs of the Holy Synod who help him govern our Church. He is the Head of the Synod and would not tolerate them if they were the kind you assume they are.

"My mother's dear cousin, Metropolitan Nestor, who is a member of the Synod, can tell you how much all the ecclesiastics and all the *cosmos*, as well, respect Archbishop Theoclitos for his high moral and spiritual values, and for his brilliance. He has studied abroad, you know, and people esteem him for the tremendous learning he has acquired. Constantine admires him, especially, as he knows him better than most people do."

Alexandra reminded Nicholas that his brother had been a student and had graduated—with honors, too, she could not resist adding, even though at the moment she was annoyed with her husband—from the Tripolis Seminary while Theoclitos was the Director of the school. His Beatitude had not forgotten his student through the years. He had honored their home more than once by a visit when he came near by on occasions such as a special celebration at the Monastery of Saint John the Prodromos— "where you remember, Nicholas, your brother served as a novice when he was a young boy; so, you see, we know him at close range, so to speak.

"And let me tell you he is no doddering old man," Alexandra declared, "even though he is considerably older than you are, I daresay he could pass for a man close to your years. But I must say, Nicholas, you look wonderfully young for your age," she added hastily, fearing she had wounded his vanity. "Why, your hair is still that lovely reddish color, and Constantine who is only a few years older than you is getting so gray—almost white now."

Nicholas was cut to the quick by Alexandra's last remarks. It was not what she said or how she said it. But the mere reminder of his age made Nicholas exceedingly uneasy. Even though he was an attractive, vigorous man in his early forties, his ladylove was, he believed, somewhere in her twenties; and Nicholas was haunted with the fear that this irreversible disparity in years might very well prove the undoing of his courtship. Here in Greece his age would be no barrier to his marrying a young girl; indeed, if he had money and was not concerned with the size of a dowry, he would be most acceptable, in fact highly sought-after. But America was the land of youth and romance where matches and dowries did not prevail over "eros," where a man was expected to marry the woman he loved rather than expected to love the woman he married.

But Nicholas may have been needlessly worried since Tilly's practical Teutonic mind was more likely concerned with the number of his dollars than the number of his years.

Constantine was neither surprised nor perturbed by his brother's derisive remarks or at his wife's dismay on hearing them, since their respective attitudes were more or less typical. Greek women vigorously profess their devotion to the Church and their respect for its dogmas and tenets. The Greek male, however, accepts them but not without some reservations, even though they may be merely token ones, as to their wisdom or worth. He is far less conscientious in attending church than the womenfolk whose presence at the lengthy Sunday services he attributes more to social interests than to religious considerations. He looks upon the ministry as a worthy calling but judges its value according to the merits of those who follow it.

The Greeks like to believe that their tendency towards skepticism is part of the legacy from their philosophically inclined forebears who had developed the detached examination of man's feelings, his thoughts and actions into an intellectual art. The ancient Greeks had gone, in fact, beyond the secular world into the sacred realm of the gods. They examined the manifold deities they worshipped; they analyzed and criticized them—going as far as to expose their weaknesses on the stage to the amusement of the theatre-loving populace of ancient Greece.

But the philosophers were in deadly earnest when it came to destroying false idols and demolishing false ideals even at a great risk—a risk so great, in fact, as to cost one of the world's supreme iconoclasts his very life.

But whatever the exterior stance the Greeks may assume regarding their religion, the fact remains that Orthodoxy is a potent force that pervades their existence from beginning to end. The rites and rituals of the Church are not only observed in some way or other in the ordinary course of life, but are concommitants to a variety of minor and major activities as well as undertakings of a personal or public nature.

One is unlikely to find a Greek home that lacks an *iconostasis* which invariably holds, besides the ubiquitous icons, a *candili*, the votive vessel which is faithfully lit each day and burns through the night—a vestigal ritual that can be romantically if not historically connected with the "holy fire" that burned ceaselessly in the early pagan Greek hearth. Unlike their ancient progenitors whose religious formulas were practised strictly within the intimacy of the family, the Christian Greek glories in witnessing and sharing with his fellowmen the ritual riches which Orthodoxy offers its adherents. Whether it be the inauguration of a new political administration or that of a civic building, laying the cornerstone of a village home or a city mansion, the launching of a ship or a fisherman's dory, the planting of newly acquired farmland or the start of a million dollar enterprise and even, as a calumnious cynic profanely quipped, the establishment of a bordello, the religious traditions are not overlooked. At such and numerous other occasions the priest is invariably on hand to perform an *agiasmos*, the aspersion of holy water, and to ask for the Almighty's blessing and to seek the guidance of Divine Providence.

"I must say, Nicholas," remarked Constantine, "that a decade of absence from our motherland has not altered your native characteristics. I confess your appearance in those fine American clothes, in which you are splendidly attired, misled me to believe at first glance that you had become quite 'Anglo-Saxonized.' Your spirited attack on our Orthodox churchmen, however, is adequate proof that you are still a true Greek who feels it is his right, if not his duty, to express his opinions on each and every subject under the sun whether it be secular or sacrosanct. But I am willing to wager that despite your anti-

186

clerical views, you did not open the Arcadia Ice Cream Parlor without a proper *agiasmos.*"

Why, of course, the store was blessed on the very morning of its opening, in fact, and before the eyes of some early customers that had straggled in. He referred to them as *aladotoi,* the "unanointed" as the Greeks call those who have not been baptized according to the rites of the Greek Orthodox Church. And the way they were gaping at the priest—a good-looking chap with a flowing black beard and black robe and his *kalimafki*—you would think he was an aboriginal medicine man performing voodoo incantations to judge from the look on their faces. "But all he was doing," Nicholas went on, "was chanting some prayers while he sprinkled holy water all over the place. He didn't have or he forgot to bring an aspergillum with him, but we had a few sprigs of rosemary in the kitchen which came in handy for sprinkling the holy water around."

"That's what they often use in the villages," said Alexandra, "instead of the good ones usually made of silver which the priest keeps in the church and uses for important occasions only—not that the opening of your ice cream parlor was unimportant," she added tactfully, "but from what you say, Nicholas, I gather that the priest who blessed your store did not come from a nearby parish."

"When we started the business there was no Greek church close by," Nicholas explained, "and there are still only a few of them spread here and there around the country. But now the Greeks in Washington have formed a parish and they've brought a monk-priest from the old country called Seraphim Alenopoulos. They say he's a well-educated fellow but I can't warm up to the likes of him. He's a moth-eaten, scrawny-like creature with a huge hooked nose and a pious air . . . bah! the more pious these monks look, the more impious they are, let me tell you."

Dionysios was getting restless. His uncle's naive audacity was entertaining, but he wanted to hear about America and he feared that this fresh disparagment of the clergy might offend his mother and provoke another tiresome harangue.

Constantine apparently shared his son's uneasiness for he ignored Nicholas' benighted view of celibate priesthood and

187

hastened to ask, "But where did he come from, this priest who blessed your new enterprise?"

"I don't know. Our brother John found him somewhere or other but he never told me. You know how closemouthed he can be. I don't understand it, Constantine, and I never will. He's the only Greek in the world, I'd swear—and he would be in our family—whose vocabulary consists mainly of two little words, 'yes' and 'no.' In fact most of the time he doesn't even *say* them. He only jerks his head up or down." (The Greek gesture of affirmation is expressed by the usual downward nod, but to indicate 'no' the head and eyebrows are raised decidedly upwards.) "It doesn't seem normal," he muttered, "no, it doesn't," he repeated uneasily.

Constantine couldn't help smiling. John was, to be sure, a quiet, serious, steady man of few words but to his voluble, effervescent brother he appeared nothing less than pathologically laconic.

"Well, Nicholas, the fact remains," remarked Constantine, "that John did find a priest. Our brother may not be talkative but you must admit he is dependable."

"Yes, he found one all right. But John is not as dependable as you think. He didn't find a Greek priest but a Russian one, if you please!"

"That doesn't really matter, Uncle Nicholas," said Dionysios, "the Russians are Orthodox Christians, too, and they recognize the Greek Patriarch in Constantinople as their Head just as we do; and if your ice cream parlor is making money, it proves, doesn't it, Uncle Nicholas, that the priest Uncle John found performed the same *agiasmos* and said the same prayers a Greek priest would say—the only difference is that it's all done in Russian."

"Ah, now you've struck it, my lad—*the difference*—that's the whole point! God only knows what he was babbling. How could I tell if he was reciting the right prayers or if the holy water had been properly blessed by a bishop or was just ordinary tap water from any old faucet. I don't trust those Russians. They're an odd lot.

"Anyway I paid him well enough and even gave him a box

188

of our best chocolates though I didn't have to. Not that I regret it. Yes, I must say that from the day we opened the store we have done well. But I can't help feeling that if that fellow had been a Greek priest, we would have done even better!''

Chapter Nineteen

Dionysios could no longer contain his curiosity. "You haven't told us anything about America, Uncle Nicholas. Every day we hear of people who have left or are planning to go to the States—hundreds of them from all parts of Greece. But we haven't had the chance to talk to anyone who has been there as long as you have and has come back here for a visit."

Nicholas was flattered by his nephew's interest. He paused for a moment or two in studied thoughtfulness before he spoke.

"Ah, my boy, I hardly know where to begin, how to describe it. It's so strange, so vast! Why, someone I met on the boat told me that Greece could fit in one of the smaller states of America called Alabama! The fellow who said this was an American archeologist, coming to our 'little country,' I gathered, to see what he could find in the way of antiquities, statues and the like. I could have told him but good manners towards a stranger prevented me from saying that he was wasting his time. He'd find mighty little considering how many times our poor *patrida*, our country, has been sacked and plundered by hordes of barbarians, including, I'm sorry to say, his own supposedly highly civilized English ancestors sneaked off with huge chunks of the Parthenon. You can be sure they would have taken all of it if they had big enough boats to bring it to their own country. *Na!*" he sputtered, as he raised and then lowered his hands

190

with palms facing outwards and fingers extended in the unmistakable Greek gesture of utter disgust.

His nephew groaned inwardly at this fresh digression, but at the risk of furthering it he could not help saying, "Yes, it was very sad that Lord Elgin stole all those marble friezes from the Parthenon, but another lord, one of the great poets of England, Lord Byron, gave his life for the cause of Greek freedom."

"Hm, poets—the world's full of them, my boy, and a useless lot they are, poor wretches, but where, I'd like to know, can you find another Acropolis and what good is it now, pray tell me, that sacred place with a denuded Parthenon stuck on top of it?—thanks to that damnable Englishman, who carted off what he could from the greatest achievement of *our* ancestors and had the gall to sell *our* marbles to the British Museum and God knows where else, besides!"

The mere mention of the "Elgin Marbles" is likely to raise the Greek's blood pressure alarmingly high and Constantine noticed with uneasiness that his brother's naturally ruddy color had assumed a tone of apoplectic purple.

"You are quite right, Nicholas," he said soothingly, "it was an infamous act for which the Turks were to blame, as well, by issuing one of their most despicable firmans to Elgin so that he could do as he pleased with our priceless treasures. But that is all part of the past to which we can return in thought whenever we wish—for the past is fixed unalterably, eternally in time. So let's deal with the present while you are here to share it with us. We want to hear about you and John and the life you lead in America. Your nephew is particularly anxious to learn about the New World. He has become quite an Anglophile, I must say."

"What do you mean—'Anglophile'?" asked Nicholas.

"I should have said 'Amerikanophilos' for our young man is certainly enamored with America," replied Constantine, "but what I meant by 'Anglophile' is that he has been learning English and speaks it quite well I'm told, by those who have knowledge of the language, which unfortunately I lack. But his mother," he added with a delicately ironic smile, "seems to have some esoteric or intuitive knowledge of English, since she claims that our son speaks it fluently."

191

"I never made such a statement," declared Alexandra, "but anyone who reads as many books in English as Dionysios does, in his spare time, should certainly be able to speak English, and speak it well, I must say."

"If I may correct you, mother," said Dionysios in a markedly polite tone which he hoped would cover his discomfort at this new digression, "that isn't the way it works. If you know some English grammar—and it's very much easier than the Greek—then all you need is a good English-Greek dictionary to do pretty well in reading and in writing, too. But I don't speak English decently at all. I hardly ever come across anyone who knows it well enough to converse in it—which is the only way really to learn how to speak a language. The Greeks consider French the only tongue besides their own worth learning, and the scholarly ones take up German; so there isn't much of a chance that I shall ever speak it fluently."

"Well, here's a chance, Dionysios, to exchange at least a few words with your uncle. By now, Nicholas, I suppose you speak quite a bit of *Amerikanika* don't you?"

It was a painful question but Nicholas faced it squarely, compelled not so much from a sense of honesty but from fear that even an exchange of a few words would expose his dire ignorance of the English language. He admitted with a disarmingly deprecatory little laugh that he was a dunce as far as English was concerned. But he had acquired enough of it to get along quite well. He knew what each kind of candy and what all the ice cream flavors in the store were called—no little feat, considering the variety of delectables which the *Arcadia* afforded. He made a point, too, of memorizing the names of his regular customers— that was good for business—even though it was practically impossible to pronounce some of those weird-sounding names Americans have.

Despite Nicholas' modest summary of his English vocabulary, he nevertheless believed that he spoke *Amerikanika* better than most of his fellow immigrants who worked in some "hole-in-the-wall" next to another foreigner who couldn't speak a word of it, either. "So, where in God's name," he asked, "can those poor devils find the chance or the time, to learn how to speak

192

English?

"It makes me laugh or want to cry how people think, the ones back home, I mean, that in America 'money grows on trees' and 'sidewalks are paved with gold.' Well, they'll find out, these hordes that are pouring in from all over Europe to the States, they'll find out soon enough that they have to work—and put their little children to work, too, if they've brought them along—to work, so help me God, like slaves and live like troglodytes if they're to survive. I know . . . I've been through it all . . . the pain, the poverty, the humiliation of the immigrant's life.

"I'm not complaining, you understand—just letting off steam—America has been good to me all the same. And I bless her, I salute her, a great and mighty country! And I thank the Lord for guiding me to her shores!

"But, now I hope, God willing, I'll come home for good some day—home to our beloved *patrida*, to our beautiful Hellas."

Dionysios moved uneasily in his chair more from embarrassment than ennui when his loquacious uncle expressed what sounded like sheer maukishness regarding his beloved *"patrida."* But his uncle was revealing a genuine emotion he shared with the rest of his compatriots who left their country to live in the *xenitiá*, which to the Greeks means any land other than their own.

This heightened ardor which the expatriated Greek feels for his motherland is expressed by C. P. Cavafy, an internationally recognized twentieth-century poet. He was born of Greek parents in Alexandria, where he was destined to remain most of his life. With poetic grandeur he reveals the exaltation he feels in being a *Hellene* (he decried the use of the word "Greek" as being aurally unpleasant):

He had that superlative virtue: Hellenism—
mankind has no quality more valuable; anything beyond
that belongs to the gods.*

---

*Edmund Keeley, " 'Latest' Poems Increase Cavafy's Appeal to Students," in University: *A Princeton Quarterly*, No. 48 (1971) pp. 33-37.

In another of his poems, "Poseidonians," Cavafy identifies his own deep sense of expatriation with those ". . . living and speaking like barbarians, excluded—what a catastrophe—from the Hellenic way of life. . . ."

"Something of Odysseus' spirit persists in the Greek," commented Constantine after his brother had expressed the nostalgia he felt for his native land. "The joyous climax for our famous Homeric adventurer apparently was his safe return to Greece. Let us hope, Nicholas, you will not be waylaid as he was in coming back to our *patrida*, that is, *if* you decide to return home for good."

"But why do you say *if* your brother comes back for good to Greece when he just said that is what he wants to do?" asked Alexandra.

Constantine replied that Nicholas had expressed the *hope* to do so. Hope was one thing, fulfillment another matter. He went on to say that Greeks were known to have reached various parts of the New World from the time of its discovery, but hardly anything is known as to how many of those early wanderers returned to their country. As for emigration to the New World in the more recent times, records indicate that approximately 300 Greeks, all males, left for America from the period beginning with the second quarter of the 1800s up to 1880.

"Surely, they must have gone there," said Constantine, "with that obsessive longing to return to their own country after accomplishing what they had set out to do—to get as little or as large a share of America's blessings as the other immigrants who were coming like locusts to 'the land of bread and honey.' Yet, outside of a few exceptions, these early Greek pioneers disappeared among the millions of New World immigrants who were coming mostly from Northern Europe and whose ethnicity had considerable affinity with that of the original Anglo-Saxon settlers in the New World. In order to survive, that relatively tiny number of Greeks had to assimilate rapidly. Circumstances forced them to forego the use of their native tongue, their adherence to Greek customs and traditions and their loyalty to Orthodoxy . . .

"Even their names were forever lost or altered beyond

194

recognition—the result of marriage to non-Greek women since none of their own nationality were available. The progeny of these exogamous alliances tended to change their family name to suit—not only as they claimed—more readily the English phonetics, but undoubtedly for social advantage since an Anglo-sounding appellation implied a higher status than a strange-sounding one—a Greek one, at that.''*

Her husband's remarks gave Alexandra the impression that in the New World something pejorative was connected to a Greek name or, in other words, to the Greeks, themselves. She was more baffled than incensed at the idea that a Greek could be considered a "persona non grata" wherever he might be. Alexandra dismissed the whole matter as quite absurd but not without making a comment.

"It seems that people in America have forgotten who gave them the 'lights.' " (This expression "the lights"—a great favorite with the Greeks—is an elliptical metaphor which refers to "the lights of Hellenic civilization and culture.")

"Who cares any more about 'the lights'?" asked Nicholas with a hollow laugh, "You'd be surprised, dear sister, what bright light those shiny new American dollars shed!"

"Well, then," retorted Alexandra, "you should have enough of them by now to light your way home—where you belong," she added with asperity.

Constantine took exception to his wife's remark. He felt that an individual belonged wherever he could fulfill his needs, wherever he could earn an honest living and assume the responsibilities expected of a decent man in a civilized society so long as he did not leave his country in disgrace or out of disloyalty. He reminded Alexandra that several of her relatives including

*A side light on Greek nomenclature was cited by the late Raphael Demos, Professor of Philosophy at Harvard University. He noted in one of his classes an unmistakable specimen of Nordic youth who bore an unmistakably Greek name—one of those polysyllabic names which require heroic effort to pronounce, let alone spell. When the Professor asked the student about this curious phenomenon, he replied that as far as he knew the name had come from an ancestor of his who had settled in Saint Augustine during the 1700's. To the further question as to how so cumbersome a foreign name had not been altered through the years, the youth replied, "One doesn't change one's name . . . regardless."

two of her brothers had gone to Russia to make their living as wheat merchants—a prosperous living they were not likely to achieve in Greece, which was still in economic upheaval following the Revolution of 1821 when people gave their fortunes and their lives to free the land from more than 400 years of Turkish tyranny.

They had indeed gone far and wide from home, admitted his wife, but they never forgot Greece or Zatouna, the village in Arcadia where they were born. She repeated the story of her granduncle, Barba* Berios, who had gone to Tunis as a youth in search of his fortune. He became a very wealthy man and when he returned to Zatouna in his later years he built that beautiful church right across from her father's house—as fine a church as can be found in all of Arcadia. He was a man of noble spirit, for he asked every man, woman and child in Zatouna to bring a stone to the building site so that it could be truthully engraved on the cornerstone of the church that this House of God was "ERECTED BY PUBLIC ASSISTANCE." She wondered if those who were going to America now would remember their birthplace as much as those who years before had left for distant lands but returned to enrich their country—and to be buried in it.

Given the time and a good measure of success, I have no doubt they will do as much, if not more, for the Greek can never forget Greece," replied Constantine, "but as for their returning home for good, I believe that is a hope based more on sentimentality than reality."

Constantine went on to say that the few thousand Greeks that were already settled in America—and the thousands more arriving each year in this first decade of the new century—were laying the foundations of a new life as close as possible to the one they left behind as far as their Faith, their language, their customs and traditions were concerned. Those who had come without their wives and children were sending for them even if it meant existing on hardly more than bread and water in order to save enough money for their passage. The single men who constituted the greatest number of expatriates were bringing over younger bro-

*A commonly-used idiomatic form of "uncle."

thers and unmarried sisters. Therse young girls were especially welcome to their unattached country men. The supply of brides was still scarce in comparison to the number of available bachelors, who were therefore willing to marry them without a dowry—indeed, more than glad to marry one of their own kind who was disposed to share the harsh lot of the immigrant's life.

"The elimination of the dowry," concluded Constantine, "is undoubtedly one of America's greater blessings, for it relieves fathers—and brothers, no less, of a heavy burden imposed on Greek and other European societies, as well. It is also a boon for a woman's self-respect which is bound to suffer when her marriage is based on financial considerations rather than her own personal worth."

Alexandra knew that her husband's condemnation of the "dowry system" was not an indirect expression of his own apprehension at having five daughters to provide for—with two of them already on the verge of womanhood. Constantine was merely expressing a principle in which he believed. Alexandra was proud of the fact that her dowry had not been a factor in his desire to marry her. He had not bothered to find out nor had he asked anyone else to ascertain its value. Another indication of his indifference was his lack of concern as to whether or not the dowry contract would be prepared well enough in advance so that it could be officially appraised as to its worth before taking the then practically irrevocable step of marriage.

No one who knew her husband could possibly accuse him of feeling the bitterness or even the disappointment that most men would feel if their wives presented them with so many daughters in a row. His only concern in each of her pregnancies was her welfare and after she had given birth, he never failed to give thanks to the Almighty for her astonishing vitality which made it possible for her to bear with utmost ease perfectly formed, perfectly healthy children save for one infant that was stillborn.

She had also lost a little girl, named Matina, who had died from diptheria at the age of two. Alexandra seldom spoke of her but she secretly mourned for that lovely, fair-haired child with deep blue eyes—a coloration that was not uncommon in her

197

husband's family. She had found the way to her father's heart by nestling in his lap every chance she could get. She would point to the pocket where he kept his watch—a sign that she wanted him to place it close to her ear. Her eyes would sparkle with that naive delight which only the innocent possess, as she listened to its ticking, blissfully unaware that each passing moment was bringing her young life nearer to its end.

Alexandra was no less aware than her husband of the difficulties most parents faced in conforming with the custom of providing their daughters with a decent dowry. She was not overly disturbed by this matter, however. Her natural optimism and her inviolate trust in the benignity of Divine Providence eased her concerns and lightened her anxieties. "God hath," she would say, meaning God has infinite kindness and mercy. But she did not believe that those who were in need of help should wait in fatalistic passivity until the Almighty found the time to come to their aid. She considered it the moral duty of good Christians to help themselves and their fellowmen as much as was humanly possible. In support of this attitude Alexandra would quote—as Greeks are likely to do—an injunction from the distant pagan past rather than a biblical one: "Pray to Athena, and give her a helping hand."

Within the limits of her own world, and often beyond them, Alexandra was willing to give a helping hand to those whose lot could be improved even to a small extent by her intercession. Her desire to do good was not a means by which to display her altruism and to receive any plaudits for it. Her concern for others was essentially due to her love of humanity and her faith in its worth. It did not matter to her whether or not those who were in need of aid—whatever their need might be—were people of consequence whose tributes to her kindness would carry weight—or were merely insignificant members of society who sang her praises but whose voices were hardly ever heard. What mattered to Alexandra was that they were all *anthropoi*, people, all of them God's creatures.

Her love of mankind was sincere, for she shared the Sophoclean view that man is the most wonderful of all the many wonderful things in nature.

198

"I can't help wondering, Nicholas," said his sister-in-law, "how you have managed so far to escape the snares of those young girls who go to America to find their mates. Don't misunderstand me; I'm not deploring or condemning them for doing so. They are, indeed, admirable for trying to relieve their parents from the burden of supplying them with a dowry. They are doing their expatriated countrymen a favor by giving them the chance to marry one of their own kind rather than a *xeni*—a foreign female. Apparently there are quite a few mixed marriages taking place over there but we don't hear too much about these alliances . . . well, the less we know about them, so much the better. Yet those girls are certainly courageous to cross the ocean far from the protective eye of a father or a mother."

Alexandra stopped her dissertation long enough to give a sympathetic little sigh and then went on to say that was why some of the nicest girls from fine old families, which unfortunately were in straitened circumstances, did not take the drastic step of going alone to America. Out of fear or desperation these inexperienced young women might make unsuitable marriages—something not likely to happen here where parents, relatives and friends strive to make sure that prospective couples are well matched—in more ways than one," she added significantly.

"I would think," remarked Constantine, "that the chances of these sheltered females remaining spinsters is rather high while the adventurous ones who go to the New World will get their man without too much trouble."

Yes, that was generally true, acknowledged his wife, but lately "Greek-Americans" were returning to their *patrida* ostensibly for a visit but with the purpose of marrying and taking back with them a wife with breeding—"an angel of a wife"—they were not likely to find in America. Constantine responded rather dryly that he hoped these superior specimens of Greek womanhood would not be disappointed in the kind of life they would live as wives of immigrants; at least the ones already there knew what they were getting into. But these protected, well-bred, young women, he feared, were bound to suffer and suffer badly.

Little did Constantine Douropoulos imagine that he and his

199

wife would see for themselves in the not too distant future the sorrowful lot of their countrywomen during those early years of immigration when the Douropoulos family came to America.

It behooved Nicholas to avoid the subject of marriage while he was at his brother's house. But within an hour of his visit, he had been caught unwittingly in the midst of this very topic.

He was at a loss as how to brush aside Alexandra's innuendoes without exposing the secret tender hopes he was nurturing for Tilly Hinckle's plump little hand. He might have been able to rebuff his sister-in-law had she been less genuinely solicitous of his welfare. Besides, she was a perceptive woman who would see through any simulated excuses or arguments he might offer against his marrying one of those "nicest girls from a fine old family," one of which no doubt Alexandra had already chosen for him—as though any one of them could compare with the fair Fraulein he had left behind. But the greatest threat to Nicholas was Alexandra's formidable determination commonly evident in the truly sincere, the truly selfless well-doers the world over. He was, therefore, justified in fearing that Alexandra's persuasive powers would lead him to be slaughtered like a sacrificial lamb on the altar of marriage. That such a calamity might overtake him made Nicholas tug with pitiless ferocity on his walrus moustache as he sent silent messages to the Lord for immediate help.

Help came not from above but from a corner in the room where his nephew had been sitting, quietly listening to the conversation which had just taken place. Dionysios had noticed but, at first, did not quite fathon his uncle's sudden perturbation. He sensed, however, that Uncle Nicholas felt threatened or intimidated by his mother's views which apparently differed significantly from his uncle's, but he lacked the courage, it seemed, to uphold his own convictions.

Dionysios' sympathy was aroused and his youthful idealism was affronted by what he considered an attempt to influence an obviously weaker individual's opinions and beliefs . . . not that his mother was deliberately guilty of such an intention; she meant well, of course. But still, any attempt to influence a grown man—a middle-aged one at that—was absurd, preposterous. . . .

200

Though he was aware that the younger members in a Greek family were not expected to question or contradict the views of their elders, Dionysios nevertheless felt he must speak out in defense of his uncle.

"Why," he asked, "should Uncle Nicholas consider marrying 'an angel of a wife'—one of those elegant Greek young ladies who were waiting for a prosperous immigrant from America or one of those available brides already in America?" Maybe, he continued, throwing Nicholas a knowing smile, his uncle had someone in mind . . . some foreigner perhaps . . . there were all kinds of nationalities settling in the New World . . . some girl he might really 'like'—and want to marry. (Dionysios refrained from using the word "love" since in his parents' time, love was not looked upon as a sound criterion for choosing a mate.)

Alexandra seemed disconcerted by her son's remarks. She wanted to comment on their unsuitability but lapsed into silence when her husband said, "Well, of course, this is a matter which your uncle should decide for himself."

The woebegone expression on Nicholas' face changed instanteously to one of utter elation. God love him, that mere slip of a boy who could make his heart grow light again! Oh, if only he had a son like that! Deeply stirred, Nicholas turned towards his precious nephew with open arms. Dionysios steeled himself for a fervid empressement but, to his infinite relief, Uncle Nicholas was suddenly overwhelmed by a tidal wave of emotion and barely managed to say, "Bless you, my boy," before a fierce flood of tears broke loose, which he tried in vain to stem with Tilly's little masterpiece.

"Po, po, po! The poor man," cried Alexandra. "Hurry, Constantine, give him your handkerchief, and I'll go for some water."

"Never mind the water—there's more than enough of it flowing around here," said her husband, as he handed his brother an ample handkerchief. "We need something more than that to celebrate Nicholas' visit." (Friends, relatives or strangers visiting a Greek home are customarily served a sweet and some kind of drink—clear, cold water in a spotless glass, if no other potion is available, which one drinks or sips following the traditional

201

expressions of mutual wishes for good health.)

"Oh, yes, of course, in all the excitement I completely forgot," confessed Alexandra, "but I will bring some refreshments right now."

"No, you stay here and comfort Nicholas and I'll go and get a bottle of cognac. Some 'Seven Star Metaxa' should improve his spirits—and ours, as well."

Dionysios, who had been looking on in grim silence, saw his chance to escape—be it only for a few minutes—from the painful atmosphere of the parlor. "I'll get it, Father," he exclaimed eagerly.

"You don't know where it is—at least, I hope you don't," remarked his father. "No, you stay here and help your mother console your uncle."

"But I can find it," insisted Dionysios.

"Why are you two just standing there and arguing?" asked Alexandra. "I think both of you should stay here while *I* go and get the brandy and make some coffee besides."

"I can make coffee, Mother; you know that; and Father can make it, too" declared Dionysios eagerly.

"Indeed I can," agreed Constantine, "I've made many a fine cup in my day from the time I was a young boy earning my keep at Saint John's monastery. The old abbot whom I served thought so highly of my coffee, he would not allow any one else to make it for him."

Alexandra looked at her husband and her son with amused reproach. How transparent they were! To avoid hearing poor Nicholas caterwauling, they were willing to assume a task which along with all other domestic duties and responsibilities were considered by Greek males as being below their dignity to perform.

"Don't worry," her son reassured her, "we'll manage better than you think."

"Well, then, go ahead but don't dawdle," she admonished them. As they headed for the kitchen she reminded them to let the water boil before adding the coffee and then to be sure to let the brew come to a full boil again otherwise they wouldn't get a *kaïmaki*—the slightly foamy film which forms on the top of properly made Greek coffee. The lack of it does not detract from the coffee's taste but it does indicate a disregard for the little niceties, which in their small way give a measure of grace to the Greek way of life.

Alexandra took hold of Nicholas' limp hand and patted it assiduously. Her compassionate nature was stirred by Nicholas' distress. Although she was aware he was the kind that "keeps tears in the pocket," as the Greeks say of those who weep readily, she believed in this instance that his paroxysms were sincerely generated by the intense emotions he felt in finding himself in his beloved brother's home and enjoying once again the comforting warmth of family life, which had been denied him the last ten years. How hard those years must have been for him—years without a home, for no place could be honored with that blessed name that lacked a wife and children to fill it with life and love. But it was time now, she said to him gently, time to forget the misery of the past, to put an end to his bachelorhood before it reached an intractable stage.

The remedy to normalize his life was simple, yes, so very simple, she remarked, with a gay little laugh; all he need do was to get married here and now and take back to America a bride that would be the envy of his countrymen. Offhand, she could think of at least a half a dozen of lovely, sweet, young women who—Alexandra stopped speaking as she heard her brother-in-law making fearful gasping sounds such as those one makes who is choking to death.

"Oh! Nicholas, what has happened to you!" she cried.

Nicholas seemed unable to reply. For a moment or two that seemed an eternity to his sister-in-law, he struggled valiantly until he caught his breath and was able to say with a wan but reassuring little smile that he was all right. It was nothing but a phlegm caught in his throat, that's all it was.

It did not occur to Alexandra that Nicholas had simulated a coughing spell in order to distract her from the topic of matrimony. She had no capacity for guile and, therefore, failed to recognize it in others. Her only thought at that moment was to make him comfortable. She insisted he lie back in his chair and relax while she would run into the kitchen to hurry things

203

along. A little brandy and coffee, she declared, would do him a world of good. She couldn't imagine why her husband and her son were taking so long, you'd think they were preparing a banquet instead of a cup of coffee.

"Let them alone, they'll manage," advised Nicholas in a firm voice that indicated a complete recovery from his sudden seizure. "In America men are expected to help around the house. Here you women wait on your menfolk hand and foot like slaves. You make them helpless, then you complain that they can't even make a cup of coffee!"

"Oh, Nicholas, how you exaggerate. I admit we cater to our men—not that we are forced to do so—but because it pleases us to please them. I don't consider that being servile. If anybody is a slave I would think it is the American husband. I imagine he works hard as a man must work in order to support his family but he is also *expected*, you say, to do chores around the house. Is that the way to treat the head of the house—like a servant who has to earn his keep?

"You cannot convince me, Nicholas, that your male ego or that of any Greek would ever tolerate such a humiliation."

Alexandra saw a flush of color spread over Nicholas' face. As far as she could determine he was not choking again, thank God! But had she said something that hit a tender nerve and caused this painful reaction? She tried to recall her words but the ones her son had spoken came to her mind instead . . . maybe his uncle had someone in mind, Dionysios said, perhaps a girl who was not Greek that he wanted to marry.

She had considered it unduly forward of her son to express himself so openly on an intimate matter concerning his uncle. But if she had given him credit for his keen insight she would not have beset Nicholas with advice to marry here and now while the one—the very one who, no doubt, had given him that fancy handkerchief, and was waiting for him on the other side of the ocean! No wonder the poor man felt strangled one moment and apopletic the next.

Whatever failings Alexandra may have possessed, neither meanness nor malice could be found among them. She, therefore, felt compelled to make amends at once for her insensitive blunder-

204

ing by saying, "Oh, of course, there are always exceptions. And in a country so vast as America, I would be surprised if there are not a good many fine women whose first consideration is to show devotion and respect for their husbands just as Greek women do."

Nicholas' distress completely disappeared. Alexandra's remarks clearly indicated to him her willingness to accept a wife of his choice—and to accept her without reservations. What a magnanimous spirit she possessed! He was tempted to pour into that sympathetic ear of hers the hopes and dreams, the doubts and fears his love for Tilly aroused in him but he restrained his impluse. The deep-rooted strictures of his provincial upbringing inhibited him from disclosing matters of an amatory nature, especially with a member of the opposite sex.

"Where are the girls?" he asked, quickly changing the subject. "I haven't yet caught sight of even one of them. They're not hiding from their old uncle, are they?"

"Of course not! They would be swarming all over you with kisses and questions if they were here. They will be coming home soon and you will have only yourself to blame—bringing all those sweets for them from your candy store—if you are caught in the midst of a pandemonium. The three older ones are in school and the two younger ones are at my sister's house playing with her children," Alexandra explained.

"So, I have five nieces now. I confess I've lost track. May God keep them well," said Nicholas offering a customary good wish for the young.

"There were two more," murmured Alexandra and went on quickly to say with a little smile, "we cannot complain for lack of daughters."

Nicholas looked admiringly at his brother's wife. She seemed as vigorous and handsome as she had appeared to him ten years ago. Any other woman who had given birth to one child after another—and all of them but the first, females— would be or should be, at least, somewhat worn-out physically and worn-down emotionally from frustration, not to say despair. As for her equanimity—and his brother's, too, in face of an unrelieved row of daughters, it came, no doubt, from the satisfaction of

205

having as their first-born a son like Dionysios! Nicholas would have been willing to endure a dozen daughters if he had but *one* such son. He could barely refrain from weeping at the thought of the understanding and the courage his nephew had shown in upholding him. He must do something, something that would show the boy how much he loved him. He began to stroke his mustache rhythmically—an indication that he was absorbed in deep thought.

Suddenly he snapped his fingers. "Aha!" he cried, "I found it!"

"You sound like Archimedes," said Alexandra. "Tell me, what have you found so unexpectedly?"

"A gift for my nephew—a perfect gift—a trip, a vacation for the boy—all expenses on me, of course! I'm going to take Dionysios to America with me when I go back."

"Take Dionysios to America?" she asked blankly. "What do you mean 'take Dionysios to America'?" She repeated the phrase slowly as though she had been mesmerized by it.

"Just what I said," replied Nicholas.

Having shot his bolt, Nicholas waited with admirable restraint to see its effect on his sister-in-law. He searched through his pockets unhurriedly until he found a slim rectangular box from which he extracted a cigarette and then lit it with elaborate care. He smoked these particular cigarettes more out of patriotism than preference since they were made by the Stephano brothers who had come to America approximately the same time as the Douropoulos brothers. A warm friendship had developed between John and these ambitious young Greeks, and when the Stephano brothers decided to manufacture an elegant kind of Egyptian cigarettes they asked John to join them in their undertaking. Nicholas had no faith in the success of such an enterprise. He felt it was his duty as an older brother to dissuade John from investing any of his hard-earned money in a frivolous business venture doomed sooner or later "to go up in smoke." John followed this fraternal advice—to his everlasting regret. Well before and long after Nicholas and John and the Arcadia Ice Cream Parlor had come to an obscure end, the "Stephano Cigarettes" caught the fancy of sophisticated smokers—and made it possible for the

Stephano family to secure life membership in the plutocracy of the New World.

As soon as Alexandra fully grasped Nicholas' notion, her immediate reaction was to dismiss it as absurd. Yet she refrained from openly disparaging it. For although it affirmed the limitations of Nicholas' common sense, it re-affirmed the kindness of his heart. It was so good of him, she said, to think of such a generous gift—but a gift that involved a great deal of money, far more than was sensible or wise to spend on one so young. In Alexandra's eyes, her son was still a mere boy despite his apparent physical and mental maturity. It was out of the question; no, they could not possibly allow Dionysios to accept so costly a gift.

"Not nearly as costly, my dear little sister, as it would be if I took back to America one of those fine young ladies you so highly recommend—not unless I am expected to outfit Dionysios with a 'frou-frou' wardrobe and bedeck him with laces and feathers and all those geegaws and furbelows that a Greek bride would demand for making a proper appearance in America."

Ignoring Nicholas' ludicrous remarks, Alexandra glanced anxiously toward the hallway. She now hoped her son and husband would delay a bit longer in the kitchen so that she could settle this unsettling proposal before it reached their ears.

"Now listen to me, Nicholas," she said hurriedly, "Dionysios is going to spend the next few months studying in the hope of entering the University this coming fall. He has so much to do! You should look into his room and just see the books the poor boy has to read."

"Hang the books! He's read more than enough of them already, too many of them, judging from the way his shoulders stoop."

"Well, yes, he does stoop a little. My first cousin, Dr. Keninis, who is highly regarded in all of Arcadia, says its simply because Dionysios has grown so fast. He told us to keep reminding him to straighten his shoulders, that's all there is to it, so you needn't worry about it, Nicholas," said Alexandra in a crisp tone.

Nicholas may have lacked sagacity but not shrewdness. He

surmised that his sister-in-law was more apprehensive about her son than she would admit. Come to think of it, the boy did look a bit peaked. He needed more color in his cheeks and more flesh on that lean frame of his. If Dionysios' mother wanted to pussyfoot around the facts, Nicholas did not intend to do so. Prompted by a sudden sense of avuncular duty, he spoke out bluntly.

"Your smart cousin-doctor, Alexandra, is nothing but a fool; he doesn't know what he's talking about. Mark my words, that boy will become a nervous wreck if you remind him every other minute to straighten his shoulders; and how the devil can he keep them straight, I'd like to know, if he has his nose in a book all the time? And what's the rush to get him into the University this fall anyway? He's young enough to wait a year or two or more. What he needs now is a rest, a change, a chance to breathe freely a bit, and he'll do that in America when he gets far enough away from that infernal reading and studying you expect him to do all summer!"

For a moment or two Alexandra said nothing and then quietly replied, "You may be right, Nicholas. To tell the truth, I am a little worried about Dionysios. He's not as robust as he should be. But I don't know what to say to you about taking him to America. Let me talk it over with his father, and if he—" she stopped abruptly and put her finger on her lips. "Sh! They're coming," she whispered. "Don't say another word."

Nicholas complied with her request but not before he had whispered back, "Better get the boy ready: we're sailing in two weeks."

Chapter Twenty

To see a new world, and to see it through the eyes of a visitor—in the "glad season of life," was Dionysios' singular luck. He was, indeed, a rare exception among the hundreds of thousands of youths emigrating to America during the early part of the century in search of a living. Dionysios, or Dion as he was "rechristened" since his arrival from Greece, was grateful for his good fortune and especially for the unexpected opportunity to spend a few months in America's capital—the first of its kind in the world to be built exclusively for the purpose of serving as a seat of government.

The letters Dion sent home began and ended in the epistolary style observed by well-bred Greek youths in the yesteryears of the present century but which now seem as remote as those of another millennium. They were addressed to "My esteemed Mother and Father" and signed "With reverence, your son, Dionysios." The contents between these filial proprieties were, however, lengthy and lively. They revealed a keenness of mind and a sharpness of pen. Those qualities would soon be recognized and rewarded in an unexpected way. Washington, which its illustrious founder had envisioned as a "Federal City, with a magnitude inferior to few others in Europe," had captivated Dion from the start. He had felt more at home in it than he had anticipated; for it reminded him, in a way, of Athens where he had spent the early years of his adolescence.

He was surprised, he wrote home, to find so many of Washington's buildings following the Greek classical architecture. And he noted with chauvinistic satisfaction that the portico which had been added to the White House within the last few years was a gem of pure Ionic design. As for the Presidential residence, occupied at the time by Mr. Taft, it was elegantly simple—a far cry from those monstrous European *palatia* where royal personages lived amidst opulent reminders of the pomp and glory of their sovereignty.

The restrained grandeur of the nation's capital impressed the young visitor but it was his uncle's establishment, *The Arcadia*, that excited him. Ice cream parlors, originally called "soda parlors," were not uncommon in the towns and cities of America during the early decades of the nineteen-hundreds. Whether or not they were noteworthy depended on the means and the imagination of their respective proprietors. The Douropoulos brothers, Nicholas and John, agreed that a store in the nation's capital should be worthy of its exalted location and should do honor, as well, to America's immigrant sons from Greece. Stirred by this sense of dual fealty, they borrowed heavily—too heavily as time eventually would prove—to produce an establishment which according to the aesthetic standards of the time had "class."

Although *The Arcadia Ice Cream Parlor* was of average size, its mirrored walls created an illusion of spaciousness; the reflection of its glistening chandeliers, the long glass counters and tall glass jars miraculously filled each day with an extraordinary variety of candy, appeared to Dion as nothing less than a crystalline fairyland created for the sole purpose of satisfying the Americans' sweet tooth.

But the wondrous strangeness of it all centered on the white marble soda fountain that appeared to stretch more than half the length of the store. This indispensible fixture of the ice cream parlor, which contained the makings of a staggering number of frosty concoctions, was for Dion a prime example of American ingenuity. Such ambrosial delights as ice cream cones, sundaes and sodas had no counterpart or even faintest semblance to anything that could be had in Greece or in any part of Europe

210

for that matter. How pitifully paltry it seemed to him now—
that little shop in Athens, called *The Helvetia* whose main at-
traction was a plate of hot *loukoumathes*,* a kind of fried cakes
served with honey syrup and a sprinkling of ground walnuts and
cinnamon.

How well he remembered the way the Rizarios seminarians
would head *en masse* for *The Helvetia* during those few precious
times they were permitted to go beyond the Seminary grounds.
These few hours of freedom were granted only on days when certain religious events of prime significance in Greek Orthodox
history are celebrated as national holidays.

On such occasions, and only after the students were well
beyond the school territory and the eagle eye of their mentors
did they dare release the animal vigor of early youth. Hoisting
their trailing cassocks and clutching their pill-box caps (truncated
versions of the cylindrical-shaped headgear worn by the Greek
clergy) they would dash with unseemly haste toward *The Helvetia*
in the hope of gratifying their juvenile craving for sugar—an in-
gredient conspicuously missing from Greek seminary fare.
Reaching their destination was, however, only the beginning of
the battle to gain a foothold as close as possible to the shop which
followed the age-old caveat: "First come, first served." But
however prepared *The Helvetia* may have been for these periodic
invasions, there were never quite enough of the *loukoumathes*
to satisfy the entire mob of sugar-starved seminarians.

The Athenians taking their customary Sunday stroll—more
to see each other in their Sabbath finery than the sights about
them—merely glanced with blasé amusement at the incongruous
mob of sedately garbed seminarians shoving, punching and kick-
ing each other without mercy in order to gain an inch or two of
ground toward their goal.

Among the anonymous passersby Dion remembered an old
woman who was dressed in black from her neatly tied kerchief

---

*According to Theresa Karas Yianilos, author of *The Complete Greek Cookbook*,
these feathery-light, puffed, fried cakes were given in ancient time as prizes to the win-
ners of the night festivals in the games. "They were called *charisioi*, meaning little gifts
or tokens," and according to Callimachos, the ancient Greek poet who mentioned them
in *The Vigil*, the athletes were "delighted to get them."

to her sturdy shoes—the traditional attire of elderly provincial females. These somber habiliments were in the past, and still are in rustic areas of Greece, also the insignia of widows and bereaved mothers who express the magnitude of their loss in a perpetuity of mourning.

She stopped and peered at the scene across the street outside of the confectionary shop. Her curiosity was apparently stronger than her eyesight, for she hobbled across to the opposite side with the help of a stout shepherd's crook she used in place of a cane; brandishing it right and left she thrust herself into the center of the fray.

At the sudden appearance of this ancient, crow-like creature in their midst, the seminarians forgot their contentions and united in a chorus of uncontrollable laughter.

The old woman waited with peasant stolidity until they had exhausted their derision before she began to upbraid them in a voice that quavered more with indignation than senility.

"Shame! Shame on all of you! Any street urchin could teach you better manners—you who would wear a priest's mantle some day or maybe you'd prefer a bishop's mitre . . . eh? Well, I won't be around to see the likes of you in front of the Holy Altar; I'm an old woman on my way to the 'other world'—the world of the dead.'' And she cackled with morbid relish.

A few ripples of tittering followed the old woman's words but she gave no indication of having heard them. She no longer seemed angry or pretended to be as Dion had suspected all along. For he noted that while she rebuked them, a hint of a sly smile had hovered around her toothless mouth.

She was obviously satisfied that she had done her "duty" as any worthy elder member of a Greek society would do—to reprimand, to advise, to instruct the young depending on the nature and the degree of their transgressions. She recognized that their infantile feuding for sweets and their ill-mannered means of acquiring them were relatively minor infractions, yet she felt duty bound to decry them. But God bless them, these fresh-faced youths, if satisfying a sweet tooth remained their only sin! The old woman had lived long enough to be well aware of far less innocent indulgences to which men, and men of the cloth, no less, were incorrigibly addicted.

Dion did not waste the precious hours of his vacation in America by being idle. An inveterate walker like most of his countrymen, he explored Washington on foot and became well acquainted with the fair sights of the nation's capital. But what interested him as much if not more than the city itself, were the human beings who inhabited it. He was particularly intrigued with the "native" Americans whose forebears had settled in the New World and had transferred to it the essence of their Anglo-Saxon ethnicity.

To come in contact with this particular breed of Americans Dion did not need to go out of his way. The majority of his uncles' steady customers were middle-class Americans attracted to The Arcadia Ice Cream Parlor by the quality and quantity of its confections. "Always give a little extra, a little more than they expect," Nicholas would regularly remind his "fountain clerks"—an appelation he considered more befitting *The Arcadia* employees than the less genteel expression "soda jerkers." But it was his brother John who showed them how to scoop out an ice cream ball so that a billowing collar would cling to it. If nature had endowed Dion's kindly uncles with as much acuity as generosity, they would have realized that these "little extras" such as clouds of whipped cream instead of the usual dollop, or a raining of nuts rather than a fine sprinkling of them—to name a few of these extravagances—would in the long run make the difference between the success or failure of their enterprise.

After his daily exploration of the capital, Dion returned towards late afternoon to *The Arcadia* where Nicholas would greet his nephew with emotion. "As though," thought Dion, "I had just come back from some dangerous expedition."

"Thank God, my boy, you've returned safe and sound! Where have you been all this time? Never mind telling me now—I can see you are exhausted—sit down and rest a while—order something to refresh yourself—don't be bashful—the place is yours—have whatever your heart desires—and not just an orangeade or a lemonade you usually drink—that won't put any flesh on you—we're not going to let you go back home as you

213

came—thin as a rail! Your mother will never forgive me!"

Nicholas' insistent largesse did not have the effect on Dion that his well-meaning uncle expected. It served only to make his nephew, who possessed an innate sense of delicacy, feel that it would be vulgarly opportunistic of him to take advantage of this unlimited hospitality—no, he simply could not accept it. He would stick to orangeade or lemonade. But it was Uncle John who managed in his quiet way to break down Dion's resolve. And it was John, no less, who would alter in due time Dion's uncomfortable status from that of a pampered guest to an ordinary employee in *The Arcadia Ice Cream Parlor.*

John greeted Dion in his usual fashion by merely nodding his head. But no sooner had Dion settled into a chair—or rather been forced into it by Nicholas—when John would appear with an ice cream soda, a huge, heavenly, strawberry concoction which he had personally prepared. His nephew could no more resist grasping its straw then a drowning man would have resisted it.

Without saying a word or waiting to hear one, John would walk away with his habitual faint smile.

This little vignette which took place regularly at *The Arcadia* never failed to touch Dion. It must be painful, he thought, for his Uncle John to display so openly his avuncular, affectionate concern. In the short time he had known him, Dion became aware that this uncle of his was an extremely shy man who was loathe to express his feelings—not that he had reason to be ashamed of them, for he had kindly, decent instincts—but simply because he did not believe they could be of any particular interest to anyone; and even if they were, he had no desire to reveal them. Unlike his ebullient older brother, Nicholas, who did not shrink from attention but which, in fact, his ego relished, the younger brother's morbid dread of calling attention to himself amounted to autophobia—a rare affliction among the Greeks.

Despite his taciturnity, John Douropoulos did not have a saturnine disposition or a forbidding presence. He was, in fact, a pleasant-looking man on the stocky side with a fine head of light curly hair and bright blue eyes which he had inherited from his mother's side. He was, to put it simply, one of those nice, quiet, polite individuals who are easily liked and readily forgotten. But nature had tried to compensate somewhat for the blandness of his personality by giving him a mind of his own which was reinforced by stubbornness, "a mulish stubbornness" as his brother Nicholas called it.

On one of his daily walks about the capital, Dion came across Washington's first public library which had been established in 1897. He could hardly believe that from the myriads of books in this sanctuary consecrated to bibliophiles, he could pick and choose whichever ones he desired and take them with him merely by having a return date stamped on an ordinary card! Dion remembered seeing a stone sign in the Athenian museum which once was affixed to some ancient library reminding its patrons that NO BOOK SHALL BE REMOVED. How marvelously different were these American libraries than the Greek ones that still followed that age-old dictum. Nicholas did not share, however, his nephew's enthusiasm for this particular American institution.

"It was a 'bad hour' when the boy found that library," he muttered uneasily to his brother John. "I took him away from those confounded books so he could rest his eyes and straighten his shoulders and now he's hitting them again like a drunkard hits the bottle."

Nicholas and John were having a cup of coffee in their living quarters above the store. Dion was still asleep (or reading in bed, Nicholas suspected) but his two hard-working uncles were early risers long inured to the immigrants' lot of meager sleep and rest. Before the cares of the day took hold of them, the two brothers were drawn together in fraternal intimacy despite the disparity of their temperaments.

"What can we do about this 'book business'?" asked Nicholas plaintively.

"Let's think about it," suggested John.

"I've already done that," responded his brother testily, "and I could solve it, of course, but I have other important matters to consider just now, what with the wedding coming on. I'd like the boy to stay a while longer, to be here for the ceremony at least—but not if he wrecks his health in the meantime. Tilly has taken a great fancy to him, you know, and wants him to be our *koumparos* (best man or sponsor). I love the boy, but you will be the *koumparos*—you, dear brother, whose blood is exactly the same as that which flows in my veins. The date is set—the last Sunday in September, God be willing.''

"God be willing," repeated John silently. He had had his fill for more than a year now of finding Nicholas and Tilly locked in amorous embraces where he least expected to find anyone, let alone a pair of lovers—in places such as the storage room, the kitchen pantry, the broom closet, even in the cellar where he would go occasionally to bring up coal for the stove. He was forced, therefore, to make a habit of coughing loudly or whistling foolishly in advance of reaching any dark, little corner as a forewarning of his presence. Even at that, they would be so engrossed in their furtive love-making, they never seemed to hear him. And when he suddenly came up on them, Tilly would giggle and say, "Oh, John, you've caught us again!" John felt sorry for Nicholas but felt constrained as a younger brother to tell him he was making a fool of himself.

The poor fellow had been badly wounded by the arrows of *Eros*, as the Greeks call "romantic love"—so much so that he failed to see how simple it was to wean his nephew from reading by giving him something more exciting to do than keeping his nose in those "confounded books."

John did not have his usual second serving of Greek coffee but went to the sink and rinsed out his cup.

"What's the hurry?" asked Nicholas. "It's still early."

John murmured something about the store needing more tidying up than usual. Sam, one of the two soda jerkers, had not shown up yesterday and with only one helper at the fountain—a lazy one at that—the place had been left in a helter-skelter state. Sam's father had come by last night to report that his son had broken his ankle playing tennis and would be laid up the rest of the summer.

"Serves him right," said Nicholas, "a university man, if you please, wasting his time throwing balls over a net, then running like a madman all over the lot to hit them back to another madman on the opposite side, who had just hit them back to *him*.

216

I watched them one Sunday morning—grown men playing that silly game, and I couldn't make any sense out of it. Sometimes I wonder about these Americans—nice people, friendly, kind, good people but a little childish when you come right down to it.

"But we'll have to get someone in Sam's place—the sooner the better. We can't do with only one fountain clerk in the summer season. So, see what you can do about it, John. I can't attend to it, you understand . . . too much on my mind now."

John was aware that getting a reliable helper was not as simple as his brother apparently thought it would be. The dependable ones were already preparing to go back to school in a few weeks.

"Why not give Dionysios the job?" he asked quietly.

Nicholas give his brother a startled look which quickly changed into a stern one. "John, have you forgotten? I brought the boy here for a vacation—not to put him to work."

John picked up his cup again and began once more to wash and rinse it.

"He's not a boy any longer, Nicholas, but a full-grown man now—all of six feet tall—but let's forget the whole business. It wouldn't work, anyhow. So let's forget it," he repeated.

Although John had surrendered without any display of his usual stubbornness, Nicholas, nevertheless, felt uncomfortable. Perhaps his brother's suggestion was not so absurd after all. "Why," he asked, "do you say it won't work?"

"They'll object," was John's brief reply.

"Who will object?" Nicholas wanted to know. John did not bother to respond. He was satisfied to have shot his bolt and had no intention of allowing his brother to cross-examine him in regard to it.

"Well, I'm not going to coax you for an answer. It's easy enough to guess; of course, it's Alexandra and Costas." (Among themselves the brothers referred to Constantine by his nickname but in his presence they addressed him by his full given name as was only proper for the educated, dignified, oldest living member of their family.)

"So they'll object, will they?" mused Nicholas as he stroked his moustache. "Well, let me tell you something—those poor,

217

proud countrymen of ours make virtue out of necessity. They try to cover their genteel poverty by pretending their educated sons are too fine for common labor; but here in this great democracy, those who labor with their hands are as good as those who live by their brains. In this blessed land, even the rich don't pamper their sons. Take Sam's father, a big-shot lawyer, who lives in a house a Prime Minister of Greece would envy. Yet, he lets his son, a student at the University, mind you, go to work in the summer for two Greek immigrants who run an ice cream parlor!

"But don't worry, I'll take care of this matter personally. You go ahead and do your work without concerning yourself about it, *adelphaki mou*, my little brother," declared Nicholas in a lofty tone, as he waved his hand in an aristocratic manner of dismissal.

Nicholas' gesture went wasted, however, for John had already left the room. He did not want his brother to think he was gloating over his facile victory—which, in fact, he was doing with a broad smile on his face.

Chapter Twenty-one

Dion wished his former classmates could see him now—no longer garbed as he was a short while ago in the somber vesture of a seminarian, but sporting an immaculate white linen jacket and trousers. How astonished they would be at his deft manipulation of levers and taps, buttons and faucets that would produce at his command ambrosial and nectarous delights fit for the Gods of Olympus! And how incredible it would seem to them, as, indeed, it seemed to him, that he was getting paid in sound, American money for doing what was incomparably less tedious and far more exciting than those hours of everlasting study demanded of the Rizarios seminarians.

Dion was delighted that his parents had not overruled his request for a few months' postponement of his return to Greece. He had written for their permission and assured them he would not waste this extra time but use it profitably to enlarge his knowledge of the English language and to acquire a broader perspective of the New World. His uncles were kind enough to say repeatedly that they wanted him to stay a while longer.

He assured his parents he had not been a nuisance to them. If anything, he was a help by working now—at their request—as a "soda jerker" whose duties he described impressively, as being indispensable to the operation of an ice cream parlor. As a final argument for protracting his visit, he had written, "If I leave now, I will miss Uncle Nicholas' wedding which is to take place in a few weeks and which I am sure you would want me to attend as a representative of the family.''

Dion's parents might not have acquiesced so readily to their son's request had they not been intensely preoccupied with the significant changes that were about to take place in their own lives. Dion had forgotten that he had heard his parents discussing the changes they anticipated when his father completed twenty-five years in the teaching profession. That time had now come, and it had completely slipped Dion's mind. Here he was in America enjoying himself while his father was facing problems about starting a new career when he was no longer young, but a man nearly fifty years of age.

Constantine's decision to resign from his profession was not due to any dissatisfaction with his work or the quality of life in Zatouna. Indeed, it was a place that left nothing to be desired in the way of scenic grandeur, or in the matter of a splendid climate that was temperate yet invigorating. As for the water that gushed ceaselessly from the mountainside, it was truly an elixir and the envy of those who did not live in Zatouna. But above all, it was the place that had provided Constantine with a wife such as his.

Up to the last century, Zatouna could not be considered a village. More than a few of its residents were cultivated and prosperous and had left sizeable portions of their wealth for the improvement of their birthplace. For generations these merchants had made their fortune in commerce not only in mainland Greece and the Greek islands, but in Europe, the Middle East, Russia and other parts of the world. Their well-educated offspring, who had studied in Greece, and often abroad, as well, had settled mainly in Athens to pursue their chosen professions. But they did not neglect their contact or concern for the land of their birth, and contributed generously for its needs like their forefathers before them. However, by the beginning of the present century, the population of Zatouna had diminished to the point where it could be properly called a ''village''—a quiet, beautiful little village basking in the afterglow of its significant past.

The decimation of Zatouna's inhabitants was undoubtedly another reason for Constantine's decision to leave the place where he had spent the happiest years of his life thus far. In the letter to his son in America regarding his plans he writes: "Your sisters, who are growing up rapidly, deserve a broader view of life than they have here. As for your mother, she is capable of making a worthwhile life wherever she may be; yet it is only fair that she should have the opportunity to exercise her many talents in a fresh environment. I must say, we are fortunate in having many relatives and friends who are concerned about us. Your mother's relatives, especially, are held in high esteem in the professional, as well as in the business and industrial world, and I have received through their kind offices several appealing offers."

However, Constantine did not consider any of the opportunities that came his way. He made the irrevocable decision to take the vows of priesthood. The love of the Church which he first felt during his early years in the monastery had remained latent until he met Bishop Nektarios. Constantine's son, Dionysios, was the youngest student in the Rizarios Seminary in Athens during the tenure of Bishop Nektarios as Director of the school. The saintly hierarch's interest and affection for the young seminarian soon expanded to encompass Dionysios' parents and this friendship reawakened Constantine's dormant desire to serve God and His Church.

In his letter to Dionysios, Constantine Douropoulos informs his son that he will be taking the vows of priesthood—God be willing, in two months or so at the Metropolitan Church of Athens. "Our beloved Nektarios* at his own request will perform the ordination—an honor I did not expect, nor do I deserve. I have already been assigned, following my ordination, to serve as pastor at the fine parish at Saint Eirene in Athens, as the priest of that church will be resigning soon because of poor health." That, too, he writes, is an unexpected honor, but he feels it is only fair to state his desire to serve in America as one of the pioneer priests, and to that end he has disclosed his intention of petitioning the Holy Synod of Greece over which Archbishop Theoclitos presides as Head of the Church of Greece.

---

*Greek Orthodox hierarchs are often referred to by the religious names they acquire when taking the vows of celibacy, or become known by the diocese they administer. This is not a matter of disrespect but rather a manner of speaking.

Constantine Douropoulos was no stranger to the Archbishop. During his years as a bishop, Theoclitos was Director of the Tripolis Seminary from which Constantine had graduated with honors. The Archbishop had kept in touch with his former seminarian, and when he was informed of Constantine's decision to take holy orders, he requested his presence at the Archdiocese.

"He greeted me with warmth," Constantine writes to his son, "and expressed the happiness he feels when one of his former seminarians decides to put to use his rigorous preparation as a servant of Christ and steward of the mysteries of God. He remarked that it had taken me longer than he had hoped, 'but if I may use a cliché,' the Archbishop had added with a smile, 'better late than never.' No mention was made, of course, regarding my petition since that matter is under the jurisdiction of the Holy Synod, which will convene by next month. The Archbishop embraced me and wished me Godspeed in all my endeavors and I left strengthened by his blessing. Indeed, I felt more confident than ever of replacing successfully the secular responsibilities of a lay teacher by the hieratic duties of a priest.

"Some may consider the events in my life which have led me to take holy vows as simply fortuitous. But I believe that the various occurrences, the complications, and those mysterious, inexplicable coincidences in life have not come about through mindless chance but result from the providential power that governs our temporal destiny."

Constantine expressed regret that his son was not with them in person at this time to express his thoughts and feelings about plans which in one way or another would affect all the members of the family. But he expected that Dionysios would be home for the ordination which would take place more than a month after his uncle's wedding, so there would be adequate time for his return to Greece. "By the way," his father added, "I have been told through an unsolicited source, and, therefore, cannot vouch as to its veracity, that a small number of compatriots have settled in Baltimore. They have formed a community and have applied, or intend to apply, to the Holy Synod for a priest to help them establish a church. If my petition to serve in the United States is granted, I will look into the matter, for this particular

222

location close to Washington would be an excellent one all around."

When Dion finished reading his father's startling letter, his reaction to it was not so much a feeling of surprise as an acute attack of homesickness. He would leave at once and gladly forego his uncle's wedding and his glamorous "position" as a soda jerker, and forget the New World with all its wonders and go home to those he dearly loved. Besides, as an only son it was his duty to be present at his father's ordination, but he had no sooner made up his mind when he abruptly changed it. No, oh, no! That would be only self-serving to show that he was a dutiful son and to satisfy his longing to see his parents and his little sisters—a longing that he felt only now when he received his father's letter. He had missed them, of course, but he was having such a good time enjoying his visit to America that he could not honestly say that he had missed them greatly. His going home now would only increase his father's financial burden by the additional expense of another fare—his own fare for coming back to the country he had left just a few months ago.

Obviously, his father's decision to serve as a priest in America was unequivocal. He had already been offered the post as pastor of the "fine" Church of Saint Eirene—as his father modestly referred to the most elegant church and wealthy parish at that time in Athens. But he would accept this assignment, his father had written, with the proviso that he could resign if and when his petition to come to the United States was granted.* Dion had faith in the soundness of his father's judgment and the strength of his conscience. Some ineluctable force in his heart and mind must have compelled him to make this precarious decision.

Dion's thoughts turned to his mother. How pleased she would be that her husband was soon to take holy orders, and Bishop Nektarios, whom she revered as a saint, would officiate at her husband's ordination! As to the drastic step of settling in America, Dion had no doubt that his mother had not only assented to it

---

*Shortly after his ordination Father Douropoulos' petition was granted. Nevertheless, he remained as pastor of Saint Eirene church for several months until a priest could be found to replace him.

223

but had wholeheartedly endorsed it. She would have no qualms about the staggering logistics of moving an ample-sized family from one continent to another, nor fearful of the manifold adjustments which would inevitably follow. She would meet the trials that were in store for her and her family with high courage, and with her sense of excitement which was as "continuous as the stars that shine"—the excitement she invariably felt at being alive in any part of God's wondrous world.

While John, Constantine's youngest brother, was still in Greece, Alexandra tried to "make a match" for him. To her surprise she discovered that her younger brother-in-law was, indeed, "stubborn as a mule." John was in his mid-twenties at the time—a relatively early age for most Greek males to consider matrimony unless they had fulfilled their familial obligations. John was fortunate in that his only sister was happily settled and his twice-widowed father was living with her. He had a nice little business in Megalopolis—a *taverna* which he and his cousin operated. It was not until this enterprise collapsed due to his partner's systematic looting of the profits that John decided to join his brother Nicholas in America.

Didn't he agree, Alexandra asked her husband, that his brother should get married since there was nothing in the way now to hinder him?

"Yes," he acknowledged, "there is nothing standing in the way—nothing except his refusal to do so—which would not surprise me in the least."

Alexandra was startled at the thought of such a possibility. In her world, men espoused either marriage or monkhood and those who failed to embrace one or the other were suspect. For a few moments Alexandra said nothing and then gravely asked, "Why haven't you told me before that there is something *wrong* with your poor brother?" Constantine looked at his wife with affectionate amusement.

"Ah, you women! How readily you say that a man is impotent simply because—"

"I said nothing of the sort, Costa," she interrupted, using his nickname by which she addressed him in their conjugal

224

privacy.

"Not in so many words, but your implication is not only obvious but typical of the conclusion women usually reach regarding men who avoid wedlock. It is understandable, of course, this indiscriminate condemnation of any male who is unwilling to take a wife and help her feather a nest and fill it with her nestlings."

"And *his*," added Alexandra most emphatically.

"His? . . . That, my dear, is simply a matter of faith."

This response incensed his wife. How could he make so gross an aspersion on wives and mothers! Constantine protested that she had misconstrued an indisputable statement as demeaning to motherhood but failed to appreciate that it was at the same time absolute proof of the complete trust men had in their wives.

"But let's not waste time," he said, "on extraneous issues and go back to John's matrimonial prospects. I suppose—in fact, I'm willing to wager—you have already decided on a bride for my brother."

"It's not for me to decide, only to suggest. But, as a matter of fact, I do have someone in mind—a jewel, a perfect jewel!"

"Perfect jewels are very rare, my dear, though I was lucky enough to find one."

She gave no indication she had heard his spontaneous compliment but it pleased her nonetheless, for her husband was not in the habit of externalizing the deep love he had for her by words of praise and phrases of endearment.

"And who, may I ask, is the treasure you have in store for my little brother?"

"She is a treasure, indeed," replied Alexandra, "and I am not thinking of her sizeable dowry either, but the heart of gold that girl has! She has spent more time helping her friends sew and crochet and embroider their dowry linens than she has on her own. It shows how unselfish, how thoughtful she is—thanks to her mother. Any other woman with dear Amalia's means and an elegant townhouse in Dimitsana would have spoiled her only daughter, but my cousin is a sensible woman; she hasn't pampered the girl one bit but has, in fact, instructed her in all the household arts."

225

"Ah, so it's your cousin Amalia's daughter, Aphrodite, you have in mind for John."

"Of course! Who else, I'd like you to tell me, Costa, could make a more suitable wife for your brother?"

"Not a bad choice, I must admit. Aphrodite is a clever girl and a brave one, I might add, heavily burdened as she is with the name of the glorious Goddess of Love and Beauty. Not that she is to blame for being a bit short and stubby and bearing a name that doesn't remotely suit her. But we Hellenes—"

"Let me remind you," interrupted Alexandra, "that your brother John is no tall or slim Apollo, either."

"Granted—but at least he's been spared the irony of bearing the handsome sun-god's name. And to finish my thought, if I may, we Hellenes are so intensely ethnocentric that we hoist on helpless infants not only the antiquated names of our renowned ancestors but those of their pagan deities and their mythological personages, as well."

"What is all this talk about names, Costa? I haven't heard you complain about them before. Every race or country has its own peculiar ones handed down through the generations, and I don't see why the Greeks shouldn't have theirs and use them as they like. I find nothing wrong with Aphrodite's name. She may not be a raving beauty like her namesake but she has other fine qualities that the goddess of Love and Beauty lacked. I doubt if *she* could cook and prepare a meal such as Amalia's daughter is capable of doing. Oh, lucky is the man who marries her!

Constantine nodded in agreement. "I think you are right on that score. I, too, am inclined to suspect that the triumphs of this particular goddess did not take place in the kitchen."

John was coming for a few days to spend Eastertide at his brother's house.

"Here's your chance," Constantine said to his wife, "to arrange the momentous meeting between my brother and your cousin's daughter."

"I don't want it to appear 'momentous,' thought it may very well turn out to be, God willing. This meeting ought to be more like a chance encounter or a casual visit, if you know what I mean—otherwise Aphrodite will be dreadfully self-conscious. Any shy, sensitive girl is bound to be at her worst when she knows she in on display as a potential bride. Matchmaking is more delicately handled nowadays than it used to be when the *first* 'meeting' was tantamount to a bethrothal, you know.''

"That was because those old-time matchmakers like the legendary *Kyra* Nicoletta, my mother's great-grandaunt, I believe she was, did their homework and did it well. They checked and rechecked all the vital statistics concerning the two parties and if the numbers tallied—give or take a few points here and there—that was *it*. So, there was no need to waste time in pretenses such as chance encounters or other coy subterfuges. Everybody involved (including possibly the entire population of a small village where weddings are a main source of entertainment) had but one object in mind: to hear the peal of wedding bells. And, as you say, the betrothal was in past years the first and practically inextricable step towards that goal—and the sooner it took place so much the better.''

He noticed the vague look in his wife's eyes. "You haven't heard a word I said," he complained.

"Oh, yes, I have. You were talking about that old matchmaker Kyra Nicoletta. I know her story inside out; she was, if you remember, your father's favorite subject. But that has nothing to do with John's matter and that is what concerns me now.''

Alexanda had a special attachment to her husband's younger brother from the time she married. She felt sorry for the quiet, motherless boy with a shy sweet smile. She induced him to come and live with them in Zatouna where he stayed until he felt secure and mature enough to leave for Megalopolis in order to earn his own living.

"I'm glad he is coming to stay for a few days," she went on to say, "he certainly needs a rest, holed up as he is in that *taverna* of his, day and night. And there will be time enough while he is here in Zatouna to arrange an 'impromptu' meeting. I think it would be too obvious to ask Amalia and her daughter to come here. They would be more at ease, I believe, in their own domain, under the circumstances. And I will find some excuse for getting John to take 'a little jaunt' with me to Dimitsana.

227

Wouldn't that be a good way to handle the matter?''

"That is for you to decide. The whole idea was yours from the start and I want no part in it,'' said Constantine firmly. "Matchmaking is your forte, not mine; besides, I have no practical experience in that area since I asked directly for your hand without resorting to matchmakers.''

Chapter Twenty-two

"You talk about taking the matter of marriage—our marriage—in your own hands with a certain pride. But others considered it a very irregular procedure that you would approach my grandfather directly to ask for my hand rather than sending an emissary to my parents, which was the proper thing to do."

Her husband, however, believed that his approach was sensible and forthright, and he had achieved his mission, hadn't he? His wife had forgotten, it seems, that when he came to Zatouna as a schoolmaster, he had no time, at first, to make friends who could act as "matchmakers," nor would he entrust such a delicate, personal matter to some distant, elderly relative on his maternal grandmother's side that still lived in Zatouna. "You remember, of course, that my grandmother was born here," remarked Constantine, "and was so attached to her birthplace that when the time came near for her to give birth to her first child, she returned to her father's house here in Zatouna in order that the child would be born in the same place where *she* was born.

"And that child was—"

"Your mother . . . I know that, of course, but I can't understand how your grandfather ever allowed your grandmother to leave Vancon and come here to give birth to their first child."

"I have no idea how that happened. You see, I didn't show up until seventeen or eighteen years later. But let's get back to your grandfather, Costakis Thanopoulos—he told me at our first meeting that he knew my grandmother from the time she was a little girl; her parents apparently were friends of the family. He was one of the few left from that era, he said sadly. Yet, I caught a tone of pride in his voice when he referred indirectly to his longevity. I must say he was remarkably fit both physically and mentally for a man his age.

"As president of the community at the time, your grandfather had interviewed me—I should say grilled me—on my qualifications as though I had applied for a professorship at the University of Athens rather than a teaching job in a village (forgive me, I should refer to it as a *town* as you often remind me). He finally seemed satisfied with the inquisition he had put me through and hired me on the spot without bothering to consult with the other elders of the council. I thought that was quite imperious of him but I confess I changed my mind, however, when—"

Alexandra hastily interrupted her husband in defense of the family patriarch. Hadn't Constantine forgotten that her maternal grandfather, Captain Thanopoulos, had been honored for his valor in the "Revolution"? If he appeared somewhat autocratic it was because he had been accustomed to making swift decisions without wasting time on arguments and dissensions. "And," she continued, "as you well know, he was a man of means with the finest house in the town—a house that any Athenian would be proud to own. Yet, he was an unassuming, benevolent man highly regarded—a man whose wisdom was never questioned."

"If you had let me finish my thought—I started to tell you that I had changed my mind about him by the end of our interview. He became most agreeable and asked me to come and see him whenever I had the desire and the time. He was a widower, he remarked, an old man in his eighties and it did his heart good to have young people around him. 'Thank God,' he added, 'I have most of my grandchildren, and great-grandchildren close by. So, you see, I'm used to young people and I enjoy them, but, if they enjoy me, that's a different matter.' "

"I certainly enjoyed him," said Alexandra, "and I loved him as far back as I can remember." That was not surprising to her

230

husband who reminded her that she was his acknowledged favorite.

Following his customary habit on the Sabbath, Constantine went to church the Sunday following his arrival in Zatouna. He had not expected to find so impressive a church in a relatively small town nor had he expected to see such a large number of worshipers, who had come to church hoping to get a glimpse of the new schoolmaster rather than from religious fervor. After the service the priest introduced "Mr. Constantine Douropoulos, our new teacher" to the parishioners as they filed past the church door. Mr. Costakis Thanopoulos, as befitted the president of the community, was the first to greet Constantine and he introduced his daughter, Angeliki, her husband, Panos Regas, and their young daughter, Alexandra.

Constantine barely had time to notice the Captain's granddaughter, yet, she must have made an unconscious impression on him, for later that day she suddenly came to his mind. He recalled her face clearly—a lovely, fresh, young face. But, something about her seemed to trouble him. After a moment's thought it came to his mind; ah, yes, those bangs—a salient row of them that practically covered her forehead. He had never seen another girl with bangs except a hussy at some cabaret to which he had gone for the first and last time, at the urging of a classmate, during his student days in Athens.

As a teacher Constantine automatically held a position of respect and, therefore, was invited to the significant events and occasions in the town. He soon had the opportunity to see Alexandra Regas again at the engagement party of her first cousin, Ketty Thanopoulos, whose father was Mrs. Regas' brother and one of the Captain's sons. Ketty was an only child who was brought up like a "princess," the *cosmos* said. Instead of attending the only girls' school in the nearby town of Dimitsana, Ketty was tutored at home; moreover, her dresses were not entrusted to a local dressmaker but made to order in Athens. She was, nevertheless, a sweet, warmhearted girl who dearly loved her cousin, Alexandra, and whenever she had a fancy dress made for herself, she saw to it that another one, no less fashionable than her own, was made for Alexandra.

When Constantine entered the *sala* in Demetrios Thanopoulos' house, he caught sight of Alexandra among a line of lively, youthful dancers. He noticed at once that her hair had been swept away from her forhead and combed in a stylish pompadour that was the fashion of the day. She seemed older and prettier than when he had last seen her. Then he realized that the bangs were gone, and he was pleased. But what had happened, he wondered, that she was no longer wearing them?

After his initial meeting with Constantine Douropoulos, *Capetan* Costakis Thanopoulos had gone directly to his son-in-law's house to inform his daughter, Angeliki, and her husband, Panos Regas, about the schoolmaster he had just interviewed for the vacant teaching post in Zatouna.

"He's a fine young fellow, and I hired him at once," reported the president of the community. "His recommendations were excellent, even so, I cross-examined him closely, and came to the conclusion that Constantine Douropoulos is an intelligent, serious, modest young man. Ah, yes, he's also a graduate from the Tripolis Seminary—a devout Christian, I'm glad to say. And by the way, his grandmother was a native of Zatouna—from the Laganis family; few of them are left now, but in years long past I knew her parents well; they came from good Arcadian stock, and the girl who became our schoolmaster's grandmother—her name was Katerina. I remember that she was mighty pretty, which accounts for her grandson's good looks.

"From what you tell us, the townfolk should be very pleased with your choice, and grateful, as well, I daresay, Captain," remarked Panos Regas who always addressed his wife's father with his military title.

The Captain shook his head. He did not expect gratitude, nor did he want it; what he expected was dissension. "We Greeks are a contentious lot—not viciously so, but as a means of stirring up excitement to satisfy our volatile nature, and as a way of asserting our precious little egos. Not many among us are as kind and selfless as you, my good Panos."

"Now that you've found a fine teacher, Father, I hope he'll stay here," remarked Angeliki, unaware that she was giving him

232

an opening to say what was on the Captain's mind. He settled himself comfortably in the chair and brought forth his *kombologi*—a string of large, oval-shaped, amber beads. As he played with them, clicking one bead against the other, he began speaking casually. No, he was not the kind who would leave them in the lurch. "He likes the place. It's in his blood, you see; his maternal grandparents and, in fact, his own mother, he told me, were born here. I am sure he'd stay if he found a wife to his liking in Zatouna."

"That's no problem," rejoined his son-in-law. "There are plenty of fine girls in the town."

"One girl—the right girl—is all a man needs, Panos, to settle down in contentment. And, I believe the one girl who would suit that young man, and suit *her*, no less, is the youngest, the finest of my granddaughters—Alexandra."

Angeliki glanced at her father and saw a look of determination on his face. "But Father, she's still a child—only fourteen years old," she exclaimed.

"She looks more like a grown woman than a child," he retorted.

Angeliki admitted that Alexandra looked grown-up because she had probably reached her full height by now. But . . . well, . . . she was still immature in some ways. Yes, she did look older—she wasn't old enough to get married. She was not ready yet, and would not be; no, not for a while, anyway. "Don't you understand what I'm trying to say, Father?" she asked in exasperation, for he had put her in the indelicate position of having to explain female maturation—a matter which women did not discuss with men. (Girls reached maturity in the past century several years later than it is reached in the present century.) Yes, he had understood her, he said, but she had misunderstood him. What he was talking about was not marriage but an engagement for as long as it was necessary. Protracted engagements were common occurrences; his own father had waited three years before his marriage took place. But long or short, an engagement was the only guarantee that a marriage would sooner or later take place.

"But what's all the hurry about?" Panos asked. "The schoolteacher has just arrived, and has yet to find a place to live, let alone find a wife.''

In a well-practiced, conspiratorial gesture, which invariably flattered his audience, the old man drew his chair closer to his daughter and her husband and addressed them in a confidential tone. ''Let me tell you something: parents with a marriageable daughter will in no time enlist relatives and friends to approach the new schoolmaster with proposals. And I can't blame them. It's seldom we see a young bachelor such as Constantine Douropoulos in the respected position of a teacher—a profession paying a steady salary that is guaranteed month in and month out by the government. Desperate mothers will go to the length of hiring professional matchmakers—those vultures who swoop down on some hapless man just to make a few paltry drachmas.''

''Oh, Father,'' laughed Angeliki, ''How you exaggerate! If the schoolmaster is half as good as you say, surely he'll ward off those 'vultures.' ''

''Ah, my child, in my long lifetime I have seen men, some of the bravest in battle, break down if they are plagued by a harpy day and night. Now, I want to save this young man from being hounded into a disastrous marriage. All he needs is to get a glimpse of our Alexandra—not that I put any stock in that silly notion of 'love at first sight,' but I believe that he will instinctively know the right woman for him when he sees her. And that's all there is to it.''

But that was not all there was to it, for the old man had more to say to his daughter concerning an impropriety he would no longer tolerate: ''Those bangs of Alexandra's must go,'' he ordered. ''No decent girl should wear them. She's had them long enough, since she was five or six, if I remember rightly.''

''Yes, she's worn them since then to hide the scar on her forehead from the time she fell down the stairs at your house.''

''Nonsense! Nothing is left of that scar by now. Even if there's a vestige of it, better to let it show than go around looking like one of those unbridled females who go about arousing . . . well, never mind what they do. Just see to it that she gets rid of them.''

''But no one thinks of it that way, Father. Why, she's been wearing them since she was a tot.''

He glared at her. "Don't *you* tell *me* what decent men think of such matters!"

Angeliki responded meekly that she would try. "It may take a bit of doing; Alexandra is stubborn—I mean, determined—as you are, Father." The Captain accepted the comparison as a compliment. "Well, there's no need to rush the girl. Wait 'til Ketty's engagement party, that's soon enough. Be kind but firm—just tell Alexandra she'll look like a lady without those bangs. That will do the trick." He then quoted an old saying: "You can catch more flies with honey than with vinegar."

He got up to leave, and as his daughter went to fetch his cap from the hallway, he lowered his voice: "Listen, Panos, that fellow is a healthy, virile man, twenty-six years old. He needs a wife that will satisfy him. And Alexandra will suit him well."

But they had not reckoned with Alexandra who rebelled against any plans for a meeting with the schoolmaster until her grandfather took it upon himself to bring the girl to her senses— *sta kala tis*—as the Greeks would say.

Chapter Twenty-three

The day after John arrived to spend Easter in Zatouna, Constantine left the house early to attend to his work and left Alexandra to attend to his brother.

"It's such a lovely day," said Alexandra, "why don't we take a little jaunt to Dimitsana? I can do some shopping and it will give me a chance to return an embroidery pattern I borrowed from my cousin. I should have returned it well before now, and you can get some Athenian newspapers. They are delivered regularly there but they'll be several days old, of course, what with the Easter holidays." To a Greek a stale newspaper is far better than none. So, John went along with his sister-in-law unaware of her determination to save him from the bleak existence of his bachelorhood.

The children were fast asleep and John had gone to bed. Constantine wished he could do the same. His day had been tiring but he knew Alexandra was anxious to relate the results of the "little jaunt" she had taken with his brother to the nearby town of Dimitsana.

"How did it go?" he asked directly when they were alone.

Alexandra's immediate response was in the way of a drawnout sigh. Greeks are prone to sighing and through their sighs they convey a variety of subtle and complex feelings. Constantine recognized in his wife's dispirited sigh an undertone of perplexed resignation rather than downright defeat. Out of consideration for her present state of mind he refrained from reminding her that he had warned her that any matchmaking schemes involving his brother were foredoomed. He asked her instead in a sympathetic tone of voice what had gone wrong with her plans.

"Nothing had gone wrong with *them*," she said defensively. In fact, her plans had fallen into place better than she had expected. John was most agreeable about going to Dimitsana; and when she had finished her shopping and John had bought an armload of newspapers, they headed for Amalia's house, which fortunately is just around the corner from the main street, so John was not a bit inconvenienced by her errand. Alexandra caught sight of Amalia and Aphrodite through the lattice gate leading to the garden where they were watering the plants.

"Do come in," Amalia had cried out to them.

"And so we went into the garden," recounted Alexandra. "I could see John was surprised by its size. You don't find many town houses with such a grand one—and that view! That panorama with our little town snuggled against the side of the opposite mountain. I pointed out to him where our house is—you can't see it distinctly, of course, from where we were, but I could show John exactly where it is—by the two cypress trees you planted right beside it as soon as we were married. They have grown so tall that they can be seen clearly, the both of them standing side by side like sentinels—the way we stand, you and I, close together with God's help, guarding our home and our children."

Constantine smiled at her reference to the cypress trees.

"Ah, you seem to find my story amusing," she remarked, "well, when you hear the rest of it. . . ."

"No, it was just your remark about the trees that pleased me. But it's getting late," he reminded her, "and let's not get waylaid with irrelevancies, so, please, simply give me the facts about your thwarted mission. That's all I want to know."

"But Costa *mou*,*" she protested, "the facts *never* give a true picture. It's the little touches, the small details, a slight

---

*The Greeks use the possessive pronoun *mou* (my or mine) following a noun in the same casual or affectionate way that the French tend to use it before a noun.

gesture or expression. *They* tell the whole truth, not your *facts*!''

Constantine burst into laughter. "This little theory of yours could revolutionize the judicial system! You must tell your uncles about it. It will make those preeminent jurists in Athens think twice before depending on *facts* in making their legal decisions.''

Constantine's hilarity at her expense did not restrain his wife from continuing her narrative in her usual meandering style. Amalia, she went on to say, insisted that they sit on the terrace to rest a bit before going their way—and Aphrodite brought out a tray of refreshments. "I wish you could have seen her, Costa—you can't imagine how pretty she looked.''

"No, I can't,'' he admitted.

She ignored his remark but reaffirmed hers by murmuring, "Ah, yes, pretty as a picture, and she was adorable the way she kept giving John quick little side glances; she didn't look at him directly or say a word. You know how shy she is, but it was written all over her face that she was taken with him, poor girl, and when we left she embraced me even more warmly than usual and dear Amalia pressed my hand ever so tightly.''

"Well, I'm glad to know that John made such a good impression on your relatives.''

"The good impression your brother made on my relatives,'' retorted Alexandra, "was due not to *his* good manners but to *theirs*. They were kind enough to overlook his discourtesy when he declined to take a spoonful of *glyko* (a sweet, usually a conserve of some kind) or even a little sip of water to wish them *Kalo Pascha*—a good Easter. I know he's not fond of sweets, but even so, it's considered an affront to a hostess to refuse this common gesture of hospitality. What's more, he refused by shaking his head like a mute would do! But Amalia was gracious enough to pretend she hadn't noticed and chatted about this and that. What a gift she has for making conversation! She's never at a loss for words, you know.''

"Yes, indeed, I know, and so does everybody else who has heard her. Naturally in front of such a gifted and tireless talker like Amalia, John would be more tongue-tied than ever. As for his refusing to partake of the *glyko*, you must remember that he is the kind of man who would rather violate a conventional gesture than his own principles, and one of them is his disavowal of sweets on the grounds that their consumption is a form of weakness indulged in by women and children.''

It was now Alexandra's turn to break into laughter. "How absurd! And all the while I thought he simply didn't care for sweets.''

"I wouldn't call it absurd—just a little peculiar, perhaps.''

"Don't try to defend him, Costa! Wait till you hear what he had to say after we left Amalia's house.''

On their way back, related Alexandra, she was anxious to get John's impression of Aphrodite. She decided not to beat around the bush and asked him outright what he thought of her. "She won't do," he replied. Alexandra was greatly upset by this terse statement and she wanted to know exactly what he meant by it. "Just what I said," he replied, "she won't do, and if you must know why—she's a prattler, that's why.'' Oh, how could he say such a thing, Alexandra had cried out, why, Aphrodite hardly spoke a word!

John was not perturbed by his sister-in-law's indignation. He calmly remarked that *they all* put on the same act—shy and quietlike before a "prospect" but once they get hold of a man, God help him escape from their senseless prattle . . . like mother, like daughter . . . it never fails . . . he added grimly.

"Really, Costa, I was taken aback by your brother's verbal attack. He is always kind and gentle and this was so unlike him. Besides, what he said made no sense and I thought it was wiser not to take any further notice of these strange notions of his. I concentrated instead on Aphrodite's domestic virtues which I expected would appeal to him—knowing how meticulous your brother is. 'John,' I said, 'that girl is a marvel around the house; you have no idea what a perfect little housekeeper she is!' But before I had a chance to tell him more about her capabilities, he interrupted me—and guess what he had to say?''

"It's too late for guessing games,'' said Constantine, "so you better tell me before I fall asleep.''

"Well, he said—and I repeat his exact words: 'I am not interested in marrying a *housekeeper*. I can hire one any time I need to, and I can fire her any time I want to. I know you mean

239

well, Alexandra, but why don't you forget the whole thing?' ''

"So you found out that John has a mind of his own—and a romantic one at that.'' Constantine gave a little chuckle. "Besides, he gave you some good advice which I heartily second—to forget the whole business.''

"That's easy enough for you and your brother to say,'' exclaimed Alexandra in an aggrieved tone of voice, "but what am *I* to say to poor Aphrodite?''

"Don't worry about that. Aphrodite is more capable than you think and less innocent than you suppose. I have an idea that she will need neither your help nor her mother's to find a man for herself.'' And rising from his chair Constantine gave a long, deep yawn which put an end to their tête-a-tête.

When they went to bed, Alexandra fell asleep at once despite the frustration she felt at her brother-in-law's rejection of her matchmaking scheme. This enviable capacity for solid slumber was one of the means by which her immense vigor was regularly revitalized.

Sleep did not come as readily to Constantine as it came to his wife. Although he was a man of disciplined habits, his biological clock had a tyrannical will of its own. He, therefore, did not make the futile attempt to dispel his wakefulness; sooner or later Morpheus would take pity on him and gently close his eyes. His thoughts wandered aimlessly and the remarks Alexandra had made about the cypress trees came to his mind. He had merely smiled when she mentioned them but he had, in fact, been no less touched than pleased by her words, for they revealed the tender, symbolic meaning she gave to them now.

He remembered how painstakingly he had planted those two cypress trees—the finest specimens he could find to commemorate the most fortunate event of his life. But his wife had shown no particular interest in them at first . . . nor in their marriage, if the truth be told, which had taken place two years after their betrothal when she had turned sixteen and he had reached his twenty-eighth year. In the interim, they had met regularly but formally in the presence of others as the inflexible proprieties of their time demanded. She, therefore, did not have the opportunity to know him, let alone love him. And when they married, she performed her uxorial duties in so perfunctory a way as to hurt him deeply, but he was patient and kind and her love had slowly unfolded, and by the time Dionysios was born he no longer had cause to doubt it. He had come, in fact, to consider himself a most fortunate man with a devoted wife who was superior to any woman he had ever met—and who had given him a brilliant son and five lovely daughters.

Remembrances from the early years of his married life began to drift past his mind, led by the ever-bright recollection of Dionysios' birth—his first child and the only son he had been blessed with, thus far. He would never forget that moment—the wonder, the awe of it as the midwife placed the newborn infant in his arms. "You have a fine, healthy boy," she declared, "and a fine, healthy wife," she added admiringly. "It was the easiest first delivery I've come across in a long time, though I must confess I thought she'd have a hard time with those lean hips and that small waist of hers. But she's a strong one, all right, even though she looks like a delicate flower.

"Well, I must say it's a mighty good start, Kyr* Costa. When the next ones come along she won't even know she's giving birth; she'll drop 'em like eggs—if she's had the help of a good rooster to start with. . . ." The midwife made a clucking sound with her tongue and then broke into blatant laughter.

Cradling the baby with awkward tenderness, Constantine went to his wife's bedside. Never had she seemed lovelier to him than at that moment. Were it not for the tiny creature in his arms, he would have found it hard to believe she had just gone through the travail of childbirth. He kissed her gently and said, "We have a new bond between us now that will strengthen, I hope, whatever love you have for me."

She gave him no answer—only a smile. He felt his heart flooding with happiness as he laid the child at her breast and went to tell the world of his son's arrival; most of all he wanted his father to know. He would write to him at once.

As soon as his wife could travel they would go to Vancon, his native village. He could see his father's worn face, the

---

*The colloquial form of *Kyrios*, the Greek title for "Mr."

241

weary eyes, and how they would light up at the sight of his first grandchild—his first *grandson*! Yet, anxious as Constantine was to make this visit, he could not do so until his wife had fulfilled an ancient religious rite which was faithfully observed by the women of Alexandra's generation. A Greek Orthodox mother was not expected to leave the confines of her home until forty days had elapsed since the time of her accouchement. She then would take her infant to a special church service to seek through prayer and supplication the aid of Divine Providence and the Almighty's blessing for the well-being of the new life which had been entrusted to her. This appealing rite is still observed by some Greek women but the proscriptions which preceded it in the past are now considered impractical and are, on the whole, disregarded.

As soon as Alexandra could travel, Constantine had taken her and the child to his father's home in Vancon. He had not been there since the time following his marriage, which had taken place two years before at his wife's domicile in the village of Zatouna.

In accordance with the provincial customs of bygone times, a bride's *first* visit to her husband's homestead takes place directly after the wedding celebrations were exhausted. (They could last as long as three days depending on the importance of the union.) The newlyweds were then escorted by the relatives of the groom to his own village. In this particular instance, the distance between the two places required a journey of several hours, and the wedding party therefore travelled by horse with the bride and groom leading the way.

As the entourage headed for its destination, it stopped at various villages en route which were prepared for its arrival, thanks to the efficiency of the "grapevine" system of communication. To refuse the hospitality of the good villagers would be deemed an unforgivable affront to their generous offerings of sweetmeats and wine with which they expressed their heartfelt wishes for a long life full of health and happiness to the young couple—and for good measure they would add a toast or two for those who accompanied them. The felicitations of these simple folks were more exuberant than usual, for the bridegroom was a *didaskalos*—a member of the teaching profession which is highly

242

respected among the Greeks. As for his bride, both her father and her mother came from well-known Arcadian families—and, besides, she was a joy to behold!

Alexandra was attired in her nuptial finery, which a bride was expected to wear on the traditional visit to her husband's homestead. Her wedding dress was made of a handwoven raw silk in her favorite color—a deep shade of red (the "all-white" bridal outfit had not yet come into vogue), which enhanced her fair, flawless complexion. The long, slightly flared skirt emphasized her slim waist and the snug-fitting bodice revealed the firm lines of a young and vigorous body. A sheer, shoulder-length mantilla—dyed to match the color of her dress—lightly covered a little "cap" which was crushed to one side by a tassle; it was similar in style to the headgear worn by the *Evzones*, the Greek army's elite infantry corps traditionally recruited from the mountain regions.

Only in one respect did her appearance differ from the one she presented on the day of her wedding. She then had worn her husband's wedding gift—a wide gold bracelet wrought in the shape of ten miniature pyramids whose peaks were adorned by ten diamonds—a prophetic symbol of the number of children Alexandra would bear. And just before the wedding ceremony took place, Alexandra's father placed his mother's massive ruby ring on the finger of his daughter who had been named after her paternal grandmother, Alexandra Regas. This jewel must have been exceedingly valuable and beautiful for it had caused an irreparable rift between the two sisters. Alexandra's grandmother had a younger sister, Antigone, who fiercely coveted the ring and when it was given to the older sister as part of her dowry, Antigone's envy was so unremittingly bitter that she never spoke to her only sister again.

Alexandra wore no jewelry on her wedding trip. Her mother, Angeliki Regas, had advised against it. Concern for her daughter's safety was due not only to the likelihood of robbery by brigands, who roamed at large in the mountain areas, but to the dreaded superstition known the world over as the Evil Eye.

The display of material wealth along with God-given gifts was a means of attracting envy—the impulse which generates the lethal

243

force of the Evil Eye. "And who can tell," said Mrs. Regas, "if some wretched being who chanced to see a pretty bride, bedecked and bejewelled, might not bring her great or even fatal harm by a single glance from an evil eye?" Mrs. Regas dreaded this sinister power for she had witnessed it in all its horror. One day she had gone to the local meat market and while chatting with the proprietor as he filled her order, a stranger quietly entered the store. He was a peddler of sorts, judging from the dented kettles and pans and the broken or mended odds and ends hanging from a dilapidated wagon. He failed to extend the customary greeting, *kalimera*, good morning, but glanced directly at the poultry rack.

"I'll take that one," he said, pointing to one of the chickens, "without its shanks."

The butcher brought it down from the hook and laid it on a huge round of wood which had been cut from the trunk of a massive sycamore and served as a butchering block. It was darkened with age yet hardly dented despite the blows it had endured from a long line of butchers, who had dismembered on its surface a variety of ponderous beasts.

The stranger noticed the butcher's block and seemed stunned by its size. "Where," he asked as he stared at it increduously, "did that piece of wood come from?" He had never seen anything like it!

It came to him, the butcher replied, from his father, and as far as he knew his forefathers had practised their trade on this very piece of wood . . . "as I do now," he declared with pride. And to display his skill, the butcher tossed a small thin cleaver in the air with a well-practised flourish of his hand; twirling gently downward it landed on its cutting edge and neatly severed the chicken's scrawny shanks.

Alexandra's mother had seen the butcher perform this legerdemain more than once and she could not resist smiling at his childish desire to impress an itinerant peddler.

The smile froze on her lips as the small cleaver hit its mark. A strange sound like the sibilation of a thousand snakes seemed to rise from the very bowels of the wood. Suddenly the terrifying noise stopped and in the silence that followed the butcher block soundlessly split in two.

She would never forget that moment nor the moment after—when the peddler began to pound his eyes with his fists and moaned, "Oh, God! Would that You had blinded me than let Satan curse me with the Evil Eye!"

It would not have mattered whether or nor Alexandra had worn jewelry that would have aroused envy or an amulet that was supposed to counteract it. For she possessed a natural antidote for such malevolence—a radiance which obliterated the fearful shadow cast by the Evil Eye.

She accepted with her lovely smile the kind words of the rustic village youths and their elders who agreed to a man that she was as pretty a bride as they ever hoped to see! The village maidens, who were constrained to hide the emotions aroused in them by a newly married couple, gazed at her in silent admiration. As for the less inhibited matrons, they clearly conveyed with sly winks and nudges that the bride's glowing face indicated satisfaction with her mate. The handsome young *didaskalos* obviously knew a great deal more than teaching the school boys their letters.

Not until he came to his home ground did Constantine hear any criticism on his choice of a wife—a criticism he was in no position to refute until two years later when he had incontrovertible proof to do so. It was a direct aspersion on his judgment and it came from his own kin—from his father's Aunt Eurydice, a nonagenarian who was the oldest living member of the Douropoulos clam. *Theitsa,* "the little aunt," as she was affectionately called, had not attended the welcoming celebration in honor of the newlyweds, for her limbs were weakened by age, although her eyes were still sharp and so were her wits. She quite properly expected that Constantine and his bride would pay their respects to *her*—an obligation that the young couple duly fulfilled.

Alexandra looked particularly appealing the day she visited her husband's aged grandaunt. She was wearing one of her "trousseau" frocks; a white muslin trimmed in ruffles of delicate lace that edged its yoke, the neck and sleeves, and with a soft pink sash that tied at the back in a large, graceful bow. She had spied on the way a cluster of wild roses that matched its color, and Constantine bruised his fingers by their thorns which he removed with his penknife so that his bride might have a few blossoms to tuck at her waist. In her dainty stylish frock she was, as Constantine remembered her, a sight to brighten an old lady's eyes.

Aunt Eurydice was not interested, however, in feminine fashions but in female functions. She did not glance at Alexandra's attire but through it, so to speak, to reach the form beneath it and gauge its capacity for breeding. Her eye swiftly pierced the yards of muslin and lace to a bosom none too ample, to a midriff much too narrow and hips lean as only a lad's should be. "Where," she wondered "could that body find room for another?"

Poor Constantine . . . education hadn't done him much good; her own sons had gone only to grammar school but they had been smart enough to marry strong earthy women—not some pretty, hot flower raised among the landed gentry; and now the old lady was blessed with many descendants—how many, she could no longer remember.

A great part of Aunt Eurydice's memories lay beneath the heavy accumulations of her years. Yet, the passage of time had not effaced but enhanced some of her earliest recollections. She had unconsciously or deliberately forgotten the trials of her youth when as a little girl she had labored in the fields with her father and her brothers in order to insure their daily bread. She had preserved an illusion rather than the reality of her childhood and remembered it as a time when she had known the simple joys of childish play and laughter, of youth's sweet dreams and innocent desires—the magic time of life that was God's gift to the young and no one had the right to rob them of it. From her ancient vantage point, Constantine's bride looked infinitely young, too young to face the inescapable trials of matrimony and maternity (Alexandra was sixteen years old at the time, but then as, indeed, throughout her life, her extraordinary vivacity invariably belied her years). The critical appraisal Eurydice had just made of the young girl dissolved into sympathy. She gave Alexandra a kindly smile as one would give to a winsome child, but for Constantine she had a look of clear reproach which she made clearer still by saying: "You should have given her a doll to play with

246

instead of a wedding ring.''

Two years later when he returned to Vancon, Constantine lost no time in paying a visit ''en famille'' to the old matriarch.

When she saw the infant she offered the inevitable wish the Greeks give a child—''May it live.'' She gazed at it lovingly and declared it was a beautiful little creature . . . a *kouklaki*. . . a little doll! ''May God keep it from the Evil Eye,'' she said. And as an additional precaution she made a pretense of spitting which would help to ward off the harm that might come to so enviable a creature.

''Do you remember, Aunt Eurydice, what you said to me when we came to Vancon on our wedding trip?'' asked Cosntantine.

She shook her head. She feared she must be getting old. She couldn't even remember what she had eaten the meal before. ''For that matter neither can I,'' said her grandnephew, ''but I haven't forgotten what you told me two years ago—that I should have given Alexandra a doll to play with instead of marrying her.''

''Did I really say that? I can't imagine why!'' she exclaimed with an air of perplexity.

Constantine and Alexandra exchanged amused glances. What a sly old fox she was! Disregarding her remark, Constantine went on to say, ''Well, *Theitsa*, as you can see she has a doll, a living doll, to play with now.''

This was the last time he had seen that delightful, thorny, old woman whose generation was now extinct. He felt sorry that his children would not see the likes of her. Nor would they know how impoverished they were by the loss of that breed of simple, shrewd, kindly, rustic Arcadians. They had enriched his early years and their departure from this earth would had left a void within him—a void that no longer existed, for it had been filled by the woman who slept at his side. The wanton memories that had taken hold of his mind faded away as he listened to the tran-quil rhythm of her breathing like that of a tired child steeped in blissful slumber. The nearness and the warmth of her young strong body filled him with desire. Yet, he did not have the heart to awaken her in ''the first sweet sleep of night.'' He turned aside murmuring softly, *"Chrysi mou,* Alexandra,"* and fell asleep.

The next morning while Alexandra was busy attending to the children, the two brothers met alone at the breakfast table. When they had finished their coffee, John quietly announced that he would be leaving for Megalopolis before noon.

"You will do nothing of the sort, my good fellow," responded Constantine. "You came here to spend the Holy Week with us and you certainly cannot leave on Good Friday. It simply makes no sense, and besides, Alexandra would be very upset if you left before we celebrate Easter."

"I'm not so sure of that; I'm afraid I've already upset her. I suppose she told you what happened yesterday in Dimitsana."

"Yes, she did, before we went to bed last night."

"I couldn't seem to make her understand that I am not interested in getting married."

"That's your business, John, and I'm glad you refused to be pushed around on that score. It's not the first match that failed and it won't be the last one either. If all of them succeeded there would be no bachelors or spinsters around and since they exist it means that some people like you have doubts about that immemorial institution which matchmakers extol as the highest state of human bliss."

"I didn't mean to hurt your wife or her cousin or her cousin's daughter, but I made a mess of it."

"Come, now, let's not make a mountain out of an ant hill. Nobody has been hurt, least of all Aphrodite. Don't flatter yourself that much. I'm not denying that you are a pretty good catch what with your hearty youth, your good looks and a prospering little taverna, to boot. But if you think Aphrodite will pine over you, you're mistaken. That girl has a wicked gleam in her eye. I suspect, she'll find her own man, if she hasn't found him already. Now let's go and order the baby lamb for our Easter feast.

It did not take long before Constantine's suspicions were con-

---

*Literally, "my golden one," a phrase of endearment that may be loosely translated as "my beloved." These same words were the last ones Constantine Douropoulos murmured to his wife as his life came to an end.

248

firmed. Soon after Alexandra's matchmaking efforts had come to naught, Aphrodite eloped with the son of a local greengrocer. Amalia went into a dignified state of "semi-mourning." She kept to her garden where she could be seen through the lattice gate watering the plants—with her own tears it was said. She no longer wore gayly printed foulards or pretty paisley shawls but modest little frocks in drab greys and melancholy mauves. The only deviation from the ascetic garb to which Amalia was now committed was a black lace fichu that covered her shoulders and rose high around her neck with the aid of inflexible whalebones. Their stiffness prohibited a lowering of the chin, thereby forcing Amalia to hold her head defiantly high. By this painful means the grief and shame in the heart of a *mater dolorosa* were hidden from the public's prying eyes.

But a reconciliation between mother and daughter took place sooner than was expected when Aphrodite gave birth to a baby boy. Amalia rushed to her daughter's side, but not before she had given to each of the several churches in Dimitsana a munificent sum for prayers to be said in behalf of her daughter's safe delivery. These premature births could be highly dangerous! "But God be praised," said Amalia with delirious joy. Both her daughter and her grandson had been spared.

And all the *cosmos* marveled that an infant born well before its time could be so large and so lusty.

Chapter Twenty-four

When Constantine graduated from the Teachers' College in Athens, he needed to start earning a living as soon as possible. Upon receiving his diploma as a teacher, he was offered, due to his academic standing, the opportunity to teach in one of the Athenian suburbs. He refused this offer, however, for he wanted to get away "from the madding crowd's ignoble strife" in the burgeoning capital of Greece. He had grown up in the countryside and he hoped that he might acquire his teaching experience in a rural area near—or better still—in his native province of Arcadia, which was closer to his heart than the stilted atmosphere of the city—later on, in two or three years, he could spread his strengthened wings and find his way to a wider world.

No position was available at the time in the area he desired. Most schools in the rural areas were small and adequately manned by one or two teachers. But Constantine's finances were depleted, and he did not dare refuse the next offer which came to him through the pedagogical officialdom in Athens. (The Greek national government has the authority, with the approval of the Ministry of Education, to decide on the assignments of the public school teachers and is responsible for the payment of their salaries and pensions.)

He accepted with gratitude to teach in the outskirts of Kalamata, a prosperous Peloponnesian seaport whose deep purple, oval-shaped olives are prized for their distinctive tart flavor. It is an ancient town where the Frankish knight, Villehardouin, had built his castle in the Middle Ages.

Following the Fourth Crusade in which Villehardouin had served as a celebrated chronicler and strategist, he had conquered with the help of his compatriot, Willian Champlitte, all of *Morea* (the popular Greek name for the Peloponessus due to its geographical shape resembling a mulberry leaf). Kalamata was Villehardouin's fief and the elegant castle he built there was retained for a hundred years or so by his descendants. Its forlorn ruins, like those of others built during the Frankish occupation in Peloponessus, are reminders of the philhellenic Western conquerors whose chivalrous reign was incomparably benevolent compared to the rule imposed a few centuries later by the Oriental invaders on a proud but helpless people.

During the time Constantine Douropoulos taught school in the town of Kalamata, he was highly regarded as a teacher and esteemed as a gentleman and a scholar. And those who had marriageable daughters saw in him, as well, the makings of an exceptional husband—a view to which the matrons and maidens in the area wholeheartedly subscribed. In their intimate exchange of opinions, they considered the young handsome schoolmaster "a fine figure of a man" and not without good reason. Constantine's naturally graceful physique had been further enhanced by the training he received at the Athenian School of Gymnastics. His diploma from that institution states that "Constantine A. Douropoulos has satisfactorily completed the full course in gymnastics as required of public school teachers by the Ministry of Religious and Public Education in the Kingdom of Greece."

From a practical standpoint, which the Greeks seldom overlook—as far as matrimonial considerations are concerned—the teaching profession which Constantine had chosen offered a steady income with the added advantages of a pension plan unusually liberal at the time it was established: teachers and their widows received lifetime benefits from the accrued amount of pensions; daughters were granted a proportionate sum until they married, and if marriage did not take place, these benefits continued until their death. Sons received a similar allowance which was discontinued, however, when they became of age.

In view of Constantine's personal merits, as well as his present and future capabilities, he received many "proposals," one of which a less conscientious young man might not have been able to resist. Certain obligations he had towards the members of his family, however, especially those regarding his young unmarried sister, Theone, precluded any personal considerations for matrimony. His essential concern at the time was to see his sister happily married.

It was not, however, merely a sense of fraternal duty that led Constantine and his brothers, no less, to provide Theone with a decent dowry at the cost of their own welfare—but a sense of deep gratitude and devotion towards their little sister who had sacrificed the tender years of her childhood to take care of them since their mother's untimely death.

After teaching for two years nearby the town of Kalamata, Constantine was assigned as schoolmaster in Zatouna, a village in the heart of the Arcadian Mountains. His appointment to this particular place was purely fortuitous as far as he was concerned; yet, he knew it well by hearsay, for it was in this place his maternal grandmother, Katerina Karanicholas, was born and bred. When she married she left home to live in Vancon, her husband's village which was also located in the province of Arcadia, a few hours' ride south of Zatouna between Tripolis and Megalopolis.

Constantine was about eight or nine years old when his grandmother died. He remembered her as a sweet old lady whose faded eyes would sparkle whenever she spoke of her homeland. Badly crippled by rheumatism, Katerina had aged before her time and had given up hope of seeing her birthplace again, which she had visited regularly when her limbs were straight and strong.

Like the women of her day, she was deeply devout and accepted her suffering as a trial by which her faith and fortitude would be tested before she could be deemed worthy to pass through the gates of Heaven. She had rationalized her ailment to the point of considering it a blessing. She could no longer muster the strength needed for the tiring journey to her former home which, she rationalized, would pain her far more than it

252

could please her, for with the passing of the years Katerina would no longer find her kin but only their graves. In time she could no longer walk. She spent the hours patiently sitting in a chair or lying on her bed without a word of complaint. Yet, beneath the Christian stoicism that Katerina practised, the longing to see her homeland once again before she died, gnawed at her heart more and more each day, and when she could stand it no longer, she determined to leave her wasted, twisted body lie motionless in Vancon while her spirit and her mind returned to Zatouna.

From then on, she was no longer aware of her present surroundings. She prattled for hours on end about her native village: the crystal-clear, icy cold water that gushed ceaselessly from five mountain springs since time out of mind, the cliffs and gorges that fell from the road in sheer shafts of granite down to the Lousios River that slithered like a silver snake at the feet of the mountains. It was here, in this very river, she had been told by a learned uncle of hers, that the water nymphs bathed Zeus when he was an infant, for his mother, Rhea, had hidden him in Arcadia away from Kronos, his father, who had the unpleasant habit of eating his children.

She would often describe the houses of Zatouna—lovely old houses constructed of native stone with red tile roofs and built in the simple square or oblong Arcadian style. But the large ones, with two and three stories, boasted of arched doors made of thick oak wood with pretty little balconies above them that overflowed with fragrant flowers and sweet-smelling herbs. Many of these old houses had arched windows as well as arched doorways which, according to Katerina's learned relative, were remnants of the influence exerted by the Venetians who off and on had invaded and conquered Peloponessus in centuries past.

One of the most handsome houses, Katrina maintained, belonged to Constantine Thanopoulos who was called Captain "Costakis." It had a large *sala*—a parlor with marble walls, if you please. She had seen it more than once when she went along with her parents to wish Mr. Thanopoulos *chronia polla*—"many years" on his nameday, the feast day of Saint Constantine and Saint Helen, which holds a high place in the roster of Orthodoxy's saints.

253

The future grandfather of Alexandra, Costakis Thanopoulos, joined the guerilla forces when he was a mere youth. By the time the Revolution was over he had achieved the rank of Captain. In the interim, his father died and the young captain returned home. He soon married and as the oldest son he assumed his responsibilities as head of the family.

Costakis had inherited a substantial estate as well as a civic and social consciousness that characterized the Thanopoulos clan. The first beneficent gesture he made was to donate a piece of property to replace the small, modest graveyard that was in use at the time. It was, and still is, a choice site above the church— facing a majestic panorama of the Arcadian Mountains. Encircled by tall, somber cypress trees, the cemetery has a serene, elegaic beauty that the Captain apparently considered a befitting place of eternal rest for the dead of Zatouna.

To her dying day, Katerina Karanicholas, the maternal grand-mother of Constantine Douropoulos, could vividly recall those visits to the Captain's house. They were truly "feast days" such as she had not experienced later in her husband's village of Van-con. How could she ever forget that carved oaken sideboard ladened with a glorious array of sweetmeats, brightly lit by two enormous brass oil lamps. Each had half a dozen upturned spouts that poured forth a shimmer of golden flames.

Ah, yes, indeed, those were gracious times, peopled with gracious folk like the Captain and his genteel wife, Sophia, greeting their well-wishers, young and old, with equal cordiality.

Sophia, who came from a fine family with excellent connec-tions, was a well-bred, pretty little woman. But Katerina was not as impressed with her as much as she was with her husband. Costakis was an attractive young man, tall and spare, who wore with virile elegance the garb of the day—the white, pleated foustanella that flowed gracefully from his waist to the knee; his maroon velvet jacket was richly adorned in bands and scrolls of gilt soutache. And on his small, crimson cap jauntily crushed to one side by a heavy black silk tassle, could be seen a small gold cockade—the insignia of his military rank.

Some of the residents of Zatouna did not, however, share Katerina's admiration for the young captain. They envied rather than admired him not only because of the size of his patrimony but his ability to increase its worth.

When Costakis returned home from the Revolution he established an enterprise for the production of a bright red dye called *prinokoki* obtained from a parasite which thrives on the Mediterranean holm oak. Before chemical dyes were perfected, this product was in great demand by the Mid-Eastern countries for dying the scarlet fezzes traditionally worn by Moslem males.

Costakis' detractors hid their envy under the guise of jocular ridicule. Wasn't it comical, they said, the lengths to which the Captain would go for the sake of hygiene? It was really quite absurd—that closet-like structure he had built next to a rear corner of his house with a drain on the floor and with a piece of perforated metal on the top. It was conveniently located close to the kitchen from where a kettle or two of hot water could easily be had and poured through the roof on Kyr Thanopoulos as he performed his daily ablutions. The next thing you know, they would say laughing uproariously, he'll be building outhouses for his livestock.

Katerina's father often said that Thanopoulos did not count his money; he simply weighed it, for his venture had proven highly profitable and he was paid in gold coinage for his services. Not that her father was jealous. He was a decent, God-fearing man satisfied to make a respectable living by selling silk goods, a product of Zatouna, in all of Arcadia as well as in other Peloponessian provinces.

Sericulture had existed for centuries in Zatouna, judging from the age of some of the mulberry trees. According to reliable dendrologists, who had examined them in the early part of the twentieth century, they were more than five-hundred years old.

Several industries besides the vital ones of agriculture and animal husbandry were thriving in Katerina's village during her lifetime. When Zatouna was, indeed, a thriving town, she could recall two large tanneries, a gunpowder mill, as well as gold, silver and tin smitheries, barrel making, and a weaving factory, no less, for the production of cotton, wool and silk articles. It really wasn't a factory, Katerina said, but Kyr Sterios' grand house—all of four stories high, if you included the huge cellar which was hardly to be considered as one since it was practically on the ground level with plenty of clear light and clean air. The looms, at least sixty of them, were scattered throughout the house where the weavers worked in comfort and were even served coffee, if you please!

Needy women gathered from far and near to make a day's pay by weaving. Ah, yes, indeed, many a poor girl and destitute widow lit a candle for that good man's health and later in his blessed memory. Thanks to him, they could make from this respectable woman's work enough money to provide themselves with a dowry or a decent living and thus be saved from the curse of old maidenhood and penury. He was a saint, all right, Kyr Sterios was. May God rest his soul.

The last formal visit Katerina paid to Capetan Thanopoulos on his nameday was shortly before she left Zatouna to live in her future husband's village of Vancon, which was also located in Arcadia, south of Zatouna between Tripolis and Megalopolis.

The Captain no longer patted her on the head and saying, as he had in the past, that she was "a pretty little girl." Instead he had exclaimed in surprise that she had grown up so quickly . . . and about to be married. It seemed hardly possible! The youths in Zatouna, he remarked, must be blind to let her slip away. But their loss was her gain, for he had been informed that her fiancé, Nikos Karanicholas, was a splendid fellow and an exemplary soldier during the Revolution. He had heard this from Captain Hadjichristos, himself, who had offered to act as *koumparos*, as the sponsor at their wedding—as fine a tribute as a man could have from his former military superior.

Little did Katerina dream, as she blushingly accepted his compliments and best wishes, that in the course of time her oldest grandson, Constantine Douropoulos would choose as a wife Alexandra, the youngest granddaughter of Costakis Thanopoulos, who was in Katerina's eyes the finest gentleman in all of Zatouna.

Disoriented as her mind may have been, in her later years, Katerina did not make the mistake—an unforgivable one as far as the inhabitants of Zatouna were concerned—of referring to her birthplace as a "village." She invariably spoke of it as a

256

comopolis, a term applied to a larger than average community and possessing a degree of sophistication which is lacking in the typical provincial Greek village. These "little pockets of culture," as well as most of the Arcadian settlements, were established sometime during the pre-Byzantine epoch, for according to Pausanias, the indefatigable traveler and geographer, the Arcadia of the past no longer existed in his time. In the eighth volume of his *Descriptions of Greece*, written in the second century, A. D., he records his impression of Arcadia, the once-renowned Peloponnesian province, ruled by the legendary Pan, whose realm was famous in the ancient days for its natural beauty, its pastoral charm, and for the wealth of its political history and the riches of its mythological lore.

Pausanias did not find the Arcadia whose praises the world had sung, but an area mostly covered by a dense forest which he feared to explore. It was no longer the habitat of mortals, of gods and goddesses, of nymphs and sprites, but the dark domain of wild beasts and birds of prey.

Arcadia was eventually repopulated but the origin and names of the early settlements are not to be found in the dim annals of the recurrent invasions and conquests that befell the hapless Greeks in the centuries that followed the birth of Christ. Time and again primitive bands appeared from the north of Europe and left after they had ravished the land. The large hordes of Slavs that came in their wake remained, however, in Peloponnesus leading a pastoral life for two hundred years until 850 A. D. when the Greeks routed them and regained their territory.

Some of the historians interested in the provenance of Arcadian settlements tend to believe that those bearing Slavic names such as Zatouna, Dimitsana, Arachova, Valtetsi, etc. were very likely established during the Slavic visitation on Peloponnesian soil. Although no agreement has been reached as to the exact date of their emergence, there is no doubt, however, that most of these communities reached the peak of their prosperity in the seventeen hundreds.

The greater part of the eighteenth century was relatively less difficult for the Greeks than it may have been for their rulers, who were beset by the internal and external conflicts which faced the Ottoman empire during that period. The lessening to a limited degree of the stranglehold the Moslem suzerainty had on their Christian subjects was evident in the opportunity given them to avoid "forced labor" by contributing money in lieu of their personal services. Also, the infamous *paidomazoma*, "the tribute of children," was suspended in the last quarter of the previous century. Up to that time, Turkish overlords or their senechals toured the provinces and handpicked boys of tender age who were sent to Constantinople to be indoctrinated in the Islamic ideology and faith. After a process of thorough "de-Hellenization" they became Janissaries, the notorious infantrymen of the Turkish army.

The Greeks felt no greater horror than the sight of the white silk banners with verses from the Koran embroidered in gold which the Janissaries proudly flaunted as they slaughtered those whose blood matched their own.

Chapter Twenty-five

The villages of Arcadia, particularly those perched on remote mountainous areas, are little known beyond their periphery. Zatouna, the birthplace of Constantine Douropoulos' grandmother and wife, is located on one of the steep elevations in the Manalon Mountain Range. Access to it can be gained only by way of Dimitsana, a picturesque medieval town, about two and a half miles away. The connecting road that follows a series of vertiginous twists and turns on the edge of cliffs and gorges is more likely to arouse trepidation in the faint-hearted than admiration at the display of nature's grandeur.

Despite the poor interconnections of the cities, towns and villages in Greece before the twentieth century, travelers and visitors oftentimes came to Zatouna. One of these was William F. Leake,* an Englishman, hired by the Turkish government to survey the Peloponnesos. He reached Zatouna in 1805 and describes it as a verdant town with pretty gardens, cypress groves and a multitude of walnut, fig, sycamore, mulberry and birch trees. He notes a variety of workshops, several tanneries and leather dyeing industries—as for the climate, he endorses it as being excellent.

---

*William F. Leake (1777-1862) was an antiquarian as well as a topographer. During his assignment in Greece, he amassed an invaluable collection of antiquities, part of which was presented to the British Museum; the rest was purchased by the University of Cambridge and is displayed at the Fitzwilliam Museum in Cambridge, England.

259

By the end of the nineteenth century, the villages and towns of Peloponnesos were already in an inexorable process of decline. Since less than one-third of Greek land is arable, economic distress had forced many of the young to seek a livelihood beyond their provincial borders. The more fortunate youths with the means for a higher education went to Athens where they earned their diplomas and settled permanently in the city or in a large town to exercise their respective professions. Those who could find no work were drawn to America by the glittering vision of a fresh world that held the sweet promise of a better life.

Many of the Arcadian towns and villages were stripped of "all the bloomy flush of life." They slowly withered and finally fell into a stage of lethargy. The village of Zatouna (still referred to as a *comopolis* by its native born sons and daughters) was in its prime the "capital" of the county of Gortynia, but by the end of the second quarter of this century its entire population could have filled no more than a corner of its church. And yet, toward the end of the 1960's this now insignificant little village suddenly became the focal point of international publicity.

After the coup d'etat by the "colonels" that brought Greece under a military rule in April 21, 1967, Zatouna was chosen for the incarceration of a prominent political figure. The prisoner was Mikis Theodorakis, the eminent composer, well-known in America for his songs in *Zorba the Greek*, and for "Z," an Oscar-winning film.

The political odyssey on which Theodorakis had embarked from his early youth became increasingly turbulent through the years, and during the fascist rule of the junta leaders it reached the headlines in many of the leading European and American newspapers.

The first paragraph in one of the several articles regarding Theodorakis appeared as follows in the New York Times:

London, Sunday March 16, 1969

The Sunday Times published today what it describes as excerpts from two letters by the Greek composer, Mikis Theodorakis, denouncing the Greek military-backed regime. The letters were said to have been smuggled to a Sunday Times reporter, who had hiked to the village of Zatouna in the wild Arcadian Mountains where the 43-year-old composer had been banished with his wife and two young children . . .

Theodorakis in the same article refers to Zatouna as "the isolated village where I am detained . . ." from where he managed, nevertheless, to send to the outside world the score for "Z," which increased his fame internationally.

On August 21, 1968, Theodorakis was ordered to leave for Zatouna where his wife, Myrto, a physician, and his two children, Margarita and Yiorgos, joined him a few days later.

The heavily armed police who were bringing their prisoner to his exile, first saw Zatouna from a distance. It looked like a typical, small Arcadian village nestled snugly in the arms of Mount Bouphagion, one of the tall Menalon Mountains in the Peloponnesos. But, as they drew near, it no longer seemed like an ordinary provincial village but a veritable stronghold protected by a natural pallisade of ravines and cliffs and a gorge close to a thousand feet deep that stretched down towards the roaring waters of the Lousios River.

No one but a highly dangerous political figure would be banished to a place not only difficult to reach but from where escape would be practically impossible. Theodorakis' security guards felt a sense of heightened importance. They looked at him with fresh interest that combined respect as well as admiration. Their prisoner, a large-sized man of lofty stature, was a charismatic leader whose music and words stirred his countrymen and aroused, especially among the young, the desire to join the Resistance Movement against the evils of dictatorship.

Scores of his comrades and followers had been summarily executed, mysteriously murdered and killed by "accident" or had simply disappeared. But the colonels did not dare to order Theodorakis' liquidation for fear of repercussions within the land which would be heard, as well, by music lovers and humanitarians the world over. They did not hesitate, however, to subject the composer to intermittent arrest and imprisonment replete with brutality and torture. By these and other inhuman ordeals his tormentors succeeded in breaking down his health, but they failed to destroy his spirit.

During the fourteen months the composer and his family were detained in Zatouna, they lived under strict surveillance in a small house which was a stone's throw from the village square. On this *plateia*, as a square or plaza is called in Greek, formerly stood the home of Alexandra Douropoulos' father, Panos Regas, a direct descendant of the earliest settlers of Zatouna. Alexandra's father was deeply attached to the youngest of his offspring. All of his children were notably attractive but this, his second daughter, who was born when he was no longer young, seemed to him the most winsome, the most spirited of his brood. Besides, she bore his beloved mother's name which, according to firmly established custom, should have been given to his first-born daughter. Apparently Panos Regas was an uncommonly uxorious husband for his time; he had conceded to his wife's wishes to call their first child, Sophia, after his recently deceased mother-in-law. An interval of twenty years elapsed during which his wife gave birth to one son after another before their last child, a daughter, arrived. Overjoyed, he took the infant girl in his arms and rocking her gently he kept whispering, "You have come back, *manoula mou*, my little mother, you have come back to me at last!"

Alexandra Douropoulos returned for a visit to her birthplace in the fall of the early nineteen thirties. She wept with joy to see her aged sister and wept with sorrow for her brothers, who were but a tender memory now. And she felt her heart would break at the state in which she found her former home—the old stone house where her parents had lived until the day they died, where she and her siblings were raised, where she had given birth to all but her two American-born children, Arthur and Elly.

Before she had so much as glanced at the house, she knelt and kissed the marble stepping stone. Through her tears she saw the deep crack that ran along its breadth. Close to a quarter of a century before she left for America, that ancient piece of marble was solid and with a patina that came from the countless footsteps of her forefathers, who had known no other home but this.

The whole house seemed to sag from the weight of its

decrepitude. Wherever Alexandra looked she saw the ravages of time and neglect. The heavy boards covering the windows hung askew revealing faded shutters that were once a vivid blue, the very color of the sky. Many of the structural stones were lost. They had left ugly gaps like missing teeth through which rain and snow and wind had entered and added to the general destruction. One corner of the house from which the stones had altogether disappeared clung mid-air in naked peril. As Alexandra looked at the desolate scene, remorse began stirring within her. If she had not left her father's house to the merciless elements, would it have come to this pathetic state? But she reminded herself that she had not abandoned it. She had left it in the hands of a trustworthy caretaker whose death a few years later was beyond her control and nobody else could be found to replace him. The number of empty houses were increasing steadily as the older generation died, and the young had no desire to remain in a place where the only source of excitement was a funeral now and then.

Alexandra was so constituted as to give short shrift to past regrets and future anxieties. Her enormous vitality automatically converted them into action. She wasted no time or energy in brooding but concerned herself with what should or could be done in the immediate present. She resolved then and there to have her ancestral home razed and the property on which it stood she would deed to the village of Zatouna—not to be sold or to be built on ever again, but to be used for the common good of Zatouna's inhabitants. Let the village fathers decide what to do with it. Surely some beneficent way would be found to utilize a piece of land in the heart of the village that was double the size of the usual lot due to its large courtyard.

Ah, that lovely courtyard . . . Alexandra had grown up in it practically as an only child. Her sister, Sophia, who was twenty years older than Alexandra, had married and had a home of her own before her baby sister had learned to walk; her brothers had also left home, one by one, to make their own way by the time she had reached her early childhood. Thus, Alexandra had the courtyard to herself, so to speak, to do as she pleased without interference from older siblings. She came to feel it was her private province, a kind of pleasance, where she could play or dream and talk to herself as children often do. But she preferred the company of her numerous young cousins and friends than being alone, for she was by nature a gregarious little creature with an unusual capacity for sociability in one so young.

Many of the little girls who came to play with her lived in larger and finer houses, two and three stories high, while Alexandra lived in a very old house that had only one floor; still none of them, they admitted, had a better courtyard. Besides, Alexandra's mother, Aunt Angeliki, as the children called her, treated them like grown-ups. She always prepared a large pitcher of *soumatha*, a milky-white beverage made with almond paste and water, and a plate of fruits and nuts and raisins. After they had tired of their games, they sat beneath the old plane tree that stood in the middle of the courtyard. And Alexandra would offer her little friends refreshments from a gleaming copper tray and give them each a tea napkin of linen that was embroidered in a scallped edge all around—the kind that was reserved for special guests at *their* house. Anyone watching the eight-year-old girl serving her playmates with effortless poise would have seen in her the makings of an extraordinary hostess.

Alexandra had yet to look at the courtyard. But she had seen enough, more than enough. Why add to the pain she had already endured? She started to walk away averting her glance from its crumbling walls. She had taken no more than a few steps when she suddenly turned around and went to the courtyard's gate, impelled by the irresistible magic of the past.

Through the wrought-iron lattice Alexandra first caught sight of the old plane tree and she smiled. The "ugly-beautiful" tree she called it when she was a child. It looked no different now than when she had seen it last, a quarter of a century ago. Its thick, rough trunk was still grotesquely knotted and gnarled; the wide-spreading branches were heavy with foliage that would not wither until the end of fall. The rich green leaves looked fresh and shiny as though they had just unfurled. An early morning shower had washed away the dust from their smooth surface so that the sun caught their sparkle as they turned and twisted in the mountain breeze.

That blessed, brave, old tree defying the ruthlessness of nature! It made Alexandra forget the desolation surrounding it and brought to her mind a time when the plane tree stood proudly in a setting that did it honor. Shortly after her marriage, the courtyard had undergone a number of improvements which greatly enhanced its charm. It had become, in her mother's words, "our little paradise." And this happy state of affairs was the end result of Adam Eliades' unexpected visit.

Adams Eliades, whom Constantine had known from his student days in Athens, came to Zatouna while on a "field trip," as he called his periodic sallies into the provinces. He was an architect with a proclivity for landscape designing. Whenever he could get away from his work in Athens, he sought the countryside where he could escape the pretentious dwellings and garish gardens that proclaimed their owners' tasteless wealth. They made a travesty of Pericles' observation that the Athenians "achieve beauty at little cost" which was, however, still eminently applicable to the village folk in the provinces. With nothing more than a few old clay pots or discarded metal containers, they transformed an ordinary window sill into an enchanting bower and glorified a humble doorway. The sight of these simple aesthetic expressions never failed to move Adam and to reaffirm his faith in his countrymen's innate sense of beauty.

Alexandra clearly remembered Adam's visit that had occurred almost half a century ago. She had an implausible memory combined with the ability to recall distant events, not as dim shadows of past realities, but with the same vitality she experienced at whatever had taken place in her life.

He appeared early one Saturday morning in May. Constantine and Alexandra had returned late and tired the night before, from their nuptial journey. The next morning they sat in the courtyard having their coffee. Alexandra was relating the highlights of their visit to Vancon for her parents' benefit when they heard the peal of the dooryard bell. Constantine took one look at the figure standing by the gate and sprang from his chair. The next moment the two were locked in an exuberant embrace—the way Greeks commonly express their affection, without embarrassment or self-consciousness.

After a flurry of introductions and the verbal amenities that follow them, Constantine suggested taking his friend for a tour of Zatouna before the sun lost its softness—an idea to which his friend subscribed, "But not before I take a little tour of this lovely courtyard, if I may. . . ."

"By all means," Alexandra's father replied, somewhat taken aback by the young man's interest in the immediate surroundings. As Adam looked around, his eyes lit up with pleasure.

"It's as splendid," he remarked, "as any I've seen around these parts! Whoever planned it had a marvelous sense of landscaping."

"I'm afraid I can't enlighten you," said Mr. Regas. "All I know is that it's been here a long time. My forefathers like many others came to these highlands centuries early on during Ottoman occupation. You may be sure those Turkish blackguards thought twice before coming up to these steep mountain areas."

"Yes, of course," agreed Adam rather vaguely as he began to walk around the courtyard. "That fellow," he murmured "whoever he might have been, was truly inspired—to clear this site and yet leave a plane tree when he planned the courtyard. He was a generous, spirited man, for he chose a stripling of a tree so that it would be around long after he was gone for the enjoyments of his descendants. And he also had the foresight to make the courtyard in ample dimensions so that when the tree reached its full growth it would not shade the entire area; without direct sunlight this stone wall would not be like the fairy ring it is now, garnered with masses of marvelous saxetile flowers you can enjoy while sitting under the shade of that fine old tree. And let me tell something more about your unknown benefactor. He could have chosen to construct the wall with stones and mortar, but that would not have encouraged vegetation. Instead he made a dry wall so he could place as he went along some plants in the soil that is layered between the stones and in their crevices and grooves. As the plants rooted and multiplied they not only held the stone securely in place but swathed, as well, the whole wall with a blanket of living beauty."

"Indeed, he was our benefactor," said Mrs. Regas in her gentle way. "May God rest his soul. I have yet to see any other wall

266

so completely covered with plants.''

"And their variety," remarked Adam, "is astonishing—dittany, restharrow, centaurea, mandrake, scarlet pimpernel . . . what's it doing here, I wonder? It normally grows in a damp place not on __"

"What about our walk?" interrupted Constantine. "You haven't changed a bit, Adam. I remember we never got very far when we decided to take a stroll. We were waylaid each time by a garden, a wall, a tree or bush or even a batch of ordinary weeds and you would show off, as you're doing now, your botanical erudition."

"Let's go," cried Adam, "before you expose any more of my failings."

A few weeks later Adam sent them a sketch of the courtyard drawn precisely to scale. In place of the old wooden gate was a wrought-iron one whose curves formed the shape of an ancanthus, the ancient plant which adorns the Temple of Zeus in Athens; a set of garden chairs, carved with the same motif, surrounded a large, circular table that swept around the plane tree's trunk; the bare ground was laid with tiles in a simple geometric design. The only evidence of any structural change was a slight one in the form of a small niche in the center of the wall opposite the courtyard's entrance. Its only decoration was a bed of ivy. If you decide, wrote Adam, to make these changes and additions, I shall gladly send you detailed specifications. Fortunately they can be had or made reasonably within your own province, where I have come across some of the finest craftsmen in the Peloponnesos. As for the niche, we'll find something to put in it later.'

Alexandra was very pleased with Adam's drawing. It was not only lovely, but it showed, as well, how comfortable the courtyard could be with a few improvements. How clever of Constantine's friend to think of covering the earthen floor, that was always dusty and drab, with those handsome tiles! "But, wouldn't they be costly?" she asked her husband, "No, not if they could be made locally, as Adam had suggested," he replied. The expense was not, however, Constantine's immediate consideration, but the time and effort required to do the job was the problem and he could spare neither one. Oh, yes, Alexandra realized that, but she could see to it herself. Constantine questioned her apparent naiveté. Had it not occurred to her that women were not expected to run about the countryside for workman or artisans and making deals or contracts with them? It was another matter for a woman to hire or to supervise harvesters as her mother did on their own land. *They* came looking for work and if none showed up then it was a man's responsibility to go about finding them.

Alexandra was not to be daunted. She would get her father to go with her, she said. She had noticed he was getting listless, not active enough for a man in his early seventies—and if she could not persuade him to do what was good for his health, then she could go with her cousin, Dr. Keninis, who knew Arcadia like the palm of his hand, thanks to his reputation throughout the province. "I'm sure," she said, "he would know exactly where we could find whatever is needed. We have nothing to lose by asking him, at least."

"I think you had better ask your father first if he is willing to go along with these 'improvements' as you call them. After all, it is his house," said Constantine. But he had no doubt that before long the courtyard would be just as Adam envisioned it. He was beginning to realize that the very young, the very pretty girl he had married was a remarkable woman.

The following summer, Adam returned to Zatouna to find the courtyard a replica of his drawing—down to the bed of ivy in the "little grotto," as Alexandra called it. She had transplanted the ivy in the early spring and it was already flourishing. In the midst of its glossy foliage Adam placed the small statue he had brought with him from Athens, "A belated wedding gift," he explained apologetically. It was a terra-cotta figure playing on a reed pipe. On its head were a pair of tiny horns and pointed ears; and it had the hairy legs and the cloven hoofs of a goat. Alexandra clapped her hands in glee at this image of the droll deity the ancient Arcadians worshipped. Where had Adam ever found him! Constantine voiced the suspicion that his frined had found this "noisy merrymaker," as he was called in the *Homeric Hymn to Pan*, well before he had put the little grotto in his sketch—in fact, that was why Adam had included it.

"Yes, I confess I've had him for quite a while and could hardly bear to part with him," replied Adam, "but he really belongs here in Arcadia. One can't imagine Pan anywhere else seeking out a quiet little haunt, now and then, where he could come and regain his composure by playing on his pipes after chasing woodland nymphs all over his domain. His ardor for those lovely creatures was unrequited and understandably so, for the poor fellow was abominably ugly." Adam stopped his little dissertation to gaze fondly at the statue. He hoped they really liked it as much as he did, otherwise he would find something else to bring them. "Ah, Adam was sorry, now, wasn't he?" Constantine asked laughlingly—sorry that he had brought them his precious Pan, but his wife was obviously taken with him, so it was too late to take him back. "Indeed it is! He's going to stay," Alexandra declared adamantly, "just where he is—in the little grotto. He looks perfectly charming there."

Some of Zatouna's residents questioned the changes that had taken place in the Regas courtyard. They said it had been good enough for Alexandra's parents just as they had found it and which they had enjoyed all these years without any of those high falutin' trappings. And that shameless statue, just what was the sense of that? Well, *that* was going a bit too far. They simply could not understand how decent Christians would tolerate that indecent "goat-god" smack in the middle of their wall, may God forgive them! Undoubtedly, it was all Alexandra's doings, but to a great extent her mother and father were to blame; they had spoiled her, and now her husband was following suit—married only a year and letting her traipse around without him, mind you, twice as far to Patras and Athens—to visit her fancy relatives, and coming back each time with a new frock or two. They shook their heads and wondered what Alexandra would do next. . . .

What Alexandra did next was to start a family. Her children came along regularly and enjoyed from their earliest days the charm and comfort of the courtyard, thanks to their father's friend, Adam Eliades, who became known, in time, as a pre-eminent *architecte paysagiste*. He was commissioned to landscape the First Cemetery of Athens, where many of the illustrious citizens of Greece are buried. This oldest of Athenian cemeteries contains some of the finest examples of contemporary Greek sculpture. Among the most moving is "The Sleeping One," a Pentelic marble statue of a young gentlewoman lying in her tomb, whose tranquil features reveal the acceptance of untimely death with patrician grace.

Alexandra's gift of her patrimonial property was accepted with gratitude. In years past, native sons of Zatouna, who had prospered in the diaspora during the Turkish domination of Greece, had bequeathed impressive sums of money for the betterment of their birthplace. But land on which a domicile was established was considered a sacred legacy to be passed down from one generation to the next, even if the dwellings thereon were reduced to rubble. The council of elders voted to level the old house and wall (among themselves they spoke of the Regas place as an eyesore) and the sooner it was demolished, so much the better. They recognized, nevertheless, that Alexandra's generosity was unusual, and as a gesture of their appreciation they promised to erect a large, handsome plaque designating the area as PLAZA ALEXANDRA.

If the promised plaque had ever been placed where the Regas house once stood, it had disappeared years later when Mikis Theodorakis came to Zatouna. The so-called plaza was nothing more than a broader section of the main street, which had been enlarged since the village had acquired Alexandra's former property. Part of it was used as a parking lot for those who, for some reason or other, drove to the village on the widened yet still precarious road from Dimitsana. Alexandra would have been grieved but not greatly surprised by these developments, for the villages of Greece had undergone radical changes in the twentieth century. What would have greatly shocked her, however, was that her birthplace could be considered suitable for harboring a prisoner!

But she would have rejoiced that the same spirit of generosity characterized the new inhabitants of Zatouna as it had the citizentry of old. The villagers did not look upon Thedorakis as a renowned composer, nor did they view him as a highly controversial figure whose leftist ideology had brought him in their midst.

270

They saw him essentially as a *xenos*, a term which in Greek applies both to a stranger and a visitor or guest, and in keeping with age-old custom both are accorded an equal degree of *philoxenia*, the Greek word for hospitality.

The prisoner and the house where he lived with his wife and two children were guarded twenty-four hours a day by a convey of gendarmes. No one was permitted to speak to Theodorakis or to get near him, yet the villagers never failed to greet him though both men and women ran the risk of being summoned to the police station where they were roughly searched and handled, interrogated and threatened. No one defied the authorities more deliberately than *Kyra* Lenio, the shepherdess, who brought fresh milk regularly for the prisoner's children. Theodorakis' guards preferred to face the wrath of the authorities than to face Kyra Lenio's scornful glance.

Kyra Lenio had been gently bred and had led a life of ease in her youth. When her parents and her only sister died, she found solace in tending a flock of lambs and goats. Some people believed she had been disappointed in love when she was young and beautiful, while others shook their head sadly and tapped their temple. For a woman, especially one reared in comfort, to choose so harsh a life was beyond understanding—not that the Greeks failed to respect individuality. As a people they are decidedly individualistic, but eccentricity is another matter. Unlike the English, who look upon eccentrics with equanimity, the Greeks view them with suspicion. Even though Kyra Lenio had chosen to lead an isolated existence she did not hesitate to join her fellowmen in showing the traditional solicitude toward a newcomer in their village. And in so doing these simple folk transcended the barriers of their insularity.* For those who are gracious and courteous to strangers, says Francis Bacon, show they are citizens of the world and their hearts are not islands cut off from other lands, but a continent that joins to them.

About a decade after Mikis Theodorakis was transferred from

---

* The population of Zatouna swells considerably in the summer months. Many of the old houses have been razed and built anew or remodelled by their absentee owners. Greek villages offering scenic beauty, pure air and water are becoming increasingly popular as summer and week-end resorts.

Zatouna to the infamous Oropos prison where he could be closer to the watchful eye of the junta, Kyra Lenio entered the nunnery of Emialon in Arcadia. She did so with the proviso that she could bring along her flock.

An old friend of hers came to see her at her new habitat. "Our good sister is not with us at the present moment," said the Mother Superior. "The last twenty-four hours she had been searching the hills and valleys for one of her lambs that strayed from the flock. You are welcome to stay here until she returns."

"When is she expected back?" asked Kyra Lenio's friend.

"Not until she finds her lamb," answered the Mother Superior.

Chapter Twenty-six

The official decree of Bishop Nektarios' sainthood was issued on August 20, 1961 by the Holy Synod of the Ecumenical Patriarchate of Constantinople according to the rules of the Greek Orthodox Church, which require that canonization can take place only *after* a saint has been recognized and accepted as such *by the people*. In the official announcement which proclaims the decree of sainthood, the Holy Synod makes use of the traditional wording of "taking into account *the common conscience of our Christians* and the deserved honor which they have bestowed upon this Holy Man." It is the Greek Orthodox Faithful, therefore, who are actually responsible for the making of their saints. They had clearly discerned in this devout ascetic qualities which transcended his immense erudition and his extraordinary talents as an educator, theologian, religious philosopher, writer, and poet.

The populace had become aware during his lifetime and beyond his death that Nektarios was truly a man of God possessed with a magnitude of spirituality and the Divine Gift of healing. Alexandra Douropoulos was one of those who could personally testify as to the thaumaturgical powers of "this Holy Man."

Bishop Nektarios, Metropolitan of Pentapolis,* first became

---

*Bishops are given the title of "Metropolitan" when they govern an ecclesiastical district; the Metropolitan of Athens is also the Archbishop, Head of the Church of Greece;

acquainted with Constantine and Alexandra Douropoulos when they brought their son, Dionysios, to the Rizarios Theological Seminary in Athens, where they hoped to enroll him despite his youth.

The boy had shown at an early age an unusual intellect. By the time he was a little more than three years old he could read the newspaper, which was written during that epoch in the *katharevousa*—a "puristic" form of the Greek language that is far more abstruse than the "demotic" commonly used today. Under the tutelage of his father, who had entered the teaching profession rather than the priesthood for which he had prepared, Dionysios by the age of twelve was more advanced academically than the average older student in the *gymnasion*, the Greek secondary school.

Mrs. Douropoulos' uncles were men of stature in Athens. One was a Justice of the Supreme Court, the other a distinguished trial lawyer, both of whom served on the Board of Trustees of the prestigious Rezarios Theological Seminary. They approached Bishop Nektarios, who was then Director of the school, and asked him if a concession could be made for the boy, who was below the usual entrance age. The Bishop stated that if the lad could pass the severe entrance examinations and the rigid requirements of an irreproachable moral and ethical upbringing, he would certainly be accepted as a student despite his youth, or rather because of it, for he would be entering as one of the youngest seminarians in the annals of the school.

The matter of entrance examinations was the responsibility of the teaching staff. Bishop Nektarios felt it was his duty to ascertain the character of the applicant and the family background in which it had developed. With this aim in mind, the Director arranged for a conference with the parents of the prospective candidate.

---

the Patriarch is the Head of a see. The four original Patriarchates are located in Constantinople (Istanbul), Alexandria, Antioch, and Jerusalem. The Patriarch of Constantinople is known as Ecumenical Patriarch and is considered the spiritual head of world Orthodoxy. A title, such as "Metropolitan of Pentapolis," bestowed on Nektarios, is an honorary titular designation.

Constantine and his wife had not yet come in personal contact with Bishop Nektarios. But they had been present at liturgical services at which the Bishop had officiated and had preached the sermon.

Until the Metropolitan of Pentapolis appeared in their midst, the Athenians had become indifferent to the sermons delivered in their churches. This apathy toward an integral part of the Greek Orthodox service was due to the unfortunate appointments of clerics who were hardly more than pulpiteers when it came to preaching the Word of God. Their superannuated sermons and the uninspiring delivery of them had resulted in an alarming decline in church attendance throughout the city.

The art of homiletics has been greatly esteemed by the Orthodox Faithful since the early period of Christianity when it became a medium of exquisite perfection through the genius of John of Antioch, an illustrious Father of the Church. This remarkable hierarch is known to all of Christendom as Chrysostom, "the golden-mouthed," named thus by the Greeks in honor of his peerless talent as a homilist.

The high standards which the Greeks traditionally demand of their preachers were not only met but, in fact, exceeded by the Metropolitan of Pentapolis. The great appeal of Nektarios' sermons was clearly manifest in the throngs that followed him wherever and whenever he honored the churches of Athens by his presence. People from all levels of life gathered to refresh their thirsting souls at the fountain of words that flowed from the lips of this renowned scholar of Christology and brilliant exegete of "the treasures of the Testament." The immensity of his erudition stirred the minds of men, but it was the magnitude of his humanity that moved their hearts.

Few knew at the time, and even fewer suspected—until Nektarios' archives came to light—how fearful a price this holy man had paid for his sublime gift of eloquence.

There are men, Plato says, who have an intuitive insight, an inspiration which causes them to do good and beautiful things. Such a man was Nektarios.

But these rare beings can become victims of individuals who, limited by their spiritual impoverishment fail to recognize that those possessing a genuine purity of soul are incapable of evil thought or action. Such an individual was Sophronios, Patriarch of Alexandria, one of the four ancient sees of the Eastern Orthodox Church—and at one time the most powerful.

Nektarios' ceaseless quest for knowledge led him to the ancient city of Alexandria; this once famous metropolis was inextricably connected with some of the most renowned Greek Fathers in the early development of the Church. It was from this historic period that the unquenchable flame of Christianity spread far beyond the Alexandrian shores. This titanic light owed much of its power to the intellectual and spiritual brilliance of the early Church Fathers, who syncretized the young Christian religion with the legacy of Platonic philosophy.

Patriarch Sophronios was greatly impressed by the deep piety and the scholarly accomplishments of the unassuming and gentle cleric who came to the Patriarchate to pay his respects and to deliver a letter of introduction and recommendation to the Patriarch from John Choremi, the devoted friend of Nektarios. Despite an education that did not extend officially beyond the secondary school level, Nektarios had already started on his prolific writing that would amount to over forty books, thirty of which were published in his lifetime. Among them are two volumes dedicated to the Virgin Mary, the *Theotokos*—Bearer of God—as she is often called in Greek. They contain poetry of exalted spiritual lyricism which places the Saint in the forefront of Orthodoxy's divinely inspired souls such as John of Damascus, a pre-eminent poet of the Byzantine era.

The Patriarch of Alexandria shrewdly surmised that Nektarios' manifold abilities could be invaluable assets to the Patriarchal Court, which in essence meant Sophronios, himself. But His Holiness stipulated that he would consider admitting Nektarios to the inner circle of the Patriarchate only if he obtained a degree from the University of Athens Divinity School so that no criticism could be leveled at a member of the Patriarchate for being merely an autodidact.

276

This concern of Sophronios was not based on a desire to improve Nektarios' personal stature, but on the Patriarch's fear lest his own prestige suffer by surrounding his august person with those lacking the proper kind of label.

Chapter Twenty-seven

Anastasios Kefalas, destined to become in twentieth century Orthodoxy the greatly beloved Saint Nektarios, entered this world on October 1, 1846, in the insignificant village of Sylivria, Thrace, a northeastern sector of Greece. No portent presaged the hallowed future of the child born to humble pious folk, whose dearth of worldly goods did not lessen the plentitude of their faith in God and His Church.

The boy's first years were spent within the narrow limits of his small, peaceful place of birth. His life did not differ from that of his peers and like them he attended the rustic one-room schoolhouse until he reached the beginning of his adolescence, which coincided with the end of his early formal education.

The first indication of the youth's indomitable spirit was his desire to relieve his parents of the responsibilities of his care, and the noble ambition to aid them rather than accept their help for his own well-being.

In that interim of Nektarios' life when he was neither an adult nor a child but a highly vulnerable organism, he left for Constantinople hoping to find work with the help of a distant kinsman, who had settled years before in what was once the first and the most dazzling Christian capital the world has ever known.

The ancient site of Byzantium chosen for the establishment of "New Rome" was named Constantinople in honor of its founder and its first emperor, Constantine the Great. To the

278

Greeks, however, it was known as "The *Polis*" and to this very day they refer to it among themselves as "The City." But during the ten centuries of Byzantine civilization, the citizens of Constantinople considered their majestic domain *The Imperial City*, ruled by the Son of God—CHRISTOS BASILEUS, EMPEROR OF BYZANTIUM. These sacred words were emblazoned on sumptuous silk and velvet banners, on the bejeweled fanons of the churches, on the gold coinage of the realm—universally recognized as the finest currency of the times, and placed on any and every surface worthy of such a divine motto.

So obsessed was this theocratic society with every aspect of the religious dogmas and theological doctrines of Orthodoxy, that the Bishop of Nyssa, Saint Gregory, who visited Constantinople in the fourth century, reported in a somewhat querulous astonishment: "Everywhere, in humble homes, in the streets, in the market-place, at street corners, one finds people talking about the most unexpected subjects. If I ask for my bill, the reply is a comment about the virgin birth; if I ask the price of bread, I am told that the Father is greater than the Son; when I ask whether my bath is ready, I am told that the Son was created from nothing."

When Nektarios arrived at "The *Polis*" in the second half of the nineteenth century, the crescent had replaced the cross for more than four hundred years. No record exists of the youth's emotions at the sight of that once exalted citadel of Christianity which was raped and desecrated with a demoniacal frenzy that left in its wake an eternal stigma on the spirit of humanity and an everlasting wound on the Hellenic psyche.

Of all the abominations perpetrated by the infidel during the capture of the "Imperial City," none exceeded in the eyes of the Greeks the savage ravishment of SAINT SOPHIA, the Church of the Holy Wisdom. This renowned House of God, erected by order of Emperor Justinian in 532, with its " . . .wonderful and almost fairy-like construction which has excited the astonishment and admiration of so many critics survives, in its kind, a solitary example of Greek genius . . . (its) interior darkened and solemn, built out of solid gold and studded with figures and groups in swarthy crimsons and blues . . . and its domes in their light-

279

ness seem scarcely to rest upon the earth at all, and in their exquisite grace and variety form a singular triumph of structural art . . . a structure, the most perfect of its kind, the world has seen . . .''[*]

The Church of Saint Sophia, whose radiance had illumed the capital of the Eastern Roman Empire for nearly a millenium, was converted into a mosque following the Turkish conquest of Constantinople in 1453. Four minarets were raised on its four exterior corners; its interior was stripped of all Christian symbols, decorations and the priceless mosaics in order to accommodate the Muslim form of worship. The inestimable treasures of the church were pillaged in the first few hours of the Ottoman invasion. The triumphant conqueror of Constantinople, Mohammed the Second, had told his cohorts that whatever they plundered was theirs, but all the structures were his.

In view of Nektarios' gentle nature and his pious upbringing one could well imagine that his young heart had bled at the mutilated beauty of Saint Sophia and the savage obliteration of all reminders of the Christian Faith which had illuminated the Byzantine Empire for more than a thousand years.

From what has been gleaned concerning the future saint's early years, it was apparently here in ''The Polis'' among the haunting reminders of Orthodoxy's past glory that Nektarios recognized his affinity with the spiritual world and his desire to dedicate his life to the Greek Orthodox Church which ''considers itself to be the one, holy, catholic and apostolic Church, founded by Jesus Christ in the year of His death, 33 A. D. It is holy because its founder, Jesus Christ, is holy. It is catholic because the whole world is considered its province, and because it is universal in time and place. It is apostolic because it was established on earth by the apostles of Christ.''[**]

Young as he was, Nektarios, nevertheless, felt he was unprepared for the honor of serving the Lord. He was acutely conscious of his intellectual limitations, for in the process of labor-

[*]L. March Phillips, *Form and Color*: ed. Duckworth, London, 1925.

[**]Arthur C. Douropoulos, ''What is a Greek Orthodox?'' *Religions in America*, Ed. Leo Rosten (Simon and Schuster, 1954).

ing for his daily bread, he had been obliged to neglect his studies. But with the dauntless will that characterized the Saint throughout his life, he decided to rectify at once this negligence by starting on a course of self-education.

His natural bent toward religion led him first to the Greek Fathers of the Church, who were steeped in classical learning with which they had infused and enhanced the new religion. These renowned apologists, who had applied the principles of Greek thought in their defense of Christianity, aroused Nektarios' latent interest in his illustrious forebears—the ancient Greek philosophers and historians, the dramatists, the poets and orators. The young boy's mind was excited by their remarkable achievements which had been preserved for more than the one thousand years' existence of the Byzantine empire by the Greek scholars. After the fall of Constantinople, these learned men fled to Italy. They brought with them their Hellenic heritage which added its timeless luster to the intellectual renascence of the western world.

Although his ancient ancestors aroused in Nektarios a profound admiration, he, nevertheless, felt an instinctive kinship with the Byzantines. They had prayed to the same God and had honored the same Faith. They had taken a battle-torn area called Byzantium which time and again had been vanquished and enslaved by pagans, and had molded it into a "Celestial City" with Christ as its Ruler. And it was the Byzantines who preserved the form and substance of the early Church and glorified it with mystical beauty and spiritual grandeur—the Church that became known as the Greek Orthodox Church, the Church to which Nektarios dedicated his life and in which he was sanctified.

In his twentieth year, Nektarios left Constantinople. He went to the island of Chios and settled in the village of Lithion to teach school. The skeptics in the community (a species commonly found in all parts of Greece) questioned the competency of the young, self-taught scholar who, according to his pupils, never raised his voice and to their great joy never resorted to the use of the rod. These doubts were soon forgotten, however, in view of the improvement in the students' scholarship and deportment—

an improvement so sudden and so astonishing as to make the good folk of Lithion suspect that in their search for a schoolmaster, they had found a saint.

After seven years of teaching, Nektarios renounced secular life and entered a monastery in Chios called *Nea Moni*—the New Monastery, which is, in fact, an ancient one of renown. It was established in the middle of the eleventh century by the Byzantine Emperor Constantine Monomachos and housed as many as six-hundred Orthodox monks at a time. A dim aura from the monastery's past splendors still surround the remnants of elegant mosaics, frescoes and ikons that remain on the age-old walls. In the large refectory, an immense table of solid, multi-hued marble still stretches majestically across the entire length of the room. Its prodigious size and weight have been its salvation, so that it stands to this day—a colossal mockery of man's ephemeral strength.

A year after taking his monastic vows, Nektarios was ordained a deacon, the first order of service in the Orthodox priesthood. This primary step into a sacerdotal world enriched his life. He found greater contentment and deeper meaning in the unbroken rhythm of canonical hours devoted to prayer and meditation, in the strict observance of liturgical service, and in the daily labor which the entire brotherhood performed for the common good.

Yet this very contentment disturbed Nektarios' conscience. An ascetic by nature, he feared that the appeal of monastic life might make him insensible to his spiritual commitment. He had entered the monastery to prepare himself to serve God, not as an escape from a temporal world, rife with greed, envy, hate and lust. For he had not succumbed to, or even experienced, these brutish passions. Nor had he sought the cloister as a fulcrum to sustain his trust in God; nor had he known the "dark night of the soul"—the fearful cycle of belief and disbelief in which Luther had been trapped and tormented until he regained his faith and his spirit its serenity.

When Nektarios became aware that his soul and his faith were indestructible, he prayed for guidance how best these blessings might be used to honor Him who had bestowed them.

Nektarios had no doubt that his prayers were answered by his friendship with a devout, wealthy, cultivated Chian called John Choremi who often came as a visitor to Nea Moni. This benevolent Christian was attracted by the fragrance of pure piety that emanated from Nektarios' soul. He was quick to perceive that the gentle young monk possessed the tremendous force of quiet strength; and once his spiritual power was released beyond the cloistered walls, it would soar to the vault of Heaven and bring back to earthlings a vision of its supernal Light.

John Choremi was a pragmatist, as well as an idealist, and he was aware that Nektarios' autogenous education—remarkable as it was—might well be used as an excuse to malign him and to denigrate his spiritual mission, especially by those whose only distinction or achievement was the possession of a conventional, sterile, "higher" education; Choremi, therefore, urged Nektarios to go to Athens to acquire a diploma from a secondary school, since without it he could not proceed further academically. Nektarios accepted with deep gratitude his friend's advice and his generosity in assuming all financial responsibility.

After receiving permission from the Abbot Nicephoros to leave the monastery and with the blessings of the Metropolitan of Chios, Nektarios departed for Athens to attend the *gymnasion* (high school, in Greek).

Nothing perhaps reveals more clearly Nektarios' humble modesty, his complete lack of self-consciousness, than his willingness to attend high school among students considerably younger and far less knowledgeable than the self-taught scholar, whose learning was already greater than that which his classmates were likely to acquire in a lifetime.

After receiving his diploma from the University of Athens Divinity School, Nektarios returned to Egypt. He had fulfilled Patriarch Sophronios' requirements by obtaining his degree in Theology. And he had lived up to the expectations of his kindly benefactor, John Choremi, without burdening him any further for financial help, thanks to a full scholarship Nektarios had won and which covered his expenses during the entire time he attended the Divinity School. The Patriarch apparently was well-satisfied with Nektarios' new credentials, for he accepted him without delay in the Patriarchal circle.

Nektarios' career, under the aegis of the Patriarch of Alexandria, began auspiciously. Within the first year, His Holiness ordained him priest and shortly afterwards raised him to the rank of Archimandrite. Immediately following his elevation to this highest celibate priestly order, Nektarios was appointed Patriarchal Vicar and Director of the Patriarchal Office in Cairo. This significant appointment, which marked a major stage in Nektarios' life, began with infinite promise, but was to end ignominiously.

Some of the most secure members of Sophronios' Patriarchal Court owed their positions, or rather their sinecures, more to the exercise of their wits than the use of their minds. These favorite sons rejoiced that Nektarios was chosen to fulfill a post that demanded a relentless expenditure of time and labor toward which their indolent, irresponsible nature was not inclined. With jesuitical adroitness, they expressed effusive praises for His Holiness' infallible wisdom in his choice of a new Director. Meanwhile, they congratulated themselves on their good fortune. The new addition to the "inner circle" was a humble, pious, provincially born and bred novice who not only slaved away at his own onerous tasks but added supernumerary ones that benefitted others more than himself! Such a "noble soul" could hardly be a threat to their own method of keeping in the good graces of the Patriarchal Throne; nor would it jeopardize the delightful little entremets reserved for those who were clever enough to earn them not by hard work but by a judicious employment of cunning and adulation.

In the three years following Nektarios' assignment to the Patriarchal staff, Sophronios had ample proof of his protegé's worth. But of all his multifold duties none were more meaningful to Nektarios than his sacerdotal services. His performance as a celebrant inspired "the ascent of the mind to God" by revealing to the faithful the awesome majesty and beauty of the Orthodox liturgy—the divine drama of Resurrection and Redemption—which manifests in its mystical climax of the Eucharist, the ultimate message of Christianity.

As a preacher, Nektarios was singularly effective. As soon as he stepped into the pulpit, a deep quietude settled over the worshipers as though a hallowed presence had appeared in their midst. His gentle voice grew resonant and his eyes glowed with "the lumen Christi," the light of Christ that irradiates the whole being of the true believer.

Nektarios' sermons were governed by his faith in an irenic theology and his words did not rend the soul by fearful predictions of heavenly fury on those who sinned or transgressed the laws of God and man. He exhorted the heavy-hearted and the guilt-ridden to seek the supreme gift of salvation which Christ offered through the divine mercy of His Pardoning Grace.

Immensely pleased with the prestige Nektarios had brought to the Patriarchate in the short period of three years, Sophronios recommended him to the Holy Synod as worthy of elevation to the episcopal rank. On January 15, 1889, Archimandrite Nektarios was ordained Bishop and designated as titular Metropolitan of Pentapolis. The three-hour long service of consecration or enthronement, as it is called in Greek, faithfully adheres to the ancient Byzantine ecclesiastical tradition and is reminiscent in its pomp and pagentry of an imperial investiture.

The hierarchal corps of parasites attached to Sophronios could no longer consider Nektarios as an inconsequential member of the Patriarchate. His elevation to the hierarchal level of bishop aroused in them not only envy but fear. They were greatly alarmed lest Nektarios' productivity would make their sterility pitifully apparent—and lead the Patriarch in a moment of disastrous clarity to see them as drones to be purged from the Patriarchal premises. The instinct of self-preservation, which is especially marked in the selfish, bound together these sycophants in their determination to get rid of Nektarios once and for all.

According to religious history, the Alexandrian See, which Patriarch Sophronios ruled, extended over the Orthodox faithful of Egypt and its then vast dominions. It was established by the

Apostle Mark and was considered in centuries long past as the most dynamic of the four original patriarchates, which are located in Constantinople (Istanbul), Antioch, Jerusalem and Alexandria.

For Sophronios, the Alexandrian mitre was the symbol of his undisputed power. It was a singular mitre whose origin continues to baffle the ecclesiologists. It differs distinctly in its shape from the traditional ornate liturgical headpiece worn by Greek hierarchs. It resembles a warrior's helmet reminiscent of the close-fitting Phrygian cap or *phrygium* worn by the pagan Romans. But whatever its origin might be, it suited Sophronios eminently well, for it symbolized his readiness to battle anyone who would dare to remove it from his head.

For Sophronios, the mitre represented hierarchal prestige and temporal majesty. He felt an aura of worldly splendor when he donned the episcopal canonicals of regal brocades, of sumptuous silks and satins with their rich folds and curves shimmering like a thousand chatoyant gems in the pale radiance of candlelight. So much did this hierarch apparently cherish the mitre that he succeeded in defying the pitiful brevity of life by keeping Charon at bay until extreme old age rendered him powerless against the untimate conqueror of man.

Sophronios was now close to the ninth decade of his life, but showed no signs of senility. In fact his love of power, and the vigorous exercise of it, had not diminished nor had the tenacity with which he guarded it. In view of his lengthy years, he must have been aware that a meeting with his Maker was imminent, yet he seemed less concerned with his spiritual status than his temporal stature.

The Greek Orthodox community in Egypt looked up to Nektarios as a natural successor to the Patriarchal Throne of Alexandria. Had not the old Patriarch tacitly designated the Director and Vicar of the Patriarchate as his heir by consecrating him with his own hand as Bishop and Metropolitan of Pentapolis? And in view of Sophronios' advancing age, it was only a matter of time, a few years more at most, which the people would suffer gladly in anticipation of their good fortune.

But their hopes did not materialize. In a little over a year after

Nektarios attained episcopal rank, he was dismissed from his hierarchal post and banished from Egypt. For the craven souls who sought Nektarios' expulsion had achieved their end by slowly, persistently trickling the vitriol of fear and envy in the ear of the aged Patriarch.

Chapter Twenty-eight

Bishop Nektarios, Metropolitan of Pentapolis, arrived in Greece penniless and homeless. Sixteen months of salary for services he had rendered to the Patriarchate of Alexandria were withheld, supposedly because of a shortage of funds in the patriarchal treasury. For Nektarios the state of penury in which he found himself was incomparably less painful than his sense of homelessness. The only place he could claim as his domicile was the House of God to which he now had no access. His coming to Greece following his banishment from Egypt placed him in an anomalous position vaguely classified as a "visiting or sojourneying" cleric who was not officially recognized as a member of the hierarchy of the autocephalous Church of Greece. The Bishop bore his cross in silent prayer. Bitterness could find no room in a heart filled with *eleimosyne*, the virtue of charity and mercy, which to Nektarios' poetic cast of mind appeared as the brightest jewel in the divine diadem of the King of Kings. The Metropolitan of Pentapolis arrived in his native land unaware that his reputation as a profound scholar and homilist had preceded him.

His sudden appearance in Greece, and the nebulous rumors that surrounded it, aroused interest in the ecclesiastical circles and in secular society as well. Those who held Nektarios in high regard for his contributions to the Church were determined to ascertain the validity of his dismissal from the Patriarchate of

Alexandria on the anemic grounds that "His Grace . . . being unable to adjust to the climate of Egypt is departing therefrom. . . ."

His admirers, having made discreet inquiries through reliable sources, were convinced of Nektarios' innocence and were moved to help him gain recognition even in a limited way, at first, by the Church of Greece. Most likely it was through their efforts that Nektarios was granted the right to preach in a provincial county of Euboia—a solitary instance, perhaps, in the annals of Greek Orthodox hagiography of a Bishop, honored by the title of Metropolitan, accepting with unfeigned joy and gratitude the lowly post of a provincial preacher! The opportunity to serve in the apostolate did not demean but exalted Nektarios. It did not matter to him whether he exercised this time-honored privilege in a village church or an imposing cathedral, so long as he could preach the Word of God to his brethren and in his beloved motherland, besides.

For three years, until he was appointed Director of the Rezarios Theological Seminary in Athens, the Metropolitan of Pentapolis kept faithfully to his rounds of preaching. The large crowds that gathered to hear Nektarios proclaim the glory of the Gospel were not only attracted by his eloquence but arrested by the man, himself. They somehow sensed that this gentle preacher with the strangely luminous, deep-set eyes had attained a degree of spiritual perfection that transcended the universal weakness of men. People sought to kiss his hand, to receive his blessing and his smile—an unforgettable smile of child-like innocence that could soften the most callous heart. And those ravaged by sorrow or sickness who ventured to ask for a special benediction claimed that its bestowal brought them a sudden surge of fresh hope and renewal of courage that miraculously eased their pain.

These ineffable powers of Nektarios that came to light at this time of his life were the first apocalyptic glimmerings of his gift of healing—a divine charisma which the faithful believe that the saintly spirit of Nektarios still possesses.

When Dionysios applied for entrance to the Rizarios Seminary, Bishop Nektarios followed his usual procedure of interviewing the candidate and then arranging for a conference with his parents.

The Bishop found the quiet youth to be exceedingly bright, well-mannered and winsome. Shortly afterwards Nektarios met with Dionysios' parents. Neither Alexandra nor Constantine Douropoulos suspected at the time that this routine meeting would eventually develop into a friendship which would be of great significance in their lives.

When the Douropoulos couple came in personal contact with the Metropolitan of Pentapolis, His Grace was in his mid-fifties. Yet he gave the impression of a venerable patriarchal figure, with a prematurely white messianic beard, who might have stepped forth from a page of the Old Testament. His clear, firm skin had assumed a delicate pallor from hours of lengthy praying and days of relentless fasting. These ascetic austerities, which he faithfully practised, had not, however, lessened the gentleness or the serenity of his face. Nor had they dimmed the strange luminosity of the deep-set eyes that seemed to reflect a vision he possessd within his soul—an empyreal vision of God in all His greatness and His glory. . . .

The conference which Bishop Nektarios held with Dionysios' parents was in the nature of a pleasant social visit, for the Bishop believed that more information could be gleaned through a friendly atmosphere than could be elicited by direct cross examination.

In the course of conversation, Constantine Douropoulos remarked that he had graduated from the Tripolis Theological Seminary but instead of taking the vows of priesthood he had gone on to the Teachers College in Athens. Since receiving his diploma, he had been teaching until a few years ago when he was appointed superintendent in the school district that encompassed part of the Arcadian area in which he lived. And within five or so years he would be completing twenty-five years in the teaching profession.

"No less valuable years," the Bishop remarked, "than those you might have spent serving our Lord."

Nektarios' impression of Constantine and his wife was no less favorable than the one their son had made on His Grace. He was, in fact, instinctively drawn to them and he hoped whatever he heard about them would be commendable. Although he was an

290

astute judge of character, Nektarios, nevertheless, did not consider it fair to allow his own opinion to prevail. But he did not have to go far to corroborate his intuitive feelings in this instance through the most reliable of sources. He had made a note of Constantine's statement that he had graduated from the Theological Seminary in Tripolis—and judging from his age, the Bishop surmised that Dionysios' father must have attended that seminary while it was under the administration of Bishop Theoclitos Minopoulos. This brilliant prelate had added to his intellectual prestige by studying in Germany after obtaining his degree from the Athens University School of Theology.

Bishop Theoclitos had recently been elevated to the highest hierarchal office in the land. He was now Archbishop Theoklitos, Metropolitan of Athens, Head of the Holy Synod and the supreme ecclesiarch of the Church of Greece. As such, all ecclesiastical administration came under his jurisdiction including the proper functioning of all religious institutions in the country.

The worldly Archbishop Theoklitos of Athens, Head of the Church of Greece and the saintly Bishop Nektarios, Titular Metropolitan of Pentapolis and director of the Rezarios Theological Seminary, met regularly on a common ground of ecclesiastical concerns.

But what interested the Archbishop, as much if not more than the supervision of the Seminary, was Nektarios, himself. What manner of man was this, Theoklitos wondered, who had not defended himself, who had not uttered a word against a Patriarch whose grim accusations had reduced a Metropolitan to the lowly status of an ordinary priest! Indeed it was a source of wonderment that Nektarios had started his shattered life anew by gratefully accepting at first a preacher's post in a small provincial country and then suddenly assuming the headmastership of the outstanding religious institution in Greece with no pedagogical experience—save for a few years of teaching during his youth in some rustic village school, which was more a condemnation than a recommendation. And yet, this controversial administrator of the Rezarios Seminary had raised the school in half a dozen years or so to such a degree of academic excellence that the period of Nektarios' rule already was known as the "Golden Age" of the Seminary.

The most extraordinary matter, however, was Nektarios' method of discipline, which completely disregarded the long established custom of applying arbitrarily severe punishment for any infractions of school regulations or rules—a tried and true means of developing strength of character in the young seminarians.

Bishop Nektarios not only ignored these hallowed pedagogical principles by taking as a rule the word of the culprit rather than that of his condemner, but, *mirabile dictu*, he was known on occasions to punish himself rather than an offender on the grounds that he was the guilty party for having failed to guide or inspire a recalcitrant student in the ways of God. The most incredible of the Bishop's actions, however, was the manner in which he handled a momentous crisis that suddenly developed within the Seminary. Atheistic propagandists had insidiously penetrated the school in an attempt to destroy the seminaian's faith in God.

Nektarios withdrew to his stark, cell-like quarters, spending the days and nights in silent prayer and total fasting until the cohorts of Satan were routed, leaving behind them a student body stronger than ever in its reverence for God and its devotion to Nektarios.

Three times during his tenure, the Director resorted to the method of passive resistance which was to be used a few decades later by one of the world's great figures. The apotheosized leader of India's masses prayed and fasted to liberate his countrymen as Nektarios had done to save a few young seminarians from what he believed would otherwise result in eternal perdition of their souls.

Chapter Twenty-nine

Soon after Bishop Nektarios had interviewed Dionysios' parents, he spoke to Archbishop Theoclitos about Constantine Douropoulos. His Beatitude reacted warmly at the mention of his former pupil. He recalled him as a conscientious scholar with a splendid academic record.

"But purposeful scholarship," the Archbishop added, "is expected, of course, from those who choose to become seminarians.

"What particularly impressed me about Constantine Douropoulos," he went on to say, "was a kind of inner grace that was outwardly manifest in a dignity of mien, a certain fineness of manner seldom evident in one so young, especially in a youth whose background was typically provincial and whose finances were strictly limited. On a conscious level I believe he came to our Seminary in Tripolis mainly because he could acquire a good education less expensively than if he had gone, let us say, to the University in Athens. But I have always felt that his choice was unconsciously governed by the spiritual values and religious convictions that were ineradicably formed in the early part of his life.

"When Constantine was a boy, about the same age as his son, Dionysios, is now," related the Archbishop, "his mother died suddenly. His father, Thanasi Douropoulos, one of those simple, devout Christians who are the backbone of our country, not only lost his wife but had suffered financial reverses as well. Unable to provide properly for his son, the good man placed the boy in the Monastery of Saint John the Prodromos (Saint John the Baptist or the Forerunner). One of the few extant treasures of its kind from our glorious Byzantine epoch of Orthodoxy when our monasteries were considered jewels of the Church, radiant with pious learned monks, who were honored as men of God and respected as men of letters.''

Carried away by his subject, Theoclitos fancied himself beside the lectern or in the pulpit, and he lapsed into the fervid style of rhetoric he was accustomed to using as a pedagogue and as a preacher.

"To these erudite yet humble men," he declaimed, "we owe an incalculable debt for the perpetuation of our sublime Faith and for preserving the priceless heritage of our noble language through the vile miasma of Turkish tyranny, which for centuries polluted our beloved Hellas!

"And not a few of these gentle, selfless monks, who had consecrated their lives to the Prince of Peace, put aside the habiliments of their calling, their breviaries and books, manuscripts and pens and left the quietude of the cloister to help free their land from the infidel.

"But none served the cause of Christianity and Freedom more loyally than those who wore the cloth. They dedicated themselves to the sacramental task of keeping alive the spirit of hope and faith without which the will can falter and the heart can fail. They emboldened the weak and disburdened the weary and solaced the sick and prayed for the dying—men of God who lived by the Cross and would gladly die for it; and those who chose an agonizing death rather than deny their Faith or their country are rightfully known and rightly revered as *hieromartyrs*—holy martyrs . . . may their memory remain eternal.

"When that hour came—on the twenty-fifth of March in the eighteen hundred and twenty-first year of our Lord—the blessed hour for which a tormented people had ceaselessly prayed through thousands upon thousands of days and nights of enslavement, it befittingly fell to a devout member of the holy orders and an impassioned patriot, as well, to declare the sacred words, 'The

294

hour has come, O men of Greece!"*

"Following a solemn liturgy at the ancient Monastery of Saint Lavra near the town of Kalavryta in northern Peloponnesos, Bishop Germanos, Metropolitan of Patras, walked to the Monastery gardens and there beside a stately plane tree unfurled the standard that marked the start of the Greek Revolution— and the beginning of a 'Holy War' fought by a Christian people so that their flag which bears the Cross of Christ might wave freely once again beneath the azure glory of the Grecian sky.

"It was a moment, a speck of time, no larger, so to speak, than a grain of sand in the boundless ocean of eternity, yet a noble moment in man's history.

"We have had our share, and more, of these moments of grandeur from the ancient days of our progenitors whose ardor for liberty gave birth to democracy.

"We have fought our battles with passion and we have won them—and even when the foe's brute strength overpowered us, it was but a Pyrrhic victory that never crushed the Greek!

"No, never," he said softly, "shall the 'heroic spirit' of our forefathers perish so long as the Greek race survives, for we carry in our veins the blood of those who won with glory at Marathon and those who died with honor at Thermopylae."

Archbishop Theoclitos did not live to see his countrymen reaffirm their heroic heritage. In less than a quarter of a century after his death, when Greece was attacked by Italy on October 28, 1940, Leonidas' memorable words *"They shall not pass"* echoed and re-echoed throughout the land.

"Few expected from Greece more than a few weeks' resistance—a brave but brief gesture for freedom that would have to be recognized when the post-war settlement was made. She surprised the world, revealed Mussolini's pitiful weakness,

*The first words of the historic letter written by Alexander Ypsilanti, head of the *Philike Etaireia*, the secret "Society of Friends" organized for the preparation of Greek emancipation by the Revolution of 1821. This letter and a sketch of its recipient, Constantine Thanopoulos, was donated by his granddaughter, Alexandra Douropoulos to the Houghton Library of Harvard University, Cambridge, Massachusetts.

upset Hitler's plans. It is a poignant irony of our time that the will to resist should be so vehement in this little, half-armed nation whereas in some greater nations it hardly existed at all.

"Greece has struck her modern blow for freedom not in blind fury but with impassioned skill. She has lighted a flame as bright as that which burned at Dunkerque and London—as bright as any that lit freedom's skies over Thermopylae, Salamis and Marathon. She may go down underneath overwhelming force but it is as certain as tomorrow's dawn that she cannot be permanently enslaved." (*The New York Times*, March 25, 1941)

A furious, frustrated Hitler was forced to postpone the invasion of Russia and come to the aid of his humiliated partner. The end result of this first blow to the "Nazi-Fascist" solidarity was the German occupation of the little country that dared to defy the Axis giants.

Throughout the German occupation of Greece during the Second World War, the Greeks, despite the Nazi reign of terror, engaged in nationwide resistance movements and guerrilla warfare. Lethal penalties were inexorably exacted by the German command for any involvement in such activities. An example of the savage nature of reprisal for "local guerrilla action" was the destruction of the ancient town of Kalavryta, "The Beautiful Springs," founded before the birth of Christ, as well as the nearby historic Monastery of Agia Lavra where the Greek Revolution of 1821 was officially declared. Both were burned to the ground. The only building which miraculously escaped the inferno was the Monastery's Byzantine Church of Dormition.

The Germans, with characteristic thoroughness, rounded up the entire male population of the town and forced them to march on a fiercely cold day in December of 1941 to the top of the ice-clad Mount of Tremolo where men and boys were shot to death. Meanwhile, the women and children were herded into an empty building. Some managed to escape; the rest were riddled with gunfire and left to die.

The monastery and the town have been built anew; only the

hands of the clock on the Metropolitan Cathedral have not changed. They still point to *thirty-four minutes past two*, the time when the distant clatter of machine guns shattered the deathly silence of the town.

When the Archbishop finished his discourse, he realized he had been speaking, or rather orating, without a pause for some time, but he didn't seem abashed by his indulgence in a rather lengthy and somewhat trite monologue. After all, what could one say about the Revolution, the Church and the monasteries that was new? He felt satisfied, however, that what he said he had said well. It would not hurt to remind the head of The Rezarios Seminary—in case he had forgotten—that the Head of the Church was no mean rhetorician.

The dynamic, self-assured Theoklitos did not feel he was threatened by Nektarios' popularity as a preacher, yet he was irked by all the fuss people made over Nektarios' sermons. They came literally in droves to the Seminary Chapel to hear him preach—not just the "hoi polloi," but the elite members of Athenian society many of whom followed the tradition of sending their sons to the pre-eminent Rezarios Seminary in the hope that they would eventually attain the honor of a high ecclesiastical office.

To avoid overcrowding the chapel, a limited number of tickets were issued each Sunday except when another cleric performed the liturgy and gave the sermon. For Bishop Nektarios was invited very often to officiate at various churches in Athens and in the surrounding areas. This matter of the tickets apparently annoyed the Archbishop even though the Advisory Board of the school had resorted to this means as the only sensible way to avoid mass asphixiation whenever the Bishop preached.

"I am afraid," said the Archbishop with a disarming smile, "that I have digressed considerably from the matter of my former student, Constantine Douropoulos, who now hopes to enroll his son, Dionysios, at Rezarios Seminary. It seems hardly possible . . . I believe it was about two years ago that I saw the boy and he seemed like a mere child . . . ah, but the years even more than the days 'are swifter than a weaver's shuttle.' "

In his previous capacity as Bishop of Sparta and Monemvasia, Theoklitos would go now and then to Arcadia for various religious ceremonies or celebrations. The last time he was there since his enthronement as ecclesiarch of the Greek Church, he had officiated at Dimitsana, a small medieval town of recent historical significance as well, for it was here that the gunpowder for the Revolution was produced. The Douropoulos family lived close by in the village of Zatouna and Theoklitos had also visited their home. On one of his visits he had been invited to stay overnight with a promise from his host, Constantine Douropoulos, that on the following day he would accompany his guest to the Monastery of Saint John the Prodromos. Theoclitos made a point of visiting "this revered place," as he called it, whenever he came to this particular part of Arcadia, from where the monastery could be reached without too much difficulty.

"It is hardly possible," mused the Archbishop, "to know people except on a superficial level by paying them a mere formal call or two. One must see them in their own habitat and break bread with them if they are to be judged at all fairly. I have visited the Douropoulos home a number of times, and from what I have seen of their family life, I can unhesitantly say they are fine people, law-abiding and God-loving. Constantine still retains the qualities which as I mentioned were evident from the time he came to our Tripolis Seminary. The years have, however, added a new dimension to his personality—considerable charm—but not at the expense of his reserve and dignity, I'm glad to say."

Nektarios nodded his head in agreement. "Yes, he appears to be an admirable type—and so does his wife," he remarked.

"Ah, Mrs. Douropoulos . . . she is, indeed, a splendid woman with a dynamic personality unusual in a Greek woman or any woman, I would say. And an excellent mother, judging from the good-sized, healthy brood she had produced. Dionysios is the oldest child and the only son. He impressed me as being very bright and well-mannered. And so did the rest of the children, five or six lovely little creatures—all girls—and another was on the way. Yes, another girl I was told. Well, I hope the next one will be a boy at least for a change," added the Archbishop with a smile.

"I do not doubt," he continued, "that there will be more little ones coming along in that family. The Douropoulos couple

298

is obviously philoprogenitive. I pray God grant us more of their kind, for they offer to our ancient illustrious race the element which is vital for its survival—vigorous, intelligent, clean stock such as can be bred on those harshly beautiful mountains of Arcadia.''

Chapter Thirty

Bishop Nektarios remarked that one of the joys his return to Greece afforded him was the opportunity of becoming reacquainted with his country. "I should say 'acquainted,'" he explained, "since I have been away from Greece proper since my early days, save for a few years while pursuing my studies in Athens—and getting an education allowed no such luxury as travel.

"In youth the future seems limitless but suddenly I was no longer young and time was no longer infinite. And now, day and night combined are hardly sufficient for the work at hand let alone the time required for traveling."

The Archbishop listened with polite interest to Nektarios but offered no sympathy for his plight. As a former director of the Tripolis Seminary, he could, of course, appreciate the time and effort required to run the Rezarios institution—and to run it successfully, he had to admit, as Nektarios managed to do. But if the Metropolitan of Pentapolis did not have a moment to call his own, he had only himself to blame. Nobody compelled him to accept invitations left and right to preach in churches and chapels all over Athens, Piraeus and their environs. Nor was he forced, except by his own desire for recognition, undoubtedly, to use the hours meant for sleep or rest in order to write his numerous religious books and tracts and poetry; nor was it all necessary but, in fact, demeaning for one holding the high office of a Metropolitan Bishop to labor like a common monk in the Seminary gardens. Nektarios planted all kinds of flowers which he tended himself; as for the violets, which were his favorite flowers, he puttered and fussed over their beds as though they were shy little creatures in need of constant loving care. Theoklitos had the suspicion that the good Bishop attributed a "soul" to each and every flower.

Nektarios' love of nature is clearly evident in the minutes of the school board meetings during his tenure as Director of the Rezarios Seminary. They reveal his repeated requests, made over the years, for the appointment of an agriculturalist in the belief that the seminarians would greatly benefit by a practical knowledge of agriculture. However, according to the school records, this request was not granted. It may have appeared to the board members as too frivolous a departure from the severe curriculum requirements of the Greek Orthodox seminaries. There was also the matter of the inordinate amount of time the Bishop expended listening to his students' troubles and tribulations—as if the wealthy, sophisticated city boys, of which there were a good many at the Rezarios Seminary, knew the true meaning of hardship. Theoklitos was glad that at his Seminary in Tripolis he had dealt mainly with hardworking provincials like Constantine Douropoulos, who were sufficiently self-disciplined and required no "special" handling.

The Archbishop's thoughts were indirectly expressed by his remarking somewhat drily, "We use our time according to what *we* consider to be our priorities. I hope the good Lord will make your Grace aware that time expended on travel, with its subsequent benefits to the mind and body, is a priority that should not be overlooked by a hierarch of the Church.

If the Bishop caught the barb in the Archbishop's words, he gave no indication of it. Nor did he enlighten his host that he had traveled extensively since his early youth. He merely replied that he had not been wholly remiss in the matter of "educational" travel. He mentioned that three years ago, His All Holiness, the Ecumenical Patriarch Constantine, had given him official permission to visit the monastic and hermitic communities of Mount Athos, the *Agion Oros* or the Holy Mountain, where man and

301

nature have glorified their Maker in a setting of wondrous beauty.

Nektarios would never forget how graciously he was welcomed to this autonomous theocratic republic, considered by the Greeks as their spiritual center. He had officiated in the inspiring daily services and enjoyed the privilege of examining to his heart's content the monastery libraries with their collections of ancient manuscripts and documents; and he was greatly impressed with the inestimable thesaurus of Byzantine art and artifacts safeguarded by generations of zealous monks through four hundred years of the infidel's despotic rule. It was, Nektarios remarked, a source of spiritual comfort to him that in a radically changing world, Mount Athos faithfully adhered to the age-old religious traditions and hieratic customs of Orthodoxy. (It is the only monachal institution in Greece that has yet to allow women or any form of female species on its territory lest the sanctity of the Holy Mountain be imperiled.) The Bishop also mentioned his pilgrimage to the *Meteora*, "the Monasteries in the Air," in Thessaly, which he recalled as one of the most extraordinary sights that the eye of mortal man can see.

"Ah, yes," agreed Theoklitos, "that forest of colossal stone pillars rising over 1,000 feet above the earth is, indeed, a most awesome sight. One cannot but marvel how those ascetics in the fourteenth century ever managed to establish their colonies on the very pinnacles of these teratogenic formations, and at a time when ascent or descent on these naked monoliths was accomplished only with the help of ropes, nets, baskets and hinged ladders that were hand-operated by means of windlass from the summit of these incredible stones."

"According to Matthew," remarked Nektarios, "faith can move mountains—let alone build on them—or erect, as the monks have done on the Meteora, monasteries and hermitages, churches and chapels that seem to be scaffolded on mere air. And all this in honor of our Lord, who, it seems, created these natural refuges as a habitat for holy men who long to be as close as possible to God's 'Church Triumphant' in Heaven."

Since the Archbishop could not think of anything more to say on the subject beyond what his guest had so eloquently expressed, he began speaking of other venerable hieratic institu-

302

tions in Greece. "Not that they can possibly be compared," he remarked, "to Mount Athos or the Monasteries-in-the-air, yet, in their own small way they are moving testimonials of our Christian progenitors' passionate devotion to Orthodoxy."

"The pleasure of seeing some of them, at least, lies ahead for me," said Nektarios. "God be willing, I hope one of these days to visit the Peloponnesos where, as your Eminence well knows, a number of our ancient churches and monasteries are to be found, scattered in remote areas of that region. Our two board members, the Thanopoulos brothers, have graciously extended to me an open invitation to join them on one of their visits to their birthplace, Zatouna, a small town in Arcadia, close to Dimitsana. As Your Beatitude mentioned, it is close to Dimitsana and not far from Saint John's Monastery where Constantine Douropoulos had entered in his boyhood. I look forward to that visit, which will include, as well, a trip to the Monastery."

"We are fortunate," responded His Beatitude, "to have two such preeminent jurists on the Rezarios school board. These uncles of Mrs. Douropoulos are an inspiring example of the kind of individuals our provinces are capable of producing. There are five or six Thanopoulos brothers. One, I believe, has remained at home to take care of the family property. They come, I understand, from a long line of land owners. The rest of them have become distinguished professional men, who have risen to the very top of the economic and social ladder, so to speak. They have all married elegant, sophisticated women from the best Athenian families. These fine ladies, I suspect, deplore our villages, but they have not been able to dissuade their husbands from making a pilgrimage at least once or twice a year to pay homage to their place of birth.

"We Greeks are, on the whole, deeply devoted to our country and especially loyal to the locality where we first saw the light of our glorious Hellenic sky. But the Arcadians, I must say, are inordinately attached to their birthplace. They tend to view it in the illusory light by which romantic poets and painters are inclined to see it. Even the Arcadian peasant who knows the anguish of trying to wrest a meager living, at best, from the exhausted soil on those immemorial mountains will, nevertheless, tell you

303

that Arcadia has been unquestionably blessed by the Almighty."

"We must forgive them for their pride," said Nektarios gently, "for the excessive love of their country is not a form of hubris but an overwhelming appreciation for the blessings of natural beauty that God has bestowed on their land."

"Yes, Arcadia is, indeed, a beautiful province. I am especially fond of the area where the Douropoulos family lives. To be exact—the road that leads from Dimitsana to Zatouna, where Constantine's wife was born, is marvelously scenic. It has a wild kind of beauty—a peculiar numinous quality that hovers over the seemingly endless range of the Menalon mountains and the steep cliffs, the deep ravines that surround the sharply curved road connecting the picturesque village of Zatouna with the fascinating medieval town of Dimitsana."

"I have the impression that Saint John's Monastery is located in the same type of terrain, or am I mistaken?" asked Nektarios.

"Not at all," replied Theoklitos, "if anything, it has even a more dramatic setting," and he proceeded to describe it.

The ancient abbey of Saint John the Prodromos was built in 1167 by the Byzantine Emperor, Manuel Komnenos. It hangs like an eagle's eyrie from one of the deepest gorges in the Arcadian mountains. The outside wooden structure clings to a perpendicular surface of sheer rock but the inner areas retain the natural boundaries of catenulated grottos created eons ago. Their Stygian darkness was dispelled by the pale glow of candlelight by which nameless monks had painted haunting ikons of unearthly beauty against the dark bare granite walls.

"It was here in this hallowed place," said the Archbishop, "that my former pupil, Constantine Douropoulos, was imbued with a reverence for Orthodoxy, which I am certain he has never lost and which I feel confident he has passed on to his son, Dionysios. And I feel no less confident that this young man will be a credit to our Seminary."

The Metropolitan of Pentapolis was moved as he listened to the Archbishop. The hallowed Monastery of Saint John the Prodromos surely would seem forbidding to a motherless youth of ten or eleven. Desolation must have flooded the lad's heart and despair filled his eyes when he first sighted the strange, dark, bleak dwelling on a fearfully steep mountainside that was to be his home in the midst of bearded strangers perpetually robed in black. . . . A barely audible sigh escaped His Grace. Slight as it was, the Archbishop, nevertheless, heard the Bishop's sigh and mistook it for a stifled yawn which he considered not only a breach of etiquette, but, more significantly, an effrontery to his high office and to his own person as well.

"It seems," he remarked coldly, "that I have wearied Your Grace."

For a moment, Nektarios was perplexed by the Archbishop's comment, but he must have quickly surmised its cause for he hastened to say, "If your Beatitude heard me sigh, it was not from ennui but from the emotions which the story of your former pupil, Constantine Douropoulos, aroused in me. I must confess I sighed at the thought of the pain a youth would bear at the loss of a mother in his tender years. In the case of Constantine, he had to endure the added pain of banishment. For surely, to a young boy, it must seem like the cruelest form of exile to find himself in the austere atmosphere of a monastery, deprived of the warmth of the family hearth and the comforting companionship of his peers. . . . I hope Your Beatitude will kindly forgive my lengthy interruption and continue with a narrative which is most absorbing."

The Archbishop was obviously mollified, for he now addressed the Bishop as he would an intimate associate without using his formal ecclesiastical title.

"My good Nektarios," he remarked with an indulgent smile, "your heart, I daresay, abounds with tender susceptibilities. But let me assure you that during the years Constantine attended the Tripolis Seminary, I saw no ill effects from his experiences at the *Prodromos*. Our monastic institutions are, indeed, austere, but despite their exactitudes, the atmosphere of humanity prevails. Saint Basil the Great, who formulated our communal type of monasticism, eschewed the violent extravagances of spiritual and bodily severities. He emphasized, rather, prayer and contemplation, learning and study, and stressed the daily performance of various kinds of physical labor not only for the benefit of those

305

in the cloister, but for the needy outside of its walls . . . so the world is not closed to our monks nor our monasteries closed to the world, which sends a steady stream of visitors and pilgrims to their welcoming doors.

"For a serious, intelligent youth like Constantine there was much to see, to hear, to learn, to enjoy in a monastic environment—in all, an incomparably wider vista than his own provincial surroundings could have afforded him. Besides, he had the good fortune to enter the monastery while the Abbot Joachim was still alive—a learned, benign old man, one of those inspiring patriarchal figures who personify the ideals of Basilian monachism. The Abbot had taken Constantine under his wing, so to speak, and was concerned about his welfare and particularly about his education. Evidently a strong bond existed between them and it seems fitting that the boy was with the Abbot when he died. Like a truly devoted son, he performed a filial duty in closing the old man's eyes. I believe it was soon after the Abbot's death that Constantine left the monastery and went back to his home."

"Ah, yes, it need must be a strong bond of love that can hold together tender youth and venerable age," murmured Nektarios. "The boy apparently felt deserted by his natural parent and came to look upon the Abbot as a surrogate one. But when he returned home—older and wiser—I hope he saw his good father in a more kindly light."

"I don't know," remarked Theoclitos, "what his feelings were. I consider it impolitic for a teacher—and even more so for a headmaster—to develop such a degree of familiarity with his students so as to encourage them to divulge their intimate feelings or thoughts. As a matter of fact, it was only by chance, due to an incident involving an old silver watch, that I learned what I have just told you concerning my former pupil, Constantine. I shall not, however, tire you with that matter. Already I have unduly subjected you, as a captive audience, to a weakness of mine for longiloquence.

"If I may disagree with Your Beatitude," replied Nektarios with a smile, "I must say that I do not consider myself a 'captive audience' but a captivated one on a matter concerning the father of a candidate for our seminary—a matter of more than passing concern to me. But I confess that besides my specific interest in Constantine Douropoulos, the mention of an 'old silver watch' has aroused my curiosity and I hope Your Beatitude will be so kind as to satisfy it."

The Archbishop glanced sharply at his visitor. Since his enthronement as Head of the Church, Theoklitos had become wary of flattery, especially from those directly under his supervision. He now suspected that the Metropolitan of Pentapolis, no less than the others, was seeking his good graces by the none too subtle means of blandishment. But intently as the Archbishop scrutinized Nektarios, he found no signs of guile that belied the expression of sincerity on the Bishop's face—a serenely ascetic face framed by a silvery white rim of hair that looked—for all the world, thought Theoklitos with a start—like a glistening aureola such as a saint should wear! It was of course purely illusory. What else could it possibly be?

The Head of the Church felt a sudden inexplicable uneasiness, but he quickly quelled it by reminding himself that he was now the Ecclesiarch of the Church of Greece and that Nektarios was simply the Director of Rezarios Seminary, which placed him and the school directly under the supervision of the Archbishop.

Having thus reassured himself of his superior status, Theoklitos addressed Nektarios in a gracious manner exercising, as befitted his exalted office, the prerogative of *noblesse oblige*.

"My dear Bishop, I shall gladly satisfy your curiosity regarding the watch I mentioned. It certainly gives credence to the touching devotion which can exist between 'tender youth and venerable age' to borrow, if I may, your charming phrase. Besides," he added cryptically, "that timepiece was to prove more than a tangential connection between a student and his mentor."

The Archbishop was about to relate the story of the old silver watch when one of those violent but short, refreshing Spring showers descended suddenly on Athens. He rang for his manservant to adjust the window shutters against the pelting rain and requested him to bring some coffee and a sweet—a ubiquitous gesture of Greek hospitality.

In the few months since Theoklitos had assumed the grave

307

responsibilities that are part of the ecclesiarch's office, he had little time, and even less opportunity, to indulge in the pleasure offered by an informal meeting such as the one he was enjoying at the present moment. Besides, he found Nektarios to be an attentive listener in whose presence he could relax and let his mind and tongue wander leisurely among feelings and events that had taken place more than a quarter of a century ago and had assumed by now the appeal of old remembrances.

In this expansive mood, Theoklitos addressed Nektarios with amused mockery in his voice. "A few minutes ago, my good friend, you protested against my calling you a 'captive audience.' Now, you must admit that nature has contrived to make you one. You cannot possibly leave from here and escape from my loquacity except," he added laughingly, "if you prefer to drown in that sudden squall which is raging outside."

Chapter Thirty-one

The Archbishop settled himself comfortably in his impressive *polythrona*—an armchair which had been presented to him by the alumni of the Tripolis Seminary when he was elevated to the Archbishopric of Greece. It was made of mellow oak and covered in dark red leather. The outside frame was elegantly carved with Byzantine motifs and symbols entwined in garlands of grapes and ivy. On top of the chair's back, poised above a cross and crown, was an emblem of Orthodoxy—the dicephalous eagle with one head facing towards the East, the other towards the West—the two parts of the world which had contributed to the everlasting power and glory of Christianity.

"That silver watch," began Theoklitos, "was an unusual one, not that I consider myself an expert horologist but watches have intrigued me since I was a child and especially during my student days in Germany where some of the finest watches are made. I daresay this particular timepiece was an antique probably produced sometime in the late eighteenth or early part of the nineteenth century. It was engraved on the back and on the face with pastoral scenes which were exquisitely rendered. It had a fluted or scalloped inner rim and the outer one was rounded. The winding key was attached to a heavy silver fob—an elegant timepiece all in all.

"But I am getting ahead of my story and you are, no doubt, wondering what this valuable watch has to do with Constantine, our then young seminarian. Well, it was *his* as I found out only a few hours after he first came to the Tripolis Seminary.

"It was the opening day of school—a vital day for the teacher, whose first few hours in the classroom are decisive as to whether he gets control of the students or whether they get control of him, in which case, woe to him!" The Archbishop raised his hands toward heaven in a suppliant gesture as though invoking the Lord to help those hapless pedagogues. "Besides my responsibilities as Director of the Tripolis Seminary and my duties as Bishop of Sparta and Monemvasia, I taught part of each school day not entirely from choice, as you may do, but from necessity since we did not have the financial means which the Rezarios Seminary has, to hire an adequate teaching staff."

The disciplining of his classes was obviously no problem for Theoklitos. His manner and bearing were enough to make those who attended the Seminary in Tripolis aware they were in the presence of an unequivocal authoritarian. On the first day of their arrival, the freshmen were reminded that they were not in an ordinary school but in a seminary to which they had chosen to come in order that they be trained as servants of the Lord. And *obedience* was the prime requisite for those who would best serve their Master.

While the Director was drumming the seminary catechism into the heads of the freshmen, he heard the clatter of metal and saw Constantine getting up from his seat.

"Oh, my watch, I dropped my watch!" he cried and down he went on all fours crawling around his desk like an animal searching frantically for a bone that had slipped from him and had mysteriously disappeared.

The rest of the students were stunned not so much that Constantine had dared to interrupt the headmaster's lecture, as the startling awareness that one of their peers actually possessed a watch!

The Archbishop admitted that he, too, was taken aback. "I could not help wondering how a watch of any kind, especially as fine a watch as this one turned out to be, had fallen in the hands of a youth born and bred in the small Arcadian village of Vancon. It's a beautiful place, by the way, near the town of

Megalopolis, where Constantine contened his schooling after leaving the Monastery.

"I ordered him to get up immediately from the floor and resume his seat but in his anxiety to retrieve his treasure, he did not heed me or more likely did not even hear me."

The Head of the Tripolis Seminary was not accustomed to having his orders ignored. What this unruly provincial deserved was to be raised from the floor by the scruff of the neck and thrown into his seat or better still thrown out of the room. But before Theoklitos had time to put his thought into action, the boy stood up exclaiming jubilantly, "I found it!"

His exaltation was shattered, however, when he heard the Director's sharp command: *"Give me that watch!"*

For a moment the boy stood motionless, then looked around him and became aware of his classmates' eyes curiously fastened on him. He felt his face grow crimson and to escape their gaze, he looked at his watch. He was deeply anxious to examine it, to put it to his ear, at least, and find out if it was still ticking faithfully as it had never failed to do before he had dropped it, clumsy fool that he was! But instead he walked slowly down the aisle and laid his precious possession on the Director's outstretched hand.

"After I had finished addressing the class, I told Douropoulos to report to me before the noon recess. Meanwhile, I examined the watch carefully. It was still ticking away vigorously. I checked it against my own watch. Despite its fall, it was functioning perfectly. "When I laid the two watches side by side, it was obvious that the old timepiece was aesthetically and mechanically by far the superior one," said the Archbishop with a wry little laugh. "I found it quite ironic that a freshman seminarian carried a watch such as the head of a seminary, or even the Head of the Church, would consider himself fortunate to possess.

"When Constantine came to my office, he looked quite miserable from a sense of embarrassment, I would say, at his unintentional but nonetheless highly irregular conduct on his first day as a seminarian; and he was suffering no doubt from anxiety concerning the watch. It was still on my desk and when he saw it, he must have realized it was not damaged for he perked up considerably. I began questioning him as to how and when and where he had acquired so fine an article.

"In brief—for I have unduly taxed your patience and your curiosity—the watch originally belonged to Joachim, the abbot of Saint John's Monastery, where, as I previously mentioned, Constantine had been placed as an oblate by his father, Thanasi Douropoulos. When the abbot felt his death was near, he gave the watch to the youth, who was devoted to him and had cared for him during his final illness. The dying man had given it to him, Constantine told me, in the presence of his faithful prior, Father Nathanael, and I gather he did so in order to have a witness who could testify that he had bestowed this valuable watch to the young boy of his own free will.

"So much for the validity of Constantine's ownership of the watch, but I wondered and I suspect the same question has already occured to you as it had occurred to me at that time. Why did Joachim, a fervent adherent of the monastic vow of poverty by which all worldly effects are disavowed, violate this solemn promise by keeping to his dying day so elegant and costly a material possession?

"I put this question to Constantine, not in the same way, of course; I merely asked him if he had acquired any information about the history of the watch. Yes, he said, he had heard something about it—not from the abbot, however, who had simply given him the watch, but from Father Nathanael, who had succeeded Joachim as head of the monastery.

"Following Joachim's death, the boy decided to return home. The new abbot gave him his blessing and told him to cherish the watch as the old abbot had cherished it and then told him why it had meant so much to his predecessor."

Joachim's father was a prosperous sea captain who violently opposed his only son's espousal of monasticism. He considered a monk's existence nothing more than a life sentence—a living death in a penal institution. But when he grew old, he repented his ungodly stand. He realized he had committed a high sin against God and against his own flesh and blood. As a token of his remorse, he sent his son the finest watch that he could find with

312

a message asking for forgiveness and expressing his longing to see his son as soon as he returned to his home port.

Joachim, who had never ceased praying for a reconciliation with his father, was overjoyed at the prospect of its realization. But it never came to pass. On his way home, the penitent captain suddenly died and was buried at sea.

"You will perhaps agree that Constantine's story is a classic type of narrative replete with the same or similar elements readily found in the not uncommon but unfortunate 'father-son' conflicts. It did not strain my credulity, however, for his words had the ring of veracity."

"Truth like gold has a special radiance," remarked Nektarios "which for the discerning distinguishes it from a baser metal."

"Thank you, my friend, for the indirect compliment. Yes, I am glad I discerned that what Constantine had recounted to me on his first day at the Seminary was true. My faith in his word became, I believe, the basis of mutual trust and our subsequent friendship. Only in one respect he has not lived up to in my expectations—his failure to take the vows of priesthood."

For a moment or two the Archbishop paused in thought. "He would have made an admirable cleric, particularly in this new century when the Church must meet the radical changes already taking place in the Western world. I am not implying, God forbid, that we need or desire outright latudinarian divines who could jeopardize the nearly two-thousand-year-old doctrines and traditions of Orthodoxy, which as unbiased historians acknowledge, are incontestably connected with the original Church of Christ. If our Faith is to remain a dominant force in the lives of the Greek people, we must attract men to represent the Church who are cultivated, men of unwavering religious convictions but with vision for the future needs of Orthodoxy, with compassionate insight into the spiritual and corporeal conflicts of their fellow men. And I believe Constantine possesses these qualifications.

"But leaving aside these ideal clerical requirements—on a practical level Constantine, as a married man, would be particularly qualified to serve as a secular priest. Our parishoners prefer, and wisely so, the services of a married priest with a family—

provided, of course, that his children are paragons of good behavior and well-versed in the objectives of deontology—and his wife, like Caesar's wife, above reproach. As far as the Douropoulos offspring are concerned, from what I gather, they are reared with a strong sense of social duty and moral responsibility. As for Constantine's wife, Alexandra, she is unassailably virtuous. She is a remarkable woman. And," he added with a hint of amusement in his voice, "what a remarkable Presbytera she would be!"

The rain stopped as suddenly as it had started. Bishop Nektarios hoped it would signal the end of his lengthy visit. But he made no attempt to terminate it. According to hierarchal protocol, it was the Archbishop's privilege to detain or dismiss his guest. Nektarios had not been bored or tired by his protracted informal meeting with Theoklitos. He had, in fact, found it pleasurably restful since he had done little talking. The Archbishop had done enough for both of them. The Bishop had not only gathered considerable information on the background of Dionysios Douropoulos, the young candidate for the Rezarios Seminary, but he was gaining, as well, some insight into the Archbishop's character and personality which were not readily evident in official meetings.

But Nektarios was now concerned with the thought of the unfinished work that awaited him at the Seminary and his desire to return in time for the simple evening mean he seldom failed to partake of with his seminarians. His anxiety was relieved, however, when His Beatitude remarked that the storm had abated and now he would be able to return safely to the Seminary.

"I fear I have detained you an unconscionable length of time," said the Archbishop, "however, at least part of your confinement in my office can be fairly attributed to that sudden stormy whim of nature." He glanced at the watch he brought forth from his pocket. "But it is not so late after all," he remarked as he showed Nektarios the time. "It is, as you can see, a little after seven o'clock—time enough to reach your destination well before it gets dark."

"What a beautiful watch that is!" exclaimed Nektarios, who normally failed to take notice of personal belongings or if he

314

became aware of them he was not likely to comment on them.

"Yes, indeed it is," replied Theoklitos.

Nektarios could not resist looking at it closely, "Why, it looks like the one Your Beatitude described—the one that Abbot Joachim gave to your pupil, Constantine."

"No, my friend," said Theoklitos, "it is not *like* that watch. *It is that watch* . . . I have told you how the old Abbot's watch came into our seminarian's hands but I neglected to tell you how it came to mine. I will gladly tell you that, too, if you are willing to postpone for a few minutes more your departure."

"Most willingly," responded the Bishop. "It would be, indeed, tantalizing not to know how the Abbot's watch completed its Odyssey and finally came to rest in your Beatitude's hands."

"Well, here is the long and short of it: On the day I was enthroned as Head of the Church, I found a small box on my desk. It was an ordinary one with no sign on it to designate where it had come from and with no card or note to indicate who had sent it or placed it on the desk. I opened it with a peculiar sense of excitement, which its exterior hardly warranted—and neither did its interior at first glance. I saw only an old worn leather pouch and I thought that someone was playing a joke on me. But in that unprepossessing container was Constantine's watch—cleaned and polished and looking more elegant than I remembered it from the time I first laid eyes on it more than a quarter of a century ago."

Theoklitos escorted Nektarios to the door—a courtesy that the Head of the Church was not expected to perform.

Before bidding his visitor goodnight, the Archbishop felt compelled to say a few more words. "I do not want you to leave, my dear Nektarios, with the erroneous impression I fear I have given you concerning Constantine Douropoulos' failure to take holy orders. I am as much if not more to blame for not inspiring him sufficiently to do so. But I hope that you will succeed in guiding his son, Dionysios, to follow the worthy calling of the priesthood."

"It is the hope we all share," replied Nektarios, "the hope for those who enter our seminaries in search of religious training. But it is God, not we, who imbues in wondrous ways the

315

hearts of men with the noble passion to serve His Church.''

The ways of God are truly wondrous, thought Nektarios, when in a few years he ordained by his own hand not Dionysios but his father, Constantine Douropoulos.

Four years elapsed before Nektarios' wish to visit Arcadia materialized. He had not intended to stay away from his work at the Seminary for more than ten days or so, he remained, nevertheless, practically the whole month of August at the home of Constantine and Alexandra Douropoulos, with whom he had formed a warm relationship.

It was during this first trip to Zatouna that the Saint performed a miracle which is recorded by Archimandrite Titus Mantheakis in his book, *The Holy Nektarios Kefalas*, containing testimonials on the Saint's healing powers. This miraculous cure involving Alexandra Douropoulos was also noted in several Greek and Americann newspapers and periodicals including Newsweek (October 2, 1961) and *The New York Times* and the *Herald Tribune* (January 3, 1965) after the official canonization of Nektarios which took place on August 20, 1961.

In 1954 Alexandra Douropoulos revisited her native land. Archimandrite Titos, who was about to publish his book, interviewed her regarding the miracle which the Saint* performed during his visit to her home in Arcadia. In a footnote on the material contributed by Presbytera Douropoulos, the author states that despite her advanced years, she has retained her physical and mental vigor; he further notes that she recalls with admirable accuracy events that had taken place fifty and more years ago. During her long life, the Presbytera has extended hospitality to preeminent personalities in the secular and ecclesiastical circles. ''Among those whose friendship she especially cherishes is that of His Holiness, the late Patriarch Athenagoras, formerly Archbishop of the Greek Orthodox Church of North and South America, and that of His Eminence, the present Archbishop Iakovos of North and South America.''

*Although the Metropolitan of Pentapolis was not canonized until forty-one years after his death on November 9, 1920, the populace had intuitively recognized his sanctity and referred to him as a Saint while he was still alive.

The following is Alexandra Douropoulos' recollection of Saint Nektarios' visit and the miracle which he performed:

"My two uncles, who were trustees of the Rezarios Ecclesiastical School, my husband and our son, Dionysios, a Rezarios seminarian at the time, escorted Saint Nektarios and his devoted secretary, Mr. Saccopoulos, to our home in Zatouna.

"We felt highly honored to have as our guest this Holy Father of the Church whose loving friendship and concern was to affect, in the next two years, the course of our life.

"For several hours in the morning and at nighttime, the Saint engaged in solitary prayer. Part of each day he spent reading or writing and dictating to his secretary. He found time, as well, to walk through our verdant woodlands or followed a hidden pathway on the mountain slopes as he chanted and recited his religious hymns and poems, which are among the treasures he bequeathed to Orthodoxy. In the evening after a simple repast, for the Saint preferred the simplest of fare, we would gather around him and listen, spellbound, to his exegesis on whatever passage from the Scriptures he chose to interpret for us.

"In the middle of Saint Nektarios' visit," said Alexandra, she experienced a mild headache and a slight stiffening of her neck. She assumed that these discomforts were due to a cold and promptly dismissed them from her mind.

After a lapse of four or five days, she awoke in the morning with a rash and a violent headache accompanied by a high fever and nausea that forced her to retch time and again. This caused her great distress, for she was barely able to move her neck or to flex her chin. Alarmed at his wife's condition, Constantine sent at once for Dr. Keninis. He was Alexandra's first cousin and as dear to her as a brother. His presence never failed to give her pleasure, but, in this instance she glanced at him apathetically as though he were a total stranger. When he finished his examination, the doctor shook his head; Alexandra's symptoms were the classic ones associated with spinal meningitis.

Bishop Nektarios broke the grim silence that followed the doctor's unequivocal diagnosis. "I would like to see Mrs. Douropoulos," he said, "and I wish to see her alone."

The doctor felt it was his duty to voice a warning: "Allow

me to remind Your Eminence that this dreaded disease is highly contagious.''

"That will not deter me," His Eminence replied.

Alexandra was not aware of the dark-robed figure that knelt for several hours at her bedside in silent prayer. "Yet, I had a strange feeling," replied Alexandra, "that someone was close by, trying to help me escape from an inferno in which I had somehow been trapped. I tried to look about me to see who had come to my rescue but neither my head nor my neck would move. Later, how much later, I cannot say, I thought a hand passed lightly over my forehead and I heard a voice saying, 'The fever is gone' and suddenly I was fully awake. As I pulled myself forward in order to sit up on the bed, I saw the Saint.

"His face had never seemed more radiant or his eyes more luminous. . . . But what had happened? Why was I lying in bed? And why was Saint Nektarios gazing intently at me with that sweet gentle smile of his? He must have sensed my bewilderment. 'You were drowsy,' he said, 'and fell asleep.' That was all he said to me.

"The news of my miraculous recovery from meningitis, within a few hours from its onset, spread quickly through the countryside, and our home soon became a place of worship for relatives and friends, acquaintances and strangers. Many came just to kiss the Saint's hand and to receive his benediction. Others who had heard of his infinite humanity sought him to confess their hidden thoughts or acts of evil that racked their conscience night and day. Gently and compassionately he led penitents to seek God's pardoning grace through the true admission and the sincere repentence of their sins. Confession with Saint Nektarios was an unforgettable spiritual experience.

"But however varied were the people or the reasons which brought them to our door, they left united in an intuitive conviction that Nektarios had been preordained a saint by his Maker.''

Few knew at the time and even fewer suspected—until Nektarios' archives came to light—how fearful a price this holy man had paid for his saintliness. He had endured many a cruel blow, but it was in his later years when he faced the cruelest trial of all for a man of God who had worn the cloth for a lifetime and had kept it free from the slightest stain.

The Metropolitan of Pentapolis retired with great honors from the Rezarios Seminary. He settled in Aegina where despite overwhelming obstacles he fulfilled his lifelong dream of founding the Convent of the Holy Trinity. It is now a renowned sanctuary where Saint Nektarios is buried and where a continual procession of pilgrims come to honor the memory of Orthodoxy's beloved twentieth-century Saint, and to seek his miraculous aid in restoring to them their mental and physical health.

In this tranquil Aegean island, the Bishop hoped to fulfill his lifelong desire for an ascetic existence; at the same time he would perform the ministerial duties that are an integral part of a monastic establishment. He would labor as a humble monk with his own hands to improve the nunnery so that those who sought its shelter would find not only serenity but beauty.

One day, the quiet of the cloister was violently shattered. A government official with two policemen in tow burst unannounced into Nektarios' study and savagely accused him of unspeakble crimes of venery.

In due time and due process of law, the Metropolitan of Pentapolis was completely absolved of the vile charges brought against him.

His accuser, however, was beset by a series of appalling misfortunes. Enfeebled to a tragic degree, he asked to be brought before Nektarios, and when he came in the presence of the man he had so cruelly maligned, the pitiable wretch fell at the Bishop's feet begging forgiveness.

"My son," Nektarios told him, "from the moment I first saw you I prayed for you and for those who sent you here. . . . I prayed to our Lord in the words of His Son: "Father, forgive them; for they know not what they do.' '"

Since the canonization of Saint Nektarios, the Greek Orthodox Faithful have erected in Greece, as well as in America, a number of impressive churches and chapels bearing his name. Of a dif-

The above is a brief account of a thoroughly-documented episode in the life of Saint Nektarios.

ferent order is a wayside shrine dedicated to the Saint in the village of Zatouna. It stands close to the edge of a broad southwestern curve on the main road and commands as fine a vista as can be found in all of Arcadia—one that is most arresting from early spring to late autumn when the wild broom flourishes "yellow and bright as boullion unalloyed." The eye sweeps over the golden blossoms on the slopes down to the valleys that merge with the verdant plain of Megalopolis and beyond to the distant horizon where the mountain peaks form a violet crown against the sky.

The Saint Nektarios shrine was a gift to his birthplace, from Louis Theophilos, the youngest son of Alexandra's only sister, Sophia. He migrated to America in his youth but returned to his native land in the late years of his life with his lovely Greek-born wife, Niobe. On one of his periodic trips to Zatouna—it was to be his last—he had the inspiration to erect a shrine dedicated to the saint who in years long past had come to Zatouna more than once as a guest in the home of his Aunt Alexandra.

The shrine is a small replica of a traditional Byzantine church with a central dome and one on each of its four corners, all of which bear a simple marble cross. The walls are constructed with native stone. Each of them is meticulously fitted and symmetrically placed so that the total composition has a jewel-like quality befitting a setting of timeless beauty.

In the arch above the door of the Saint Nektarios shrine is a marble plaque. On it is inscribed:

ERECTED IN THE MEMORY OF
ALEXANDRA DOUROPOULOS

Chapter Thirty-two

October had come again and with it the fourth anniversary of Father Douropoulos' resignation from the Greek church in Boston. The priest found it hard to believe that four years had passed by since his letter to Archbishop Alexander apprising him of his decision to relinquish his duties as pastor of Boston's Greek Orthodox community.

To the Priest it now seemed that the years were growing shorter while the days were getting longer. . . . In the last few months he found that he had more hours to spare than ever before. And soon—how soon he did not know—he would have more time, infinitely more time—not on this earth but in the realm of eternity. Of late, Father Douropoulos had the feeling that his life was coming to an end. He did not attempt to deny this prescient sense of death, nor was he consciously frightened by it. As a rational being, he accepted the immutable law of nature that man was born to die. And if Divine Providence deemed that his time had come, he was prepared to say in the words of Saint Luke: "Lord, now lettest thou they servant depart in peace."

The stoicism with which Father Douropoulos accepted the premonition of his life's end must have faltered, however, when his mind turned to his family. He must have found it unbearable to think that he would soon be separated from his children, and above all, from his wife. He loved his children and loved them dearly, but they were the "by-product" of his union with

Alexandra—a blessed union for which he would be ever grateful.

Another part of his life which would arouse in him a flood of poignant memories was the village of Vancon where he was born and bred. For now that he could hear the flutter of Death's dark wings, he knew that he would not see his birthplace again— that tiny piece of Arcadia where he first sensed the sweet freshness of early life.

But Father Douropoulos' self-imposed discipline which had stood him in good stead through the years did not fail him now. He gave no indication of his thoughts and feelings as he contemplated the foreshadowing of his life's end. Only his wife seemed to be vaguely aware that something was amiss by the preoccupied, abstracted expression on her husband's face and the measured way he walked which was unlike his usual firm stride. She did not, however, appear disturbed by these indications of her husband's ebbing strength; rather, she was grateful to God that the strain to which he had been subjected during the last four years, and the stress he endured as a pioneer priest in the New World, had not been as harmful to his health as she had anticipated with grave misgivings. But beneath the rationale of her thinking lay the sublimated fears of a woman who loved her husband deeply and who had unconsciously assumed a sanguine view of his well-being.

Alexandra's deep-rooted anxieties nevertheless came quickly to the fore when her husband wanted to join her on a trip to New York. Their daughter, Sophia, had given birth to her second child a few months ago and her delivery—a difficult one in this instance—was followed by a post-partum depression.

Despite the reassurances from Sophia's husband that his wife was steadily improving and that the infant was thriving under the care of a competent nurse, the Presbytera wanted to judge these matters for herself by spending a few days at her daughter's house in New York. Father Constantine was anxious to accompany his wife but she thought it unwise for him to undertake the hurried trip she had in mind. She did not express her fear that it would tire him unduly but persuaded him to wait until they could go for a leisurely visit. He would then have more time to enjoy their first grandson, Bobby, a lively, loveable two year old and the new grandchild who was the Priest's namesake. (According to custom the first and second grandson in a Greek family bear respectively the name of their paternal and maternal grandfather.)

The Presbytera found that the situation at the Limpert house left much to be desired. She was, however, pleased to inform her husband when she called home that Sophia had, indeed, improved; she seemed not only well enough but, in fact, anxious to start taking care of her infant son. Yet, that vixen of a nurse wouldn't allow her to hold the baby. "And would you believe it, that miserable woman," Alexandra fumed, "even tried to stop me from picking up that dear little creature. Why, you'd think I had no idea how to hold and cuddle a child and give it *latra*—the tender care and love that children need—as though I hadn't raised eight of them!"

Father Constantine did not need to ask who had won *that* battle of wills, nor was he surprised at his wife's next communiqué: The nurse had left in a huff. But his wife's triumphant declaration had its downside. She would have to remain a while longer to make sure Sophia could comfortably cope with her maternal duties. She assured her husband, however, that she would be home in time to celebrate Christmas—whereupon he announced he would join his wife without fail in New York.

This time his wife did not try to dissuade him from his decision. She had no doubt that he missed her despite his good fortune in being surrounded by his children who were unfailingly solicitous of his welfare. The change, she now believed, would do him good and ease his mind about Sophia's progress; even though her husband would not admit having more affection for one daughter than the other, his wife was, nevertheless, aware that a special fondness, or what should, perhaps, be called a special "liking," existed between her second daughter, Sophia, and her father. But above all, she would see for herself how her husband was faring, for she did not trust his reassurances that he was feeling fine; perhaps it was so, perhaps she had been overly concerned about him but how could she help it—he was her husband, her beloved husband . . . may God be with him, she murmured, and made the sign of the cross.

Father Douropoulos was busy packing his bag when Elly left for school. She was well on her way when it began raining. There had been no sign of rain when she left the house otherwise Elly would have worn her bright yellow slicker and the matching fisherman's hat. But if she went back for it now she would be late for school. From the time she had entered the first grade she had never been tardy—not even once—and now that she was in junior high school she was not about to spoil her record. Thank goodness, this wasn't anything but a few drops of rain that would hardly amount to much, certainly not a nasty "north-easter" like the one a couple of weeks ago. She started to giggle as she remembered what happened to Arthur in that rainstorm. They had gone to school in the morning, both wearing their slickers and rain hats, but when her brother came home in the afternoon he was sopping wet from head to foot.

Eleni was appalled at the sight of him standing on her freshly washed kitchen floor in a pool of muddy water. "What happened to you," she cried, "and where's your raincoat?"

"I forgot it in school," he replied nonchalantly.

"Forgot it in school!" shrieked Eleni. "How stupid can you be! I wish your sisters could see you now. They're always saying how smart you are. Well, any boy who had brains wouldn't forget his raincoat on a day like this. You better get out of my way so I can mop up the floor again—after all the time I spent washing and waxing it. Go on now, go upstairs and take off those soggy clothes before you catch your death of cold; it will serve you right if you do, letting yourself get wet to the bone—po, po, po, wet to the bone," she repeated.

Whatever her thoughts and feelings might be, Eleni did not express them directly. Arthur, therefore, suspected that her attack on his intelligence was a covering for the anxiety she felt lest he catch his "death of cold." Nevertheless, he was irked by her concern. He was now old enough to be responsible for his actions rather than be told what he should have done or what he should do. But was it fair of him to expect Eleni to grasp the fact that he was no longer a little boy when his mother and sisters

324

failed to do so? No, he couldn't upbraid Eleni; he tried, instead, to assure her that he wouldn't catch a cold or get pneumonia since he hadn't gotten "wet to the bone."

"You see, Eleni," he explained, "people are really water-proof, I mean their skin is—yes, they can get 'wet to the skin' but not beyond it. That's why they don't get waterlogged and drown when they're in the water for some reason or other. That goes for fish and all the animals, too, that live in the water most or all the time. If they weren't waterproof, they'd drown in no time, wouldn't they?"

Leaving his question hanging in the air, Arthur bounded up the stairs to change his clothes and Eleni started to mop the floor with a puzzled look on her face.

By the time Elly had walked a few blocks, she had dismissed from her mind the recollection of that foolish little squabble between Eleni and Arthur. Her thought now wandered idly un-til she reached the railroad tracks that ran across Massachusetts Avenue in the center of the town from where she could hear the faint whistle of a distant train. But at night when she was still awake in her bed, the train's whistle reached her clearly with a plaintive sound that made her feel sad. She would start thinking about the people on that train. Why and where were they going in the dark hours of the night? She wondered if they were on their way to some far-away place and leaving behind them some-one they dearly loved—someone they would never see again. One of these days, she would write a story about a train and the "mysterious people" on it.

When Elly told Arthur about her literary inspiration, he had scoffed at the idea. "That's old hat stuff . . . romantic notions that amount to nothing more than sheer bathos," he remarked in a supercilious tone, "and there's all kinds of stories about people on trains going to strange places trying to escape the police (they're always called *gendarmes* in those stories) because they've murdered someone or stolen money or jewelry or what have you. Of course, its a different matter if they're well written, and about fabulous trains like the "Orient Express." But what can you write about these dinky small-town trains that start in Boston at North Station and stop at dull little suburbs like Arlington?"

325

Her brother could really be awfully annoying at times, yet Elly would forgive him because he was only teasing her. But she could always depend on him to defend her against her sisters when they rebuked her sharply. For unlike them, Arthur was never mean or nasty to her. So, how could she not love him?

Elly had no sooner passed the tracks when she remembered with a start that her father was taking the train to New York this very day. How stupid of her not to have said good-bye. Now, of course, it was much too late to go back home and return to school before the tardy bell rang . . . well, maybe it wouldn't really mean that much to her father. Lately she had noticed that he seemed more preoccupied than usual, and perhaps he wouldn't even notice that she had already left for school. Having thus rationalized her thoughtlessness, Elly continued on her way.

But she had gone no more than a few steps when suddenly she stopped. For a moment or two Elly stood motionless then abruptly turned around and began quickly retracing her steps to Palmer Street. What compelled her to do so she did not know or try to fathom. Nor did it matter that she would spoil her perfect school record for promptness. All that mattered to her now was a compelling urge to see her father—to see him before he left for New York today. The priest was coming down the stairs for breakfast when Elly burst into the house. He was surprised at her unexpected appearance. "Aren't you supposed to be in school?" her father asked as he glanced at the glass-domed clock on the hall table. Yes, but she had forgotten something—that's why she had returned, Elly replied.

"It must be something important to make you come back home." She hesitated for a moment then she blurted out: "I came back home because I forgot to say good-bye to you, Bábá. I didn't remember you were going away today until I had almost reached school."

"I'm glad to see you, of course, before I leave, but if I'm not mistaken, won't this be the first 'tardy mark' on your report card?"

She tried to make light of it; really she didn't care about that . . . she was bound to be tardy sooner or later now that she had entered junior high school, which started one hour earlier than grammar school, and besides she had to walk twice as far; so, any day now she would surely not make it on time.

She changed the subject as quickly as she could: "Will you please call us tonight, Babá, so we'll know that you arrived safe and sound?"

He thought it was unnecessary to telephone home regarding his arrival in New York. "They are expecting me, and if I do *not* arrive then you will surely get a call. This is an instance when no news is certainly good news. At any rate, I shall write in a few days. If all is going well at the Limpert household we will return home no later than the week-end of the twentieth of the month. That should allow sufficient time to prepare for the celebration of Christmas on the following Thursday—God willing."

God willing . . . Elly had often heard her father and her mother use that phrase, but now for the first time it rang ominously in her ears. What if God did *not* will that her father could come home for Christmas? What if God willed that her father would *never* come home again? Suddenly Elly became aware of an inexplicable fear that her father was going to die—and it was that fear she now realized, which had subconsciously made her return home.

Her father's voice broke into the turmoil of her thoughts. "Elly," he asked in a casual tone, "what made you come back home?"

"You asked me that already, Babá, and I told you I came back because—well, because I thought—I mean I just wanted to see you before you left for New York."

"Ah, yes, so you did. Well, I must say that I am glad that you came back, my child. I am sorry, though, that you will be penalized with a tardy mark on my account. But it shows all the more how considerate you are to be willingly late for school in order to bid your father good-bye."

But she could not say "good-bye," for the very word lodged in her throat like a stone . . . she wanted to put her arms around him, to tell him she loved him, how much they all loved him; in fact, she suspected that her sisters loved him more than their mother. But no, she mustn't tell him that; Babá loved mother

327

so much he would be hurt if he knew they loved him more.

She had better go without saying anything at all; they were not a family that made extravagant display of their feelings. Yet, she could not resist the impulse to kiss his hand as she and Arthur used to do when they were little children before going to bed—a Greek gesture of respect accorded to churchmen, and to the venerable aged by reason of their benevolence and dignity.

Neither of them spoke. Elly opened the door and closed it gently behind her. She remembered her father saying: "You can tell mannerly people by the way they close a door."

Sophia and her mother were upset because Father Douropoulos made light of the pain in his back which began a few days after he had arrived in New York. All he needed to overcome it, he assured them, was a few days' rest and a few aspirins. The pain, however, persisted and his discomfort was exacerbated by a sudden onset of abdominal pains.

Dion, who was now working in New York for the Borden Company, came every night to see his father. He had left Boston after his partnership with Hercules Petrakis was dissolved. Their heavy investment in coffee and sugar, which were scarce commodities in the First World War became abundantly available after the war. As a result their enterprise was in financial jeopardy. In the meantime, Hercules married; Dion—quixotic as ever—withdrew from the partnership leaving whatever profits could be salvaged for his partner's benefit.

Dion had become acquainted with Dr. Corillos, a distinguished Greek doctor who had recently come to New York to study the advanced procedures and techniques in American medicine. Since his condition had not improved, Father Constantine did not object to his son's arrangements for an examination by a compatriot with whom he could converse in their common mother tongue. After the examination, Dr. Corillos recommended that his patient go to the Columbia Presbyterian Hospital, with which Dr. Corillos was connected at the time, for tests, X-rays and further examinations that were necessary before an accurate diagnosis could be made. The doctor was pleased that as far as he could determine, Father Douropoulos was generally in good health, and he hoped that further tests would prove no less satisfactory.

In a letter dated Monday, December 22, 1924, addressed to his daughters and Arthur, Father Douropoulos writes: "Your mother and I are very disappointed that we will not be with you for Christmas. The doctor advises me not to travel since I still have pain and I feel weak. On the whole I am improving but rather slowly. However, I hope to feel well enough by next week so that the doctor will not object to my coming back in time for the New Year. Sophia is fine and the little ones are a delight and our visit here is enjoyable; nevertheless, we would rather be in Arlington during the coming holidays. But that is how it is, according to God's will. May my indisposition be something that will pass. Love from all of us to all of you, and may God be willing that we will soon be together again."

By the end of the week, the priest had taken a turn for the worse. At the doctor's orders he entered the hospital for the first time in his life as a patient. A series of tests, X-rays and further examinations failed to give any indication as to the cause of his alarming condition. Dr. Corillos had a consultation with his colleagues and the consensus was to perform an exploratory operation on his patient the following day, December the twenty-ninth.

The family was greatly disturbed that Father Douropoulos would be subjected to an operation to determine the nature of his illness. The Presbytera, however, found comfort that her husband would be in the hands of a surgeon by the name of Dr. St. John. Anyone with so revered a name would surely be a fine doctor. And, indeed, Dr. St. John was acknowledged in his day as one of the outstanding surgeons in New York.

Monday morning of December twenty-ninth, Mrs. Douropoulos, Dion, Sophia and her husband came early to the Columbia Presbyterian Hospital. They waited in somber silence, withholding from one another the fears that haunted their minds while the exploratory operation on Father Douropoulos was taking place.

The interminable suspense dissolved as soon as Dr. Corillos came smiling into the room. His patient, he reported, had withstood the operation splendidly, and he was happy to say that nothing of a malignant nature had been found. The Presbytera could see her husband briefly as soon as he recovered from the anesthesia. Tomorrow if all went well, the rest of the family— one or two at a time could see him, but for only a limited time. And on Thursday, New Year's Day, the doctor hoped Father Douropoulos would be feeling comfortable enough to see his family for a longer period.

Dion walked with the doctor as far as the corridor. What, he asked, was Dr. Corillos' prognosis regarding his father's full recovery? The doctor replied that he would discuss the matter with Dr. St. John before expressing an opinion. "As you well know, Dionysios, an abdominal operation is a trauma to the system. So far all we know—to the extent we could determine from the exploratory operation—is that your father' illness is not due to an abdominal malignancy which we suspected. But we do not know yet what is causing his illness. Therefore, we need more time before we attempt to make a diagnosis—let alone a prognosis."

"Yes, of course," replied Dion. He understood the doctor's position and he apologized for his inopportune question. But he was now troubled by a matter of immediate concern—the likelihood of an embolism, a hemorrhage or an infection in the wake of his father's operation.

"Those are legitimate fears," said Dr. Corillos, but made no further comment. For he noticed that his young friend's face was deeply lined with anxiety. Although the doctor was already late for his office appointments, he was reluctant to leave without trying to lighten a loving son's concern for his father. . . . "As I have already told you, Dionysios, your father is basically a healthy man and the chances for recovery are in his favor—even more so if he has the will to live, and I am sure he has the desire to survive and enjoy the years ahead with so devoted and fine a family as his. The will to live is more potent than any medication or treatment a doctor can give. So let us not dwell on the dark side. We have good reason to hope—to hope for the best."

But the best was not to be. In mid-afternoon of New Year's Day, Father Douropoulos' life came to an end.

330

The final entry on the hospital record of the Rev. Constantine A. Douropoulos was the date of his death, January 1, 1925: *Cause of death* unknown.

Within three years of her husband's death, Alexandra was faced with another tragedy. Dionysios was killed by a drunken driver. Of the many misfortunes in her lifetime the cruelest was the death of her first-born son—a son who respected and admired and adored his mother.

Chapter Thirty-three

During the nineteen-thirties, the Great Depression reached pandemic proportions throughout the country. In those fearful years, thousands of homes, including the Douropoulos house on Palmer Street, were foreclosed. The Presbytera accepted her loss with the fortitude of those who have an insuperable faith in God's will. Yet, whenever she spoke or thought of her home she would sigh, for she was no longer the mistress of a household that accommodated her large family and those who entered freely through its "open door." What troubled her most, however, was the loss of security which the house afforded her—the security which she owed to a loving husband's foresight. And now through no fault of his or hers, she no longer had a roof over her head.

Elly, meanwhile, had married and was living in Cambridge. The young couple decided to rent a larger apartment with two bedrooms which they could hardly afford. But if Elly's mother could be induced to live with them, a room of her own was indispensible. Elly and her husband, who was devoted to his mother-in-law, were finally able to persuade Mrs. Douropoulos to make her home with them.

This mutually satisfactory arrangement was terminated when Elly's husband entered the government's service in Washington during the war years as an attorney. The Presbytera refused to leave Boston; she found an apartment at a low rent, for there was no lack of inexpensive housing during those economically depressed years. She managed to live a full life despite her meager means and the fierce blows she had been dealt thus far in her life. Besides the death of her first-born son, Dion, Alexandra had cared for, and had watched in helpless anguish, her first-born daughter, the sweet, kind, gentle Angela, die of cancer.

By the early nineteen-fifties, Alexandra's four married daughters and her son had gravitated to New York. Arthur was no longer teaching, but had been appointed Director of the Press and Information Department of the Greek Archdiocese and English editor of the *Orthodox Observer*, official publication of the Archdiocese in New York.

The matriarch of the family was now eighty years old and her children urged her to join them in New York. The advantages of such a relocation were obvious. She would be at least near her offspring, near to Arthur, now her only son, to whom she was deeply attached, and to Elly, her youngest child, who was closer to her than the rest of her daughters; and she would be near her grandchildren that she dearly loved — especially Elly's daughter, the only one of her granddaughters who was her namesake.

But for Alexandra to leave Boston was a heartrending decision. She would be leaving behind Catherine, her sensitive gifted daughter who was blessed with a fine soprano voice. Following her father's death, Catherine became despondent but in a relatively short time she appeared to have regained her spirits and began again to train her voice.

The shock, however, of her brother's Dion's sudden death in an automobile accident brought on a severe depression. Despite the best medical care available at that time, Catherine's illness proved intractable, and she was indefinitely hospitalized. Had her illness occurred a few decades later, she likely would have been cured by the anti-depressants (called "miraculous" by many of those cured through their use), along with other modalities used today as needed to spur on recovery.

At the insistance of her children, Alexandra finally settled in New York with the resolve to return to Boston to see her daughter as often as possible.

With her strong spirit of independence, Alexandra decided to live by herself in a small hotel which catered mainly to a Greek clientele of transient guests and permanent lodgers. Although her children were now able to give her sufficient assistance for more comfortable quarters, their mother preferred to live as inexpensively as possible. Whatever she could save she would use to help others for whom a few dollars more a month was a godsend. She, therefore, chose an average-sized room with a "kitchenette" which amounted to nothing more than an old stove, refrigerator and sink. Yet, without any of the amenities she had in her home on Palmer Street, that ordinary room became overnight, so to speak, the center of the hotel's social activities.

One of the Presbytera's first visitors in New York was Anastasia Perris who had known the Douropoulos family from the early years in Arlington. Anastasia and her friend, Zoë, had come to America after the First World War. They were in a group of four or five young girls sent to Boston under the auspices of Queen Sophia of Greece to study "home economics" at Simmon's College.

The two friends soon became attached to the Douropoulos household where they spent most of their free time. They decided to eliminate the nuisance of transportation back and forth to Arlington by renting a room from Maggie Barry who lived a few doors away from the Douropoulos home. Maggie, bereft of her mother when she was about fourteen years old, considered it her duty to take care of her father. By the time he died during the virulent 1918 influenza epidemic, Maggie was middle-aged and unmarried, and well off—thanks to her father's success as a builder of fine houses for the carriage trade "above the tracks."

Of all people—it was a most engaging Irishman, Father Flaherty, priest at St. Agnes Catholic Church in Arlington, who found living quarters for the two Greek students that had recently come to Boston.

Since Thomas Barry's death, Father Flaherty, a Catholic priest, had kept close watch on Barry's only daughter, Maggie. Although she was not the complaining kind, the priest suspected she was lonesome in the large handsome house her father had

334

built for his family. And surely it must have seemed strangely quiet to Barry's daughter that her father's hearty voice and his lusty laughter no longer reverberated through the house.

Occasionally on a Saturday afternoon, if Father Flaherty was free of any unexpected demands, he visited as many of his parishioners as time allowed. He usually put Maggie Barry's name on top of his list for he was anxious to know how she was faring. On his way down Palmer Street he saw the Douropoulos house. He had been the first priest in Arlington to pay his respects to the Greek Orthodox cleric and his family soon after their arrival in Arlington. He had been cordially received by Father Douropoulos and his wife and they had warmly urged him to come again any time he desired. On the spur of the moment, he decided to do so. He apologized for his unexpected intrusion when he saw a group of young people gathered around a tea table. He was prepared to leave but Mrs. Douropoulos insisted that he must stay and have a cup of tea, at least—and so he stayed, and stayed much longer than he had intended.

When he finally arrived at Maggie's house, she pretended to be hurt that Father Flaherty had stopped at the Greek priest's house before coming to see her; apparently she was just an "afterthought." But what was he doing, if she might ask, all that time at the Douropoulos' house?

Well, he wasn't doing what *she* obviously had been doing—looking out of the window and keeping track of everybody's business on Palmer Street.

"Don't try to evade my question, Father. Will you please tell me just what *were* you doing there practically all afternoon?"

"Enjoying myself," he replied in the rich brogue he had yet to lose. "Now, Maggie, you don't expect an Irishman worthy of his name not to be tempted to linger a bit when he finds himself surrounded by a flock of pretty girls, and if he wears a Roman collar his hand is kissed when he enters, and when he leaves, which is what properly brought up Greeks are taught to do to those who wear the cloth. And that's more than a Catholic priest gets from his parishioners." Maggie burst out laughing. What a dear rogue he was! No wonder everyone loved him, Catholics and non-Catholics alike.

335

"Ah, Maggie, it does my heart good to hear you laugh. And now let's talk seriously about my visit to your neighbors. I believe it was Divine Providence that prompted me to ring their bell. Among the young people there were two pretty girls, very pretty girls," he added with a twinkle in his eye, "sent by the queen of Greece to study here. By the way, they speak English fluently. They're looking for a room to rent in this area.

"I thought of you living alone in this big lovely house. Maggie, take my advice and rent them a room. I know you don't need the money, but you need these nice, bright, lovely girls to give light and sound to this house."

Maggie Barry never had cause to regret Father Flaherty's advice. As for Anastasia and Zoë, their landlady was the first to dispell a misconception of theirs: In America, they had been told, and particularly in New England, they would find the attitude towards strangers cold, ungracious and inhospitable. Nothing could have been less true. The Greeks, they soon discovered, did not have a monopoly in the matter of hospitality.

When they had completed their studies in Boston, Anastasia and Zoë returned to their native land. Within a few years they both had "good fortune"—the way Greeks speak of a fine marriage.

Years later, Tom Petris, Anastasia's husband, who was a ship owner, opened a branch office in New York where he and his wife established a second home as elegant as the one they retained in Athens. When Anastasia learned that Mrs. Douropoulos had moved to New York, she went at once to see her.

Anastasia came home late from her visit to find her husband waiting for her. Tom could see that his wife was anxious to tell him about her old friend. "Why don't we have a bite to eat first," he suggested, "and then you can take your time and tell me all about your visit."

When dinner was finished, Tom lit the one cigar he allowed himself each day. "Now," he said, "let's hear your news about the Presbytera. Incidentally, how long has it been since you last saw her?"

"All of thirty-five years ago; she was a middle-aged woman

336

then, and I," sighed Anastasia, "was a young girl in my early twenties. Since I last saw her, she has endured the terrible blows of losing her husband, then Dionysios, her older son and Angela, her oldest daughter. I expected to find an elderly woman steeped in grief, and I did find her deeply grieved. But her grief was contained in front of others so as not to distress them beyond the point of consideration. She was always thoughtful of people's feelings—unlike our countrywomen, not all of them, I'm glad to say, who are wrapped in a shroud of self-pity and sorrow. They refuse to accept that their lost loved ones are hostages of fate. All they do is wring their hands and bemoan their lot *ad infinitum.*"

"Let's be thankful," remarked her husband, "at least, they don't practice 'suttee.' "

"That's barbaric—and the Greeks have never been barbarians."

"Really!" exclaimed Tom, as his eyebrows arched in sardonic amusement.

Anastasia wisely chose to overlook her husband's mockery, which she admitted to herself was justified in view of her irrational chauvinism. She went on to say that neither time nor sorrow had significantly altered the Presbytera's appearance, at least, not outwardly. She had always belied her age and she still continued to do so. Her fine features had not sagged despite the force of gravity, and her complexion had retained its freshness. "I think that was mainly due," explained Anastasia, "to the striking change in the color of her hair. She still wears it in the old style of a 'grande dame' high on her head like a coronet. Now, though it's white, all white, with an odd golden gilt to it. White hair, you know, softens the face, for it blends in with the inevitable changes in the tones of an aging skin. If the Presbytera was a vain woman, I would swear she had colored her hair in that lovely pale golden tone it now has, but she never used any cosmetics—not even a dab of face powder. And why should she when she doesn't need to?"

"It never fails to amaze me how many details women can see at a glance which men miss completely. But tell me, what was your old friend's reaction when she first saw you?"

"Well, her face lit up at first with that lovely smile of hers, then she broke down and we both wept. I'm ashamed to say she pulled herself together sooner than I did. But as she wiped the tears from her face, I saw the pain in her eyes—the pain that would never leave her, and I wept again. 'Don't cry, please, don't cry,' she said, 'we mustn't spoil this moment when we meet again after so many years!' She said nothing more but looked me up and down with approval and remarked, 'Why, you're just as petite and pretty as when I last saw you.' That pleased me, of course, though I'm afraid she was more kind than accurate. She asked about you and mentioned some very nice things she had heard about you more than once through the years."

"I hope you confirmed them," said Tom.

"Of course not," replied Anastasia with a sweet smile; and now that she had gotten even with her husband for his "sardonic mockery," she went on to say that her hostess excused herself to see how the water for their tea was coming along. She had put the kettle on before I arrived, she explained, for the stove was an old one and it took so long to heat the water. That was the only apology—an oblique one at that—which she made regarding the inconveniences she put up with in her lodgings.

"I began to glance idly about the room, but my eyes went no further than the wall opposite me where a sizeable picture in soft muted colors had been hung. As I went closer to it I saw that it was an oil painting of Father Douropoulos. He was sitting in a wicker chair reading a book on the porch of the Palmer Street house, and he was wearing his cassock which he always wore at home."

Anastasia, absorbed in the picture, did not hear her hostess lay the tea tray on a table until she asked, "Isn't it a splendid likeness?" she asked. Yes, it is, Anastasia had replied, but resemblance was a matter of technique rather than talent. What had struck Anastasia was the painterly quality of the work. The portrait was devoid of a formal or pretentious pose; so Anastasia surmised that the artist had come across Father Douropoulos by chance on that summer day with a light breeze gently ruffling the priest's hair. And the artist was inspired to re-create this moment of unfeigned beauty which seemed to possess an overtone

338

of spirituality.

"Who painted this picture?" asked Anastasia.

"An artist from Greece, who had been commissioned to do the icons in the Greek Cathedral of Boston. Those Byzantine icons are as beautiful as I've seen anywhere. His name was Evangelos Ioannides," said Mrs. Douropoulos.

"Evangelos Ioannides! Oh, I know him, or rather I knew of him. I always went to his exhibitions in Athens. He was well-known, a fine painter who had studied in Germany and one of the outstanding followers of the Munich School. The poor man died of malnutrition during the German occupation of Greece in the early forties. Please, do tell me more about him and how he came to paint your husband's picture."

"He was in America for a number of years as an iconographer. And during the time he was in Boston, he became one of our dearest friends. He was a fine-looking man, quiet, and unassuming—a gentleman in every respect. Demetra's husband, Nick, who was involved in bringing him to Boston, believed that Ioannides was not only an eminent artist but one who had a highly cultivated, brilliant mind. He was middle-aged then, and my daughters didn't bother with him; they were more interested in the group of young men that came to the house. But Elly, who was much younger than her sisters, was very fond of him and 'Don Evangelos,' as she called him, was devoted to her.

"After he returned to Greece, he corresponded faithfully with Elly. I remember that she received a letter from him—his last one—just *after* the Germans occupied Greece. Who knows how it slipped by the strict censorship of those days. Elly can tell you more about 'Don Evanglos' than the rest of us. Some day, if you like, we'll go and see Elly. She recently moved to Darien, Connecticut, which is fairly close to New York."

"I'd love to see her. I can only think of Elly as I last saw her—just a little girl. I can't quite believe that she is grown-up and married."

"I'm afraid, Anastasia dear, it's only in our memories that time stands still . . . but come now, let's have our tea before it gets cold."

"Really, Tom, nothing brought me more vividly, more

339

poignantly back to the house on Palmer Street than the *Presbytera's* lovely old Sheffield tray with two of the same English Cauldon china cups we drank tea from in Arlington. They were shaped like lilies and adorned with a gold edging. Only in those days there were usually far more than two teacups on the large mission oak table in the dining room, and the sideboard was filled with plates of sweets. Some of us would sit around the table and others would take their tea in the parlor. And Elly and Arthur, the two little ones in the family, would pass around the sweets.''

"Didn't those kids ever drop a plate of those sweets?" asked Tom. "I surely couldn't have done anything like that—going around with sweets without dropping the whole business on the floor, or on somebody's lap.''

"Tom, dear, if you were as chubby when you were a child as you are now, you would have eaten all of them up before you would pass any around. I must say those two children were well-behaved. Of course, they were used to being around older people, for they were considerably younger than their siblings and had grown up among adults. They had a lot of poise as a result, although Arthur was a shy little boy. They were sort of a family apart—the only two, by the way, that were born in America. You could see there was a strong bond between them.

"To get back to the Arlington days in my youth, I liked sitting in the Douropoulos parlor which most people would have considered old fashioned by that time; but I thought it was charming, for it had a Victorian flavor with lace curtains and green plush furniture and a green Aubusson carpet that had a rose and cream medallion in its center. How many hours we spent in that room talking about life—as though we knew all about it then—talking and philosophizing like bright young fools, like 'oximora' as the Greeks would have called us.

"Those early days in Arlington must have been the halcyon days of the Presbytera's life in America when her large family formed an unbroken circle. Zoë and I used to call it the 'magic circle.' Yet, today in that little hotel room we drank our tea and chatted like a couple of schoolgirls, and before I knew it the afternoon was gone, a most pleasant one, thanks to my hostess. She had succeeded in making me forget her deep sorrows and to

340

overlook her cramped quarters."

"Quite a feat, I must say," remarked Tom, "I certainly would like to meet that remarkable woman. Why don't you invite her over for dinner one of these days?"

"Oh, I intend to do so—not once but as often as she can come. But even if she came time and time again I could never hope to match her hospitality."

For a few moments Anastasia paused with a puzzled expression. "I wonder why—why everyone speaks of the Presbytera as a 'remarkable' woman?

"I remember when I was in Boston, what Raphael Demos had said about her way back then. He was a close friend of the Douropoulos family. I always listened carefully to what he had to say. Young as he was then, he had a brilliant analytical mind. It's no wonder that he became the head of the philosophy department at Harvard. I still have what he said written down in the diary that I faithfully kept in my student days. He spoke of the Presbytera as vital, regal, dynamic, even dominating, making an unforgettable impact in whatever group she happened to be. He recalled something Jessie Whitehead said about her. Jessie was the daughter of the English philosopher, Alfred North Whitehead, and Catherine, one of the Douropoulos girls, worked at the Harvard Widener Library as an assistant to Jessie on Greek books. She had invited Jessie for tea at home one afternoon, and Catherine must have felt uneasy about her mother who was not 'intellectual.' What Jessie Whitehead said afterwards to Raphael Demos was that Catherine's mother did not have to study history because she embodied history and tradition and the legends of Greece."

"That," said Tom, "says in a few words a great deal about Mrs. Douropoulos and about the perception of that great philosopher's daughter."

"Yes, it does, but still it doesn't explain what makes my old friend so *remarkable* a personality," persisted Anastasia.

"What you are asking for is a definition of 'personality'— something that's indefinable, I think. 'Personality' has no common denominator. One can be rich or poor, with good looks or

341

not, well-educated or practically illiterate (like Kazantzakis' *Zorba*, for instance); one can lack personal or family prestige or any number of virtues and vices, as well, and may or may not have personality. In other words, it defies definition and that's because it's a mystery.''

"A mystery," repeated Anastasia in bemusement. "Then why not call it the 'mystique of personality' and let it go at that?''

"Oh, one of those Americanisms—not a bad phrase, I must say—the mystique of personality," smiled her husband. "By all means, use it if you like even though it doesn't mean much.''

She smiled back at him. "Indeed I shall, even though you really don't approve of these fashionable words or phrases,purist that you are.''

In the dozen years or so since Anastasia Petris first visited Mrs. Douropoulos in New York, she never failed to see her during her annual trips to America. However, in 1964 Anastasia did not come to New York at her usual time in the fall. Her mother's illness kept her in Athens. In November of that year she wrote to her old friend that her mother had regained her health, and she would be coming to New York directly after the New Year. Anastasia made reservations for her return to America by boat as she disliked flying. On the second or third day of January she sailed from Piraeus, the main port of Greece. Midway on her journey, she suffered a fatal heart attack on board ship and was buried at sea.

But even if Anastasia's life had not come to so sudden and tragic an end, she would not have seen her old friend if she had been fortunate enough to reach New York. For Alexandra Douropoulos died on January 1, 1965.

On January 3, 1965, the New York and Boston newspapers, and shortly after, the Athenian press, announced the death of Alexandra Douropoulos. The Sunday edition of the *New York Herald Tribune*, January 3, 1965 (p. 34), carried the news of her death as the lead article in the obituary page. The heading stated "Widow of Greek Priest, Claimed Cure by Saint Canonized in '58.'" The following is, in essence, the information given by the

A woman who knew the most recently canonized saint of the Greek Orthodox Church, Mrs. Alexandra Douropoulos died in her 95th year at the French hospital here. Her death took place on New Year's Day, forty years to the day that her husband had died.

Mrs. Douropoulos, who lived at the Hotel Newton since 1950, claimed to have been cured of a form of meningitis in 1902 by the prayers of Bishop Nektarios, Metropolitan of Pentapolis, when she was a young woman in Greece. The bishop was canonized Saint Nektarios by the Ecumenical Patriarchate of Constantinople (Istanbul) in 1958* and his icon is in the Church of the Evangelismos here, which Mrs. Douropoulos had commissioned in Greece during one of her trips to her motherland.

Mrs. Douropoulos was the wife of the Rev. Constantine Douropoulos, a pioneer priest of the Greek Orthodox Church in the United States, who died January 1, 1925, after serving in Baltimore, Pittsburgh and Boston. These churches are now designated as cathedrals in their respectives cities.

Her husband was ordained by Saint Nektarios, a serene and holy man, who used to visit Mrs. Douropoulos' family home in the mountainous town of Zatouna, Arcadia, during summertime—where Mrs. Douropoulos was born.

The doctors had given up hope for her recovery from meningitis. It was described only as a mysterious, highly contagious disease at the time—when the saintly bishop, who was visiting at her Arcadian home at the time, came to her bedside and prayed for several hours. He had assured her family that the symptoms would leave her and that she would recover. Her recovery became evident as soon as the holy man had finished his prayers.

On New Year's Day this year, as she lay in the French Hospital—she had been hospitalized with a cardiac ailment

---

*The official date of Saint Nektarios' canonization according to the records of the Ecumenical Patriarchate in Constantinople (Istanbul) is April 20, 1961.

and poor circulation—Mrs. Douropoulos told her son, Arthur, that she did not expect to last the day. She recalled that her husband had died forty years ago on that very day.

Archbishop Iakovos, Primate of the Greek Archdiocese of North and South America will return to New York from a Florida vacation to officiate at a funeral service for Mrs. Douropoulos at 2 p.m. tomorrow in the Holy Trinity Cathedral, 319 E. 74th Street. Burial will be in Forest Hill Cemetary, Boston, at a later date.

Surviving, besides her son, Arthur, who is Director of Information for the Greek Archdiocese, are five daughters: Mrs. John H. Limpert, Mrs. Nicholas Culolias, Mrs. Stephen P. Ladas, Mrs. Harry M. Dracos, and Catherine Douropoulos.

On January 4, 1965, Elly wrote a letter to her sister, Demetra, and her husband, Nick Culolias, who were in Greece on a protracted trip at the time. Several years later, Elly came across this letter among Nick's papers which he had left in her care in the event of his death, which occurred in 1972. Most of this material is a definitive account of the inception and development of Boston's Greek community and church, now known as the Annunciation Cathedral, an edifice which is included in the National Register of Historic Places.

The *Nicholas C. Culolias Papers* are at the Houghton Library of Harvard University, Cambridge, Massachusetts.

Darien, Conn.
January 4, 1965

Dear Demetra and Nick:

We returned from Mother's funeral a short while ago. Even though I am exhausted I want to tell you—while it is still vivid in my mind—about the funeral service which took place at 2 o'clock this afternoon.

For the first time after so many hours and days we have spent in the valley of death, I feel consoled and grateful. This last tribute to Mother—enhanced by the presence of her beloved Archbishop Iakovos—truly befitted her. I cannot tell you now, drained as I am physically and emotionally, indeed, I doubt if I ever could do justice to the feelings His Eminence expressed. For his was not simply a eulogy but a paean of his respect, his admiration, his affection for Mother. The sincerity of his feelings moved us deeply and made us feel proud to have had as a mother, and others to have had as a friend, a human being of rare worth.

The Archbishop spoke from the heart when he said that in his entire life he had not known anyone who had so aroused his unreserved esteem and devotion.

He spoke of the day he first met her. He was then a young and untried priest in Boston. She approached him after the liturgy one Sunday and told him that he reminded her of her son, Dionysios. And, thus, within a few moments and with a few words he became, so to speak, her son and she, his mother.

He spoke of the time he was consecrated bishop at the Ecumenical Patriarchate in Istanbul—rather I should say Constantinople, or "The Polis" as the Greeks still call it. His mother was mortally ill and unable to be with her son at that momentous event in his life. As for Mother—she was, you remember, in her mid-eighties and weak at the time. It was only a little more than two years since she had the serious operation on her knee; the doctors doubted that she would walk again without much pain and, at best, for only short distances and with adequate support. Yet, with that extraordinary will of hers, she triumphed over her physical weakness and defied her advanced age and the fierceness of the winter in February of 1955 so as to be with him, "her son," at the time of his glory. She was not a substitute mother. She *was* his mother then and forever after.

He spoke of an instance after Angela's death when Mother went to him for confession*—a most astonishing "confes-

*In Archbishop Iakovos' book, *Faith For A Lifetime* (New York: Doubleday, 1988), p. 33, His Eminence refers to this episode as follows: ". . . the antidote for an inability to pray is more prayer and meditation. I can remember one elderly widow, who came to me early one Sunday morning for a confession while I was serving as a priest in Boston.

sion"—if he could call it such. "I need your help," she told him, "to find my faith again. Something has happened to me and I can no longer pray. I do not believe it is because I have lost my child. I have lost my husband and a son, and I have suffered many, many sorrows in my life but my faith never faltered." Soon after when she saw him she said, "All is well. You have helped me to find God again."

He spoke of that sorrowful Christmas Eve when he went to the hospital to see her. He gave her communion and a gentle radiance from some inner light suddenly illumed her face with serenity. Arthur and Sophia, who were present, were astounded at this change in Mother. (I was not there as Ted had come home from school with a high fever due to some virus or other.)

Throughout her anguish—before and after the amputation of her leg—not for a moment did she lose her faith or lament her fate. She tried but could not stifle the cries of terrible pain that I could hear as soon as I reached the long corridor leading to her room, yet the minute she saw me she would try desperately to smile. No one who saw Mother in the last days of her life could doubt the gallantry of her spirit.

I wish you could have been with us today. I know you were with us in spirit. I made sure the lovely wreath you had telegraphed for Mother was close to her along with those of the family. It could not have been a finer farewell. Archbishop Iakovos, who conducted the entire service, was joined at his request by an entourage of a dozen or so ecclesiastics including several hierarchs. His Eminence was a majestic figure in a black robe with a long pleated train bordered with wide gold and purple bands.

She knelt before me and said, 'I don't have a confession, but I do want to as you a question: Why can't I pray? I simply can't seem to pray anymore!'

"At the time, I was a young man, without a great deal of spiritual experience to draw upon. I couldn't think of a Bible passage, an apt theological reference, or a reasoned response to get her back on the pathway to communication with God. But what finally came to me was a suggestion that I don't believe was my own insight. Rather, I think it was direct guidance from God. All I said was, 'Can we pray together?'

"Our prayer together helped to open the door to a communication with God, which somehow had previously slammed shut in her life. Here, prayer itself was the pathway to prayer . . ."

346

A friend of ours, who was waiting in the church hall with many others to express sympathy, said it was the most inspiring funeral service she had ever attended. It had, she added, the grandeur of a regal medieval pageant, and she would never forget it—and neither will the rest of us.

If I have tired you with this lengthy letter, forgive me, but I wanted to share with you this sad yet beautiful day. I hope you will sleep well tonight knowing that Mother's ordeal is over and she is at rest now—and forever.

Elly

Chapter Thirty-four

More than half a century had passed before I returned once and for all to Boston. It was the only place I could call "home," and so I came back like a lemming to complete the circle of life in the old familiar haunts.

Long ago when I was a child, I had made a promise to myself: If I ever left Arlington, one day I would go back again to see the house on Palmer Street. Time, more than enough of it, had passed to efface the memories of childhood pain and the heartaches of youth. But what I had hoped for most of all—that the years would lighten the "sorrows of parting," was a vain hope; time had only served to increase them and had finally distilled them into an essence more powerful than they possessed in their original form.

But how was I to know when life stretched out endlessly before my young eyes that the flames burning bright and strong on the family hearth were bound one day to expire? And how could I have possibly guessed in my childhood years that the errant law of averages would prevail in my instance and I, the youngest, would remain the sole survivor of our family?

As for the "promise" made long ago in those moments of childish bliss, I had all but forgotten it; yet, since my return to Boston it came back to me, and along with it a saying of my father's: "To break your word is to dishonor it." But what troubled me most was the recurrence of the feeling that the house

348

on Palmer Street was aware of my promise. It was, of course, a nonsensical notion springing from an infantile fancy that the house was waiting for my promised return, waiting to be told what had happened to the people who once lived under its roof and filled its rooms with their laughter and their tears.

My mind kept reverting to the conviction that the house had a life of its own . . . that it had a special sparkle to it whenever guests, especially important ones like the bishops, came to dinner. And it seemed to me that it was pleased, as I was, by the manner my father introduced me to those impressive dignitaries. "And this," he would say, "is our Benjamin." Babá's introduction was quite a compliment, Dion told me, because "Benjamin" was his father's *favorite* child.

The bishops would smile and ask me if I knew who Benjamin was, and I would reply in my best Greek: *Malista*'—Yes, he was the youngest son of Jacob and Rachel. They would remark that I was a bright little girl and how well I spoke Greek. And I felt very important that they chatted with me as though I was a grown-up.

My sisters, except Angela, of course, were annoyed and said I was a show-off, which hurt me. I told Eleni about it and she made me feel better by saying, "Don't listen to them; they're jealous because they don't get as much attention as you do."

My juvenile promise to return to Palmer Street one day was again soon forgotten. Getting settled and readjusted to a world that was strangely new kept me occupied. Even though I had often come back to Boston through the years, I did not realize in those short visits how radically the city had changed in half a century. Another preoccupation was my reunion with old friends who welcomed me back into the fold. One of them called one morning soon after my "homecoming" and asked me to have lunch at her house. I hesitated to accept her invitation. For I had planned to spend the day in putting my home in some semblance of order. Mine was not a simple matter of the usual strain of moving. It involved the emotional trauma, as well, of returning

'The common form for "yes" in Greek is "*ne*."

to Boston as the last member of a large and vital family now forgotten, save for a handful of friends who still remembered the halcyon days of the house on Palmer Street.

"I know it's a short notice," acknowledged my friend, "but surely you can forget about getting your place in order for a few hours, at least." Better still, she advised, was to wait for some miserable rainy weather to get comfortably settled. She reminded me that it was only a short distance by car from Brookline to her house on Brattle Street in Cambridge. "Oh, do come," she urged, "it's such a glorious day!"

I glanced around the chaos that surrounded me and accepted her invitation without further ado, and before long I was on my way.

Indeed, it was a glorious day, a spring day in April that my mother would call *chara Theou*, a joy of God. The sky was tender blue, the wind was gentle, the branches of the trees were festooned with the gold-green haze of nascent leaves. The scent of moist, warm earth and a sweet fragrance—was it perhaps from blossoming acacia trees?—filled the mid-morning air.

A sadness swept over me, a bitter kind of sadness, at this loveliness, at this renascent beauty of spring after spring, eon after eon, while mortals were doomed to extinction after an infinitesimal moment of time on earth. As soon as I saw my old friend, my spirits revived. We lunched in the sunroom from where we could see a maze of forsythia bushes blooming in golden splendor. And we talked in the easy rambling fashion of two close friends who have known each other for practically a lifetime. But as the afternoon wore on, I became uneasy. A subconscious urge to cut my visit short kept coming insistently to my mind, and suddenly I heard myself saying that I must be on my way. "I just remembered," I added lamely, "an errand I have yet to do." My hostess looked at me quizzically but had the good grace not to question or to comment on my excuse. I thanked her for the splendid lunch and, bidding her goodbye hurriedly, I went to my car.

As soon as I started to drive, the compulsion which led to my abrupt departure began to take form in my mind. And by the time I reached the corner of Brattle Street and Massachusetts Avenue I had fathomed the subconscious reason behind it. Therefore, I did not make a right turn that would lead me to Brookline, but turned to the left in the northerly direction of Massachusetts Avenue. A wave of exhilaration swept over me. My pilgrimage to Palmer Street had begun at last.

The traffic was light as the onslaught of home-bound travellers had yet to begin. I drove with ease on the ancient avenue, which had been the main artery to Arlington (then called Menotomy) since before the Revolution. It was, in fact, a part of the route taken by Paul Revere on his midnight ride from Charlestown to Lexington. All along the way he aroused the citizens to warn them of the arrival of the British troops in Boston. Revere's historic ride inspired New England's poet, Longfellow, to commemorate it in verse. His poem became well-known and especially admired by his fellow New Englanders despite its inexactness of fact.

My eyes searched for signs that would bring into focus the memories of my early days. Here and there I recognized some of the old red or grey four- and five-story structures which once dominated the lower part of the avenue. Their r any small windows were covered with dust and grime that must have been permanently imbedded in their surface. These architectural relics from the Victorian era were of no interest to us when we were children. Now, however, it seemed to me they were far more intriguing than the nondescript little stores that had sprouted haphazardly beside them.

A commercial atmosphere prevailed along Massachusetts Avenue; nevertheless, many of the singles houses, and especially the two-family houses that had sprung into popularity during the turn of the century, still held their ground. But what had happened, I wondered, to the few "patrician" houses that afforded us glimpses of unexpected elegance on the trolley car ride back and forth to Harvard Square? Already landmarks in our day, we would watch eagerly for these Victorian "mansions." They had been built before the twentieth century for the wealthy townsfolk when the area was essentially a residential one. It was, no doubt, their valuable frontage on this vital thoroughfare which ultimately became the nemesis of these old "grand dames"— or, more likely, their saviour. Due to the high prices their land commanded, they were quickly sold and thus spared the humiliation of neglect and the odium of decay by being razed in the name of "progress."

As the traffic light turned red, I stopped by a house on a corner lot. It was a large house with a coat of obviously fresh, stark white paint. I looked at it and my eyes traveled idly to the upper section of the house. An arched window was framed in a sharp pitched roof whose triangular form was outlined by a curlicue border. Something about that gingerbread trimming, that single arched window seemed dimly familiar. For a few moments it tantalized my mind, but to no avail. It was, I decided, only a feeling of déja vu or a kind of paramnesia rather than a veritable recollection from the past.

Then suddenly it came to me: The vision of a handsome old house, this very house, on this very spot. I saw it again in my mind's eye as I had seen it long ago. It was then enclosed within an ornate wrought iron fence that kept it apart in solitary grandeur from the pedestrian little houses that had begun to surround it as the town's population increased. The veranda which encircled the house was gone and its facade was covered with synthetic stone. The bay windows had been replaced by an expanse of plate glass revealing draperies that were discreetly drawn.

The fence, the lawn and shrubbery, the trees and lilac bushes had given way to a flood of concrete; and the pergola with its wisteria-laden colonnade had also disappeared; where it stood was now a space reserved for a row of limousines.

Nothing whatsoever remained of the gracious charm the old house possessed. Its present ambience was one of factitious dignity apparently considered proper for a place harboring the rigid bodies of the dead within its dark panelled walls . . . walls that once reflected in their burnished glow the dancing flames of candlelight. The sun was still warm and the air was still balmy, yet, I felt a chill run through me. By the time I reached Alewife Brook, which separates North Cambridge and East Arlington, my mind had tired of its compulsive movements. It was after all, a futile exercise, this compulsion of mine, to compare and contrast the old and the new. For even if by some magic this world had not changed an iota, I would not recognize it now—now that I could no longer see it in the first sweet freshness through a child's guileless eyes.

In less than half the distance I had already traveled, I would reach my destination, and the nearer I came to it the more oblivious I became to my immediate surroundings. Suddenly I found myself in the realm of vanished time, retrieved by some archane process of the mind. Fragments and shards of memories—people and places, events and scenes long hidden beyond the reach of consciousness appeared before my inner sight. They came like fireflies, each of them illuminating for a moment remembrances from the distant past . . . mesmerized, I watched them flashing by and lost all sense of time and place.

Caught in the thrall of rekindled recollections, I was unaware that I had by now reached the final stage of my pilgrimage. Yet, like a homing pigeon, I turned automatically onto a side street and stopped at the corner. I saw the signpost with the words: PALMER STREET, two words that once encompassed the perimeters of my early life. I repeated them again and again until they sounded strange.

Chapter Thirty-five

I was startled by my cursory glance of Palmer Street. How small and commonplace it seemed—not more than an ordinary, size city block if, indeed, it was that much in length! And where were the maples I fondly remembered through the years? Each spring they were trimmed by Joe Riley, a jovial Irishman whose liquor-ladened breath was overlooked in view of his expertise as the town's tree warden. Not that the street was devoid of trees, for here and there were tall, ungainly ones whose limbs had grown all out of bounds. Interspersed unevenly between them were unsightly tree stumps that bespoke of a fatal disease, or were they victims of neglect or indifference towards one of nature's glorious gifts on the face of this earth?

Walking slowly towards "the priest's house," as the neighbors called it, I was heartened to see that the houses were in good repair and for a good reason, indeed. They were three- and four-bedroom houses, and some, like our house, had three additional dormer rooms. These old, substantial, roomy homes had increased in value during the past decades thirty to forty times and more their original worth! Yet, during the Great Depression many of them were consigned to the auctioneer's hammer. And some of the luxurious estates could then be had for a song.

They appeared to be well-cared for, yet they seemed somehow stark until I realized that most of them were devoid of the ubiquitous front porches of the past era. They had, no doubt, been condemned as anachronistic appendages by their subsequent owners. In their time, porches served a multitude of uses: a place to curl up in a padded wicker chair with a book; a place to chat and gossip with neighbors and friends, or to indulge in the fashionable game of "mah-jong"—a place where little girls on warm, rainy days played with their dolls, and noisy boys were quietly absorbed in dominoes, checkers, parcheesi, etc. for hours on end. But during the heady nights of summer, the porch became a favorite spot of the young folk. Its dark corners were well-suited to flirtation which usually progressed to "necking and petting" as these early stages of lovemaking were called in bygone days; then they speedily advanced to amatory discoveries and excitations—provided, of course, that parents had retreated to the parlor in order to listen raptly to that astonishing discovery of the nineteen-twenties called the *radio*.

When I came in sight of our old house, a few moments went by before I recognized it. How small it seemed! But what bewildered me more was the porch, if it still could be called such. The graceful wooden balusters had been removed and replaced by a wrought iron railing laid across curves and curliques lacking in quality or design.

I turned my eyes away from this travesty of good taste toward the rear of the garden with the expectation of seeing the grape arbor. Arthur and I used to call it mother's outdoor *kafenio*, "the café" where summer visitors sat and sipped little cups of Greek coffee under the arbor's shady canopy. Not a sign of it remained. All I could see was a shabby one-car garage several yards away from the back entrance to the house. Two tracks had been made by the car tires through the middle of the garden in order to facilitate an entrance and exit to that wretched structure. Not only was the sparse lawn crushed out of existence, but the circular flower bed that stood in the way of the car's wheels had been destroyed. In the springtime Mother planted gay colored annuals in the circle that surrounded the pièce de résistance of the garden—a tall, slim, perfectly symmetrical red cedar no longer to be seen. She had loved that tree, for it reminded her of the stately cyprus trees that are indigenous to Greece; she also must have been poignantly reminded of the two cypress trees her husband had planted, one for her and one for him, in the front of their home in Arcadia soon after their marriage. Whenever Mr. Riley came to prune and spray the trees on Palmer Street, he would look admiringly at the cedar. "Now, there's a fine specimen," he'd say, "I ain't seen one like it anywhere else."

The longer I looked around me, the more disillusioned I became, for nothing remained that gave rise to my cherished memories. I started walking back to the car when suddenly I stopped as the pear tree came to my mind. We had found it flourishing in the corner of our back yard. The first time I saw it in full bloom with its pale pink blossoms against a stainless blue sky, I thought it was the most beautiful sight I had ever seen—indeed, so beautiful that it inspired my first childish poem.

From where I now stood, the back yard of the house could be clearly seen, but the pear tree was gone! In its place was a shoddy tool house without a door. Inside of it was an old-fashioned lawn mower and a few garden tools. And without a further glance I turned away once and for all.

I felt a sudden anger rise within me, an anger directed against myself for the "pathetic fallacy" that the house on Palmer Street had a heart and a soul—and was waiting for my promised return to learn what happened to those who had lived under its roof more than half a century ago. But, in truth, I had not given any serious consideration to that childish promise of mine. It would come to my mind only during moments of nostalgic sentimentality. Surely, if I had taken my promise to heart, I would have revisited Palmer Street during one of the many times I had come to Boston through the years.

What was it, then, that made me suddenly decide on this sentimental journey, this irrational search for the Holy Grail of childhood, that futile desire to recapture the rapture of youth . . . as though it ever existed, save as a fragile illusion which would disintegrate in the ruthless light of reality? I could not help smiling wryly at my phrase "to recapture the rapture of youth" . . . so maudlin, so ironic.

It was, of course, absurd, this whole matter; this spontaneous decision to revisit Palmer Street that now affronted my normal sensibilities. I had failed to see the psychic dangers involved in

356

the revival of the past. Surely it was folly, if not madness, to reignite an alien child's schizophrenic world that smoldered with the guilt of conflicting loyalties and the torment of inescapable ambivalence. And again I asked myself the question: what had brought on the self-inflicted pain of this pilgrimage? It could be nothing else, I thought, but the treacherous beauty of springtime, this insidiously beguiling April day which seduced me and left me senseless.

In the slanting rays of the late afternoon sun, Palmer Street, was "paved with gold," the way the early immigrants expected to find the streets of America, the legendary land of their hopes and their dreams. And in the magic of that moment when the world around me was flooded with a golden glow, I felt like a little child once more . . . the youngest member of the family. I saw them all again: my parents and my seven siblings sitting around the large oak table in the dining room in that yet unbroken circle.

But they were mute, motionless like marble figures on an ancient frieze. And I wept as I remembered them—alive, vibrant, beautiful and now shadowy forms from the yesteryears.

The light in the sky was still glowing like a lambent flame. It was more than I could bear. I closed my eyes to shut out its radiance. For a second or two, its after-image remained and then dissolved.

I started the car, and even though the sky had not yet lost its luster, for me "the sun had set and all the ways were darkened."

By the time I was close to home, the sun had disappeared. But its afterglow colored the clouds gathered above the horizon in waves of scarlet and gold. Dusk followed swiftly and the heavens took on the chiaroscuro of an El Greco sky. As darkness deepened into night, I felt again that sense of desolation which is akin to despair. All I wanted now was to go home and sleep my cares away. As soon as I reached home I went to bed. But sleep did not come, and I lay awake reviewing my hapless pilgrimage to Palmer Street. It had led me into a labyrinth of half-lit memories from distant days when Arthur and I were the "children" in that "magic circle," and we shared the exuberant

357

dreams of youth that were swept away in the cataclysm of the Great Depression. I wept again as I remembered Arthur, for I would never see the likes of him again. I wept in the dark where no one could see or hear me. And the irony of it was what the *cosmos* said, that I was, indeed, a courageous survivor, and a lucky one at that, as though my survival, or rather my reprieve from the common doom of mankind, was my own doing. It was simply a matter of luck—a random choice Fate had made in my instance, as in any other, from the fathomless genetic grab bag of humanity.

What had I done with that fortuitous gift of a longer life which extended my time on earth beyond that of all my siblings? The question was not an existential one but merely rhetorical. For I was well aware that I had done precious little with my life since I became the survivor of my family, the keeper of its many memories: the good, the rich, the beautiful, the tender memories, and the sorrowful ones that are inescapable in life.

And now, so little time remained. Yet enough of it might still be left, deo volente, to complete the memoir I started long ago and laid aside when thought and action were paralyzed by despair. I could not think of a better way to occupy my mind in whatever time was allotted to me by my fated reprieve than to leave for my children and grandchildren the recollections of a dual world— a new one and an ancient one—thousands of miles apart that were combined in the life of a child called Elly. It was a world incredibly different from the one in which we live today and one that has vanished forever.

Finally, I fell asleep and for the first time in a long while I slept soundly, without dreams that were peopled with the dead. The long day's journey into night had not been in vain.